Pioneers of Personalized Education

Westminster Public Schools & the Pursuit of Competency-Based Learning

JENI GOTTO
OLIVER GRENHAM
BRIAN J. KOSENA
ROBERT J. MARZANO
PAMELA SWANSON

555 North Morton Street
Bloomington, IN 47404
800.733.6786 (toll free) / 812.336.7700
FAX: 812.336.7790

email: info@MarzanoResources.com
MarzanoResources.com

Printed in the United States of America

Library of Congress Cataloging-in-Publication Data

Names: Gotto, Jeni author | Grenham, Oliver author | Kosena, Brian J. author | Marzano, Robert J. author | Swanson, Pamela author
Title: Pioneers of personalized education : Westminster public schools and the pursuit of competency-based learning / Jeni Gotto, Oliver Grenham, Brian J. Kosena, Robert J. Marzano, Pamela Swanson.
Description: Bloomington, IN : Marzano Resources, 2025. | Includes bibliographical references and index.
Identifiers: LCCN 2024052623 (print) | LCCN 2024052624 (ebook) | ISBN 9781943360697 paperback | ISBN 9781943360703 ebook
Subjects: LCSH: Competency-based education--Colorado--Westminster | Individualized instruction--Colorado--Westminster | Public schools--Colorado--Westminster
Classification: LCC LC1032.5.C62 G68 2025 (print) | LCC LC1032.5.C62 (ebook) | DDC 373.01/110978884--dc23/eng/20250401
LC record available at https://lccn.loc.gov/2024052623
LC ebook record available at https://lccn.loc.gov/2024052624

Production Team
President and Publisher: Douglas M. Rife
Associate Publishers: Todd Brakke and Kendra Slayton
Editorial Director: Laurel Hecker
Art Director: Rian Anderson
Copy Chief: Jessi Finn
Copy Editor: Charlotte Jones
Proofreader: Sarah Ludwig
Text Designer: Fabiana Cochran
Cover Designer: Abigail Bowen
Acquisitions Editors: Carol Collins and Hilary Goff
Content Development Specialist: Amy Rubenstein
Associate Editors: Sarah Ludwig and Elijah Oates
Editorial Assistant: Madison Chartier

Acknowledgments

This book would not have been possible without the dedication, passion, and tireless efforts of the students, teachers, staff, school, and district leaders of Westminster Public Schools (WPS). The hard work and commitment of these individuals are at the heart of every achievement documented in these pages. It is their willingness to embrace change, take risks, and continually strive for excellence that has driven the transformative journey of WPS.

To the students, your resilience and adaptability in navigating a system designed to meet your unique needs have been nothing short of inspiring. To the teachers, your unwavering commitment to your students' success, your openness to new ideas, and your mastery of innovative instructional practices have been crucial to the success of the WPS personalized competency-based system. To the staff and support personnel, your behind-the-scenes work has provided the foundation on which this transformation was built. To the school and district leaders, your visionary leadership, strategic thinking, and ability to guide your teams through uncharted territory have made this journey possible.

The stories, examples, and successes shared in this book are a direct result of your collective efforts. This acknowledgment serves as a tribute to each of you and to the incredible work you do every day to make WPS a beacon of innovation and educational excellence.

Table of Contents

About the Authors

Jeni Gotto, EdD, brings over twenty-five years of transformative leadership to the pages of this book. As superintendent of Westminster Public Schools, Dr. Gotto leads with an unwavering commitment to equity and innovation, ensuring every student, regardless of background, has the opportunity to succeed. Her pioneering work in competency-based education (CBE) has redefined learning for countless students, blending rigor with personalized pathways to achievement.

From her early days as a vocational teacher in a small rural district to her current role as a national thought leader, Dr. Gotto has dedicated her career to reshaping education. As the superintendent of the largest districtwide implementation of competency-based education from preK–12, she oversees groundbreaking initiatives that set a new standard for personalized and equitable learning. Her efforts in curriculum design, assessment, and high-reliability organizational practices have not only improved school systems but also inspired educators worldwide. A compelling speaker and global trainer, she has shared her expertise in forums ranging from national conferences to international symposia, leaving a lasting impact on the future of learning. Her innovative approaches and dedication have earned her prestigious accolades, including the Colorado Association of Leaders in Educational Technology Dan Maas Technology Leadership Award and multiple grants to advance educational practice.

Dr. Gotto holds a doctorate of education in leadership for educational equity from the University of Colorado Denver, along with a master's in administrative leadership and policy studies.

Oliver Grenham, EdD, is a visionary educational leader dedicated to helping individuals reach their full potential. With extensive experience in leadership empowerment, effective systems design, transformative school turnaround, and continuous improvement practices, he brings a wealth of expertise to his work.

As the chief architect of a pioneering personalized, competency-based preK–12 system, Dr. Grenham transformed educational structures and practices at Westminster Public Schools in Colorado, creating a learner-centered environment where students advance at a purpose-driven pace based on demonstrated performance. Widely recognized for his work in competency-based education, he has shared insights on its challenges and successes at prominent conferences, symposia, and seminars, advocating for educational systems that better prepare students for a dynamic and diverse future.

In July 2023, Dr. Grenham received the Colbert Cushing Award, presented by the Colorado Association of School Executives, which honors individuals for outstanding professional contributions and exceptional service to the field of education. He was also named one of the Top 100 Visionaries in Education by the Global Forum for Education and Learning in June 2021, an internationally recognized organization uniting educators, innovators, and thought leaders to address complex educational challenges worldwide.

Dr. Grenham earned his bachelor of science degree and higher diploma in education from the University of Galway, Ireland. He also holds a specialist degree in educational leadership and administration and a master's degree in instructional technology from the University of Colorado Denver, as well as a doctorate in educational leadership from Nova Southeastern University, Florida.

To learn more about Dr. Grenham's work, visit www.linkedin.com/in/droliver grenham.

Brian J. Kosena, EdD, is the chief learning officer in Westminster Public Schools. Previously, he was the founding principal of John E. Flynn A Marzano Academy, a preK–8 school of innovation in Westminster Public Schools in Westminster, Colorado. The first campus of the Marzano Academy network, Flynn continues to serve as the instructional laboratory school for both Westminster Public Schools and Marzano Academies. Dr. Kosena has been an educator since 2006 and has served as a principal, instructional technology coordinator, and high school social studies teacher. His experiences in education range from teaching in a private Jesuit high school to being the principal of a predominantly minority and low-income public elementary school. He has also taught graduate-level and teacher-licensure courses in the Denver metro area.

Dr. Kosena is a strong advocate for CBE. In addition to working in Westminster Public Schools, a national leader in CBE design, Dr. Kosena has formally researched CBE instructional practices and implementation in school settings. He regularly attends and presents at CBE conferences, helping share his experiences while encouraging a wider adoption of CBE across all public school systems. His work has helped identify common challenges for CBE schooling and find practicable solutions.

Dr. Kosena received a bachelor's degree in international affairs from the University of Colorado Boulder, a master's degree in secondary education from the University of Phoenix, and a doctorate in educational leadership and equity from the University of Colorado Denver.

Robert J. Marzano, PhD, is cofounder and chief academic officer of Marzano Resources in Denver, Colorado. During his fifty years in the field of education, he has worked with educators as a speaker and trainer and has authored more than fifty books and two hundred articles on topics such as instruction, assessment, writing and implementing standards, cognition, effective leadership, and school intervention. His books include *The New Art and Science of Teaching*, *Leaders of Learning*, *Making Classroom Assessments Reliable and Valid*, *The Classroom Strategies Series*,

Managing the Inner World of Teaching, *A Handbook for High Reliability Schools*, *A Handbook for Personalized Competency-Based Education*, and *The Highly Engaged Classroom*. His practical translations of the most current research and theory into classroom strategies are known internationally and are widely practiced by both teachers and administrators.

Dr. Marzano received a bachelor's degree from Iona College in New York, a master's degree from Seattle University, and a doctorate from the University of Washington.

To learn more about Dr. Marzano, visit www.marzanoresources.com.

Pamela Swanson is an acclaimed educational leader with nearly four decades of experience spanning the United States and Europe. Most recently, she served as superintendent of Westminster Public Schools in Colorado, where she led the district's transformation to a preK–12 competency-based education system. Her leadership has been recognized with numerous accolades, including the prestigious 2020 Colorado Superintendent of the Year award and the 2019 North Metro Woman of the Year honor. Swanson is widely celebrated for spearheading a seven-year turnaround effort through a state accountability system, fostering sustained improvement and innovation. In 2025, she is launching "the entrusted," an educational leadership network and podcast dedicated to empowering leaders in education.

Swanson received a bachelor's degree in music performance from Winthrop University, a master's degree in educational administration from the University of Colorado Denver, and a doctorate in educational leadership from Nova Southeastern University. She also holds a certification as a senior professional of human resources.

To book Oliver Grenham or Brian J. Kosena for professional development, contact pd@MarzanoResources.com.

Introduction

The interest in standards-based or competency-based education (CBE) has been increasing geometrically since around 2014—the same year U.S. Department of Education announced the Experimental Sites Initiative for higher education. As reported by Robert J. Marzano, Jennifer S. Norford, Michelle Finn, and Douglas Finn (2017), the initiative was also known as *the CBE experiment*. Within this program, postsecondary institutions were encouraged to develop self-paced CBE programs. In 2015, the Department of Education expanded the experiment to focus on students learning as much as possible in the shortest amount of time without paying for additional courses.

In 2015, then secretary of education Arne Duncan (as cited in Schneider & Paul, 2015) encouraged high school principals to change their schools to competency based, explaining that "it's the right thing to do." He noted, "If you can demonstrate that you know algebra, why should you sit in that chair for nine months?" (Schneider & Paul, 2015). Secretary Duncan's remarks highlighted a basic premise of CBE at both the K–12 and higher education levels—namely, that learners should be able to move on when they have demonstrated mastery of the content.

At about that same time, Chris Sturgis (2015) from CompetencyWorks reported that nearly 90 percent of states had generated legislation that created options for competency-based innovations. Some had created "seat-time waivers" that allow districts and schools to offer competency-based credits (Sturgis, 2015). Interest in CBE continued to spread across the county. By 2020, iNACOL (now the Aurora Institute) was reporting that forty-nine states and the District of Columbia were making allowances for the implementation of competency-based initiatives (Evans, Landl, & Thompson, 2020). By 2021, the Aurora Institute estimated that "8 to 10 percent of U.S. school districts are piloting or working toward competency-based learning" (Patrick, 2021, p. 27). Finally, by 2024, it was estimated that every state in the U.S. allowed schools to implement CBE systems in which students can matriculate through the grade levels and graduate by demonstrating competency as opposed to fulfilling seat time (Stanford, 2024).

While there are a growing number of schools that have transformed to a CBE system or are in the process of doing so, there are scant few districts which have accomplished this change systemwide or who have even tried to do so. The most probable reason for so few districts undertaking the change to a CBE system is that at the district level, CBE requires a rethinking of basic structures that have been foundational to K–12 education since the turn of the 20th century. Additionally, implementing a CBE approach at the district level requires new structures and protocols that generate outcomes not possible within the current system.

The basic question this book is designed to answer is, How can an entire school district make the shift from a traditional K–12 education system to a CBE system? The book answers this question by detailing the approach employed by Westminster Public Schools (WPS) in Colorado—a shining example of what is possible when a whole district is willing to rethink its basic structures. The following pages lay out the demographics of this district, its learning model, the tenets woven throughout the WPS CBE system, and what readers will find in the chapters to come.

Westminster Public Schools Demographics

WPS is a seventeen-square-mile landlocked school district located in the north-central section of the Denver metropolitan area in Colorado. Once considered a typical suburban school district, economic and demographic shifts within the larger metropolitan area changed the face of WPS in a relatively short fifteen-year period of time to resemble an archetypical urban district. As of 2024, the district serves a diverse group of approximately 7,500 students in eighteen schools, including two early learning centers, three preK–5 schools, six preK–8 schools, one middle school (6–8), four innovation preK–8 schools, one comprehensive high school, one alternative secondary school, and a highly structured, therapeutic day treatment program (Instructional Services Center).

The district employs about 750 personnel, including 500 licensed teachers and administrators and 75 educational support professionals. Students are characterized by significant socioeconomic challenges, a high rate of mobility, and generational language barriers. Most students are Hispanic (77 percent), most qualify for free or reduced lunch (85 percent), and just under half (42 percent) are English learners. About one-fifth (18 percent) of the district's students move in or out of WPS during a given school year, from August through May.

WPS district and school administrators believe schools contribute significantly to the vibrancy and prosperity of the local community they serve. Therefore, WPS has a moral imperative to provide students an equitable education that benefits the common good. The Westminster learning model provided the infrastructure and instructional practices to fulfill this mission.

The Westminster Learning Model

School districts ready to discard the fragmented elements of the traditional industrial model of education must ensure the new structure is explicit and systemic. The traditional model of education groups students by age, with academic progression determined by time-based criteria such as course credits or grade-level completion. Students follow a fixed curriculum at a uniform pace, regardless of their individual circumstances. In contrast, a personalized competency-based system (PCBS) groups students by ability, with progression based on individual mastery of clearly defined learning targets. For example, instead of receiving a points-based letter grade at the end of the school year, students demonstrate competencies through varied assessments throughout the year and advance to the next level of instruction only when they are ready. Such a systemic structure will take time and focused energy to create. In migrating away from the traditional industrial education model, the WPS learning model has undergone substantial transformation since its inception and launch in the 2009–2010 school year. The WPS learning model as of 2024 is depicted in figure I.1 (page 4).

At the macro level, the model consists of five comprehensive and dynamic components and four validating tenets or foundational beliefs. The five components are as follows.

1. Shared vision
2. Leadership at all levels
3. Competency-based design
4. Learner-centered classrooms
5. Continuous improvement

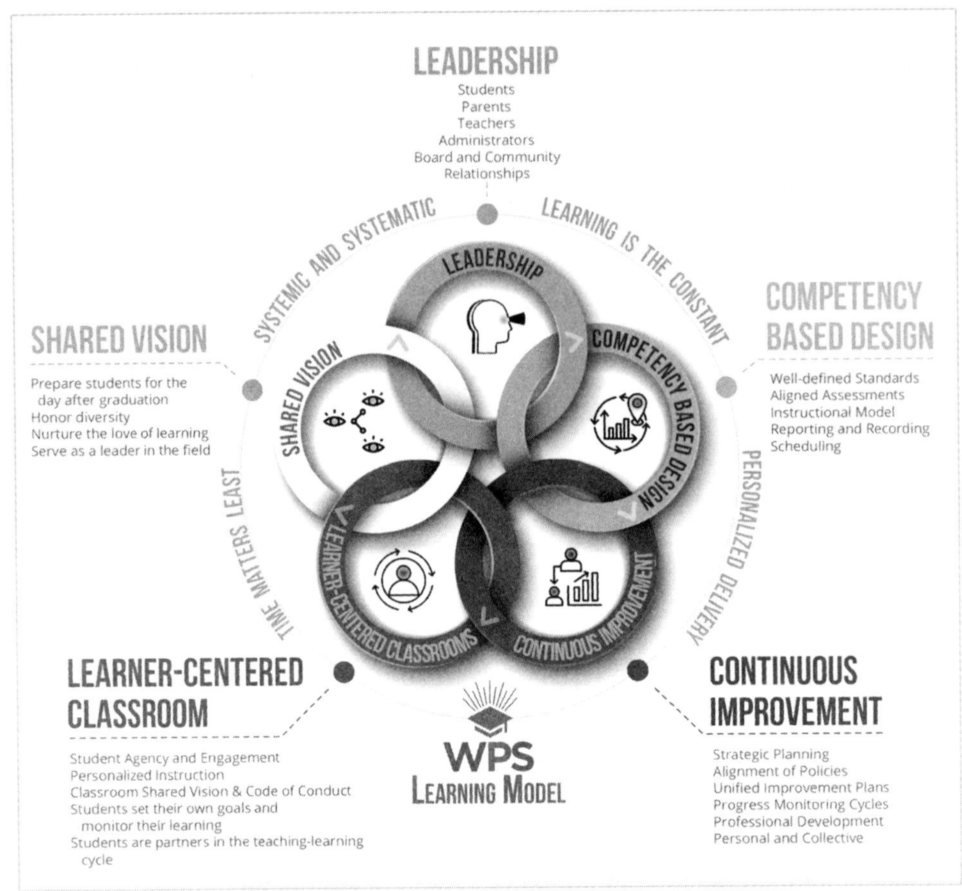

Source: © 2024 by Westminster Public Schools. Used with permission.

FIGURE I.1: Westminster Public Schools learning model.

These provide structure and support, giving the model systemic stability and providing a common foundation to build on. Each component evolves purposefully and thoughtfully over time in response to new insights and emerging realities. The smaller text beneath each component provides specific examples or subcomponents that align with and support the broader principles of each. These examples serve as illustrative pathways that districts might use to implement the components effectively. However, they are not exhaustive; rather, they act as a guide for achieving the larger goals of each component. Districts are encouraged not to adopt but instead to adapt these ideas or develop additional strategies that align with their unique context and needs.

The four validating and unchanging tenets or foundational beliefs of the WPS learning model are as follows.

1. Learning matters most (learning is the constant).

2. Time matters least (time is the variable).
3. Implementation is systemic and systematic (policy, process, and practice).
4. Delivery is personalized (learner driven).

"Learning matters most" emphasizes the constant focus on learning, while "time matters least" acknowledges the variable nature of time in the learning process from student to student, and from content to content for individual students, while recognizing that time is still a limited resource in schools. "Implementation is systemic and systematic" highlights the importance of aligning policies, processes, and practices in a cohesive manner, ensuring a systematic approach to growth in learning. "Delivery is personalized" reinforces the learner-driven aspect, capitalizing on the learners' inherent dispositions and aspirations, emphasizing the individualized and personalized nature of education within the model. These tenets provide the glue that holds the system together by serving as broad criteria for appraising improvements to the entire system. This criteria-based approach ensures any new policy, process, or practice is aligned, is connected, and meaningfully promotes system growth rather than hinder it.

The personalized competency-based system tenets are not just guiding principles—they are the framework that ensures every aspect of the district's transformation is aligned, coherent, and focused on the goal of student success. By embedding these tenets into the shared vision, leadership development, competency-based design, learner-centered classrooms, and continuous improvement processes, districts can create a sustainable and effective educational ecosystem. These tenets, when fully understood and applied, become the bedrock on which a truly personalized competency-based system is built, leading to meaningful and lasting change in education.

In summary, the Westminster learning model stands as a dynamic and evolving framework enhancing learning while meeting current challenges and adapting to future ones. Next, a brief discussion on the WPS learning model components and tenets provides context for the chapters that follow.

Crafting a Shared Vision

The PCBS tenets are foundational in the development of a shared vision that guides the district's transformation. When creating a shared vision, it is crucial to articulate how the proposed changes align with the tenets, particularly "learning matters most." This tenet emphasizes the importance of prioritizing learning above all else, guiding the shift from time-based practices to a model where students advance based on demonstrated competence. By aligning the shared vision with these tenets, stakeholders can visualize and embrace the new learning paradigm, setting the stage for systemic change.

Fostering Leadership at All Levels

Leadership within a PCBS requires a deep understanding of the tenets, especially "implementation is systemic and systematic." This tenet ensures leadership structures and practices are coherent and aligned across all levels of the district. For instance, representative leadership bodies like the teacher cabinet play a crucial role in facilitating communication and ensuring all voices contribute to the enhancement of the system. Effective leadership in a PCBS context is built on a foundation of knowledge, understanding, and systemic support, enabling leaders to guide transformative change effectively.

Ensuring Competency-Based Design

The "systemic and systematic" tenet is also central to the successful implementation of competency-based design. This tenet ensures the structures and practices supporting learners and teachers are consistent and aligned throughout the entire educational journey. By integrating the tenets into the design and implementation of competency-based structures, districts can ensure innovative solutions, products, or processes support the PCBS vision. Continuous professional learning is also critical, enabling educators to effectively incorporate these designs into their practices while staying true to the tenets.

Facilitating Learner-Centered Classrooms

"Delivery is personalized" is the key tenet in fostering learner-centered classrooms. This tenet guides the creation of environments that reflect and support each learner's unique needs, aspirations, and goals. In a learner-centered classroom, personalized delivery means providing opportunities for individual voice and choice, promoting mastery of learning, and fostering agency. By integrating technology, flexible learning pathways, and collaborative practices, teachers can create dynamic classrooms that inspire curiosity and creativity, fully embracing the spirit of personalized learning.

Promoting Continuous Improvement

The tenet of "implementation is systemic and systematic" is the driving force behind continuous improvement within the Westminster learning model. This tenet ensures the district's progress is valid, reliable, and aligned with measurable outcomes. By adopting a systemic and systematic approach, WPS has been able to develop innovative tools like the WPS High Reliability School (HRS) Playbook and the High Reliability District Level 6. These tools help maintain coherence and prevent fragmentation, ensuring continuous improvement efforts are focused, effective, and aligned with the overall PCBS vision.

What You Will Find in This Book

This book has six chapters dedicated to the five comprehensive components of the WPS learning model. These components represent the foundational elements that guided the district's approach to fostering an innovative and effective educational environment. While these components were designed for the unique needs of Westminster Public Schools, the principles underpinning them apply to any district implementing personalized competency-based education (PCBE). For example, a shared vision can help any district align its stakeholders toward a common goal, while the competency-based design component can offer a framework for personalizing a student's education. Continuous improvement, learner-centered classrooms, and inclusive leadership provide blueprints for addressing systemic challenges that, inevitably, every district will encounter. By showcasing WPS's successes and challenges, this book aims to serve as a guidebook for educators seeking PCBE implementation.

Chapter 1 delves into the importance of a clearly articulated and widely embraced shared vision within WPS. It explores how the district developed a unified vision that aligns with its PCBS and how this vision serves as the cornerstone for all strategic planning and decision-making processes across the district. The chapter also discusses the role of stakeholders, including educators, students, parents, and the community, in shaping and sustaining this vision.

Chapter 2 examines the critical role of leadership in driving the success of the WPS learning model. It outlines the qualities and strategies of effective leadership within the district, emphasizing how leaders at all levels—district, school, and classroom—are empowered to cultivate a culture of innovation and continuous improvement. The chapter provides insights into how leadership practices have evolved in WPS to support the implementation of a PCBS, including the development of leadership capacity and the alignment of leadership goals with the district's vision.

Chapter 3 focuses on the structural foundation of the WPS learning model and the principles and practices of PCBS. It explains how WPS designed and implemented a competency-based framework that allows students to progress at their own pace, based on mastery of skills and knowledge. The chapter explores the intricacies of designing curricula, assessments, and instructional strategies that align with CBE principles, as well as the challenges and successes WPS has encountered in transitioning to this model.

Chapter 4 highlights the transformation of classrooms in WPS into learner-centered environments. It details how the district shifted from traditional, teacher-centered instruction to a model where students take an active role in their learning journey. The chapter explores the strategies used to foster student agency, engagement, and personalized learning experiences, including the integration of technology, differentiated instruction, and formative assessments. It also addresses the professional development and support provided to educators to facilitate this shift.

Chapter 5 illustrates how the concept of continuous improvement has been integral to refining and realizing the goals of the WPS PCBS. It outlines the district's journey from initial, fragmented improvement efforts to a cohesive, data-driven approach that permeates all levels of the organization. The chapter discusses the tools, processes, and cycles of reflection and action WPS uses to ensure ongoing progress and adaptability. It also explores how continuous improvement practices have been institutionalized within the district's culture, leading to sustained improvements in student outcomes and organizational effectiveness.

The last chapter, chapter 6, addresses how the High Reliability Schools process can be applied as a dynamic mechanism for monitoring and enhancing the five comprehensive components of the WPS learning model. While HRS is considered a subcomponent under the continuous improvement component in figure I.1 (page 4), it warrants its own chapter due to its central role in operationalizing and sustaining the district's vision. HRS is the process used to align districtwide efforts across all five components, providing a cohesive framework to ensure systemic reliability and ongoing progress. By dedicating an entire chapter to HRS, this book highlights how WPS adapted the framework not only to achieve high reliability in its schools but also to achieve the district's broader strategic goals. The chapter provides a detailed account of how the HRS process has been operationalized within WPS, the development of district-specific indicators, and the creation of tools like the WPS HRS playbooks to drive continuous improvement and maintain high standards across all areas of the district.

The authors of this book bring direct, lived experience from working in Westminster Public Schools, a district that adopted and successfully implemented PCBE. Their roles as leaders, educators, and practitioners were instrumental in shaping and realizing the WPS learning model. From the development of a shared vision to the codification of systems like HRS into systemwide practice, they have witnessed the transformative nature of the WPS learning model. This journey wasn't without challenges, but those experiences provided deep insights into what works and what doesn't as a district dismantles traditional structures to build a student-centered, personalized education system.

The goal in sharing the WPS story is to provide readers with inspiration and concrete strategies and tools that any school district can adapt to their unique context. The authors believe PCBE holds the key to unlocking the potential of every student and are confident this book will empower your school district to take the first steps—or the next steps—in that journey. The work ahead may seem intimidating, but it is filled with the possibility to design a better way. As you dive deeper into the chapters that follow, the authors hope you'll feel the same excitement and sense of purpose that fueled WPS's own journey. When a school district is willing to innovate and try something different, they can create educational environments where all students thrive, where learning becomes personalized, and where every graduate is ready for the day after graduation.

CHAPTER 1

Shared Vision

Building a shared vision is the cornerstone of any successful transformation journey, particularly in the context of transitioning to a personalized competency-based system. At the outset, there might be a strong temptation for school districts to dive directly into familiar territories, such as competency-based design, the subject of chapter 3 (page 53). However, the experience of Westminster Public Schools has revealed that bypassing the essential step of creating a collective and coherent shared vision can jeopardize the long-term success and sustainability of transformational efforts. A well-crafted shared vision not only aligns stakeholders—both internal and external—but also fosters a deep understanding and commitment to the fundamental changes required for a PCBS.

This chapter explores the critical role of a shared vision in establishing a solid foundation for deep systemwide change, guiding school districts through the complexities of systemic transformation while ensuring all voices are heard and all actions are aligned with a common purpose.

In the following pages, we will explore readiness for change, the blueprint for creating a shared vision, creation of the WPS shared vision, accountability, preparation for second-order change, curriculum and instructional frameworks, the necessary cultural shift and professional development, continuous reflection and evolution, and ways to sustain the shared vision.

Readiness for Change

In the fall of 2006, Westminster Public Schools (formerly known as Adams County School District 50) began developing a shared vision for a PCBS. This transformative initiative was driven by a convergence of five key factors.

1. Escalating state accountability expectations and sanctions, coupled with declining student scores
2. The district's designation as "Academic Watch" for the 2006–2007 school year
3. The appointment of a new superintendent from out of state
4. A Comprehensive Appraisal for District Improvement (CADI) audit
5. The Colorado Association of School Boards (CASB) convention focusing on "Preparing Students for a Changing World"

In December 2006, the secretary of the Westminster board of education and Region 5 board director for CASB attended the 66th CASB Annual Convention. A session titled "Reinventing Our Schools" highlighted the Chugach School District's success in rural Alaska, including its recognition as the first K–12 public school system to receive the Malcolm Baldrige National Quality Award in 2001. Inspired by this session, the board secretary shared her reflections with district leadership, urging further exploration of systemic standards-based concepts. This proposal was unanimously supported, fueled by two primary drivers: heightened accountability expectations with severe sanctions and a decade of groundwork in developing robust standards, aligned assessments, and technological tools for monitoring student progress.

In fall 2006, district leaders faced mounting pressure to use state and local data to guide instruction, driven by conflicting state and federal legislative requirements, including the Colorado Accreditation Accountability Act (1998), Colorado's School Accountability Reports (2000), and No Child Left Behind (2002). The situation became critical when the Colorado Department of Education notified Westminster on November 30, 2006, that it ranked in the bottom 10 percent of Colorado school districts, earning the "Academic Watch" designation. Anticipating increased accountability challenges, district leadership proactively requested a CADI audit to address persistent performance issues. Conducted in December 2006 by a team of state-approved educational experts, the six-day audit evaluated curriculum, instruction, assessment, systems design, and leadership. Its findings provided critical insights that guided the district's response to escalating accountability demands.

By spring 2007, Westminster initiated a strategic planning process involving all stakeholders and supported by an external consultant. The district's vision was to ensure every student acquired the skills and knowledge necessary for success as a 21st century citizen. Four strategic goals were established.

1. Implement effective academic programs to raise student performance to the highest levels in the state.
2. Foster school-community and business partnerships that embrace the community's diversity and nurture student success.
3. Operate with fiscal responsibility to maximize resource effectiveness and efficiency.
4. Provide safe, secure, and adequate school facilities.

Implementation of these goals began in fall 2007, coinciding with early planning for a personalized competency-based system (then referred to as a standards-based system). By the 2008–2009 school year, the district's shared vision for a PCBS became more defined, aligning seamlessly with the first strategic goal. The full rollout of PCBS was scheduled for fall 2009, with strategies and actions evolving to align with the new learning model. In other words, Westminster Public Schools' PCBS journey began.

To transition to a PCBS, school districts should conduct a thorough needs assessment across all departments and schools to gauge the readiness level for implementing *second-order change*. Educational consultant Michael Fullan (2001) established that this type of change involves a fundamental transformation in how the organization operates, requiring alterations to the underlying structures, goals, and processes that define its work. Unlike first-order change, which typically involves incremental improvements to existing structures, second-order change demands that individuals within the organization adapt to entirely new systemic conditions. In this context, merely expecting compliance is insufficient; second-order change requires commitment from all levels of the organization.

Second-order change is difficult to achieve without a clear and compelling shared vision. For WPS, the shared vision provided the foundation for systemic transformation by aligning all stakeholders toward a shared common purpose: ensuring every student is provided a personalized competency-based education. The shared vision served as a compass heading, informing decisions and creating a commitment to the systemic changes necessary for PCBS implementation. By unifying the entire district to the vision, WPS was able to foster trust, clarity, and continual progress to navigate the inevitable challenges a second-order change brings. Without this collective purpose, the profound transformation required for PCBS would not have been possible.

The needs assessment should include executive leadership readiness, operational readiness, data readiness, technical readiness, individual school readiness, and so forth. Migrating away from traditional school practices to an explicit systemic approach that seeks a new desired state will undoubtedly disrupt the values, beliefs, and status quo of all stakeholders. Conducting the needs assessment not only communicates the desire for second-order change but also helps to create demand for transformational change. The needs assessment process should resemble the course of action used for comprehensive strategic planning. Input regarding the desired state needs to be gathered from all stakeholders (students, teachers, support staff, leaders, parents, local business owners, corporate representatives, community members at large, and the board of education) to identify the collective aspirations of the community. These aspirations can then be translated by the district administration to formulate goals, timelines, cost estimates, and success criteria as part of this articulated process.

Becoming a PCBS involves a fundamental shift in thinking and work practices for all instructional stakeholders and requires new thinking and work practices of all noninstructional support staff. All supporting departments—human resources, financial services, technology services, operations, and so on—will need to develop and align new operational protocols and procedures based on the principles of the new desired state. In the case of WPS, these tenets are reflected in the WPS learning model: shared vision, leadership, competency-based design, learner-centered classrooms, and continuous improvement. While these components are specific to WPS, they align closely with framework principles any district or school adopting a PCBS would need to consider. Given this complexity, an adept superintendent or principal will not declare the adoption of a PCBS without a thorough understanding of and detailed plan for the necessary and significant system changes that will be required for implementation.

A comprehensive implementation plan is essential to ensure readiness. This plan must outline the specific changes, responsibilities, timelines, benchmarks, and associated costs. Over time, policies, protocols, procedures, and relevant training should be developed to guide all instructional staff and leaders in adopting more effective instructional approaches that consider student voice and choice, assess ongoing progress, score and report improvement, and foster student agency to create a vibrant learning culture. Similarly, noninstructional staff and leaders should update and align their policies, protocols, procedures, and training to correspond.

The timeline for implementing second-order change to transition to a PCBS hinges on the "opportunity gap" between the current and the desired future state. School districts that have been most successful in implementing transformation from the traditional industrial model to a PCBS are often grassroots initiatives supported by leadership at all levels. This is especially true when experienced leaders are intimately familiar with the district's history and culture. These leaders can endorse as well as lead change based on their knowledge, experience, and trust within the district.

Complete system transformation is not easy. It requires the creation of collective efficacy and effort to focus on improving the right work in spite of or because of current challenges—superintendent tenure, principal turnover, teacher shortages, flawed accountability, enrollment changes, student mobility and migration, student discipline, chronic absenteeism, local politics, and the like—all of which can intensify the need to focus more urgently on the right work. The key to building and preserving collective efficacy and effort during transformation lies in creating a sustainable shared vision that is actionable, dynamic, and endorsed by all stakeholders—students, teachers, support staff, leaders, parents, local business owners, corporate representatives, community members at large, and, of course, the board of education.

The Blueprint for Creating a Shared Vision

Crafting a shared vision that propels transformative second-order change requires more than simply selecting lofty, flowery language for vision and mission statements. School districts can proudly display their statements, yet often the fundamental work and results of schools persist without substantial change. To establish an authentic shared vision, all stakeholders must witness their contributions reflected not only in its creation but also in the execution of its objectives. Once the aspirational words of the vision and mission statements are penned, they serve as a constant reminder of the *why* driving the ongoing transformative journey.

The steps that follow offer a strategic outline for district leaders to initiate and guide the transformative journey toward becoming a PCBS. Following these steps is a description of the background story of creating the WPS shared vision, which illuminates the underlying moral purpose driving and sustaining WPS's transformation.

1. Identify Why the Change Is Necessary Now

Change for the sake of change is seldom welcomed, yet it occurs frequently in school districts. Research suggests that "initiative fatigue" can occur when a clear and cohesive strategy is not present, leading to fragmented initiatives that leave staff overwhelmed by competing priorities, ultimately reducing the efficacy of the most important reforms

(Fullan & Quinn, 2016). Whether prompted by a new leader, attendance at the latest conference, or persuasive vendors, such piecemeal changes can disrupt organizational focus and erode trust among stakeholders (Kotter, 2012).

When considering the transition to a PCBS, clarity on your why is essential. What systemic issues or issues within your school district are you seeking to address? Establishing this purpose helps ensure change is intentional, aligned, and meaningful rather than reactive or superficial.

- Is there low academic achievement for all or some students?
- Are there persistent academic gaps?
- Is student apathy and chronic absenteeism high?
- Is teacher apathy and chronic absenteeism high?
- Are there rapid changes in student enrollment due to mobility?
- Are multiple systemic issues interconnected to some degree?

2. Understand the Historical Background and Extent of the Issues

Once you have found your why, you must gain a comprehensive understanding of the systemic issues and investigate the origins and ongoing presence of the current problems within the school district's context. This involves analyzing historical data and engaging in formal discussions with those most impacted by the issue. It is also imperative to consult personnel with extensive experience and trust in the district, as they can provide valuable insights into the problem's evolution over time. Often, these individuals belong to the silent majority and are not necessarily the ones who speak the loudest.

3. Determine Possibilities for a Realistic Desired State

After identifying and thoroughly understanding the systemic issues, the next question is, Will implementing a PCBS help resolve these challenges, or could it unintentionally exacerbate them? Are there specific components of a PCBS that, while initially appealing, would meaningfully address the identified issues if implemented successfully? It is essential to carefully analyze which elements of the model align with the district's unique needs and challenges to avoid investing in changes that might create additional barriers or unintended consequences.

Additionally, is the current political climate of the school district conducive to supporting second-order transformational change? Transformational change requires buy-in from key stakeholders, including school boards, administrators, teachers, parents, and the broader community. If such support is lacking, districts must identify what strategies or information is necessary to build sustainable momentum and ensure the transition is both successful and enduring.

4. Learn From the Current Body of Literature

Since WPS embarked on its journey, there has been a burgeoning growth of valuable literature regarding the implementation of PCBS policies and practices. Despite this significant growth, misconceptions and misunderstandings persist, and it is important to note that what succeeds in one district may not apply universally, as researchers Denise H. Rhoney and Susan M. Meyer (2024) have explained. District leaders are urged to connect with school districts already engaged in similar efforts to learn how they have addressed comparable systemic challenges. Additionally, several nationally recognized organizations can provide guidance and resources to districts embarking on this work, including CompetencyWorks, the Aurora Institute (formerly iNACOL), KnowledgeWorks, and the Learning Policy Institute. These organizations offer frameworks, case studies, and professional learning to help districts navigate the implementation of PCBS. Utilizing these resources will provide district leaders with best practices and tailored approaches to their unique contexts.

5. Select and Prepare Key Personnel

Once the decision to explore further steps in transitioning to a PCBS is made, gather a small coalition of willing representatives who are both trusted and respected within the organization to accomplish the following.

- Develop a broad-strokes communication plan and common message describing the desired new state and the issues that will be resolved if transformational change is implemented.
- Create a process to seek commitment and sustainable support from all stakeholders.
- Outline an initial implementation that describes the major goals and objectives for meaningful change as well as a method for achieving them.
- Determine success criteria.
- Seek approval and support from the board of education in public to move forward in sharing information with stakeholders.

6. Create Demand Within the Organization and Broader Community

Begin strategic engagement of all stakeholders, including teachers, support staff, non-instructional staff, leaders, parents, students, local business owners, corporate representatives, community members at large, homeowners' associations, Rotary Clubs, and so forth. To share information regarding the identified systemic issues and the strategy for resolution aiming for better outcomes for everyone, schedule in-person meetings with the following groups.

- **All instructional and noninstructional district and school leaders**, to ensure clarity on why transformative change is necessary to address the identified systemic issues. Provide a common information base and foster universal understanding. Gather their input and feedback as part of a SWOT (strengths, weaknesses, opportunities, threats) analysis and seek sustainable commitment for moving forward with the initiative.
- **All school and department staff**, inclusive of support and noninstructional staff, to establish a common understanding and information base. Solicit and compile their input and feedback for further analysis. Assess the level of commitment and support for advancing with the initiative.
- **Parents and guardians** at each school site during their parent-teacher organization (PTO) and parent-teacher association (PTA) meetings, accountability committee meetings, or special events. Share information, foster common understandings, and seek support and feedback for next steps. Utilize online surveys to collect input from parents who are unable to attend in person. Compile and analyze these data to gauge the level of support for moving forward with the initiative.
- **Student leaders**, to share information; cultivate common understandings; and solicit their ideas, input, and support for advancing with the initiative.

Analyze the feedback from all groups and adjust communication and initial implementation plans accordingly.

7. Solicit Broad-Based Internal Support

Before allocating resources to detailed planning, convene all internal stakeholders, including noninstructional staff, to assess their commitment to implementing transformative second-order change in pursuit of a PCBS. Establish a process for gathering everyone's voice and choice that meets or exceeds the agreed-on threshold to achieve critical mass. In WPS, the commitment threshold was 80 percent.

8. Build on Existing Expertise, Knowledge, Assets, and Processes

Based on reaching the commitment threshold and the analysis of the collected feedback for creating demand within the organization and the broader community, identify additional supportive members from the coalition of the willing who will now be needed to assist with deeper analysis of the following tasks.

- Conduct an audit of recording and reporting practices, processes, and technologies to identify gaps and omissions.
- Review all written content standards and courses. Inspect how the standards are taught and measured at the classroom, school, and district levels.
- Evaluate the alignment of standards, instruction, assessment, recording, and reporting for all content areas.
- Identify the measurable competencies needed to become a future-ready graduate, inclusive of skills (academic) and dispositions (nonacademic).
- Create a personalized competency-based pilot classroom within each school or within each school in a feeder area. If feasible, create a pilot school.

9. Develop a Multiyear Plan of Action

Be as specific as possible in the creation of a comprehensive multiyear plan of action that includes measurable quarterly benchmarks and annual outcomes. The benchmarks and annual outcomes will provide opportunities for implementing plan, do, check, and adjust (PDCA) cycles, essential for continuous improvement. The plan of action should encompass the following and is explored further in chapter 5 (page 143).

- **Identification of professional learning needs:** Address the learning requirements for all stakeholders, including students, faculty, and noninstructional staff.
- **Integration of essential technologies and learning resources:** Incorporate any new indispensable technologies and hands-on resources into the learning environment to enhance effectiveness.
- **Establishment of implementation benchmarks and annual outcomes:** Define specific benchmarks, outcomes, and goals to be achieved within designated time frames, ensuring clarity and accountability.
- **Evaluation of student learning results:** Continuously review and analyze student learning outcomes to measure the effectiveness of the plan and adjust as necessary.
- **Current and long-term budgetary needs:** Align the plan with the approved district budget, ensuring sufficient funding for both short-term implementation and long-term sustainability over multiple years.

10. Share Progress and Planning Updates Regularly

Regularly disseminate progress updates and planning reports to keep all stakeholders, such as the following, informed about the ongoing efforts, challenges faced, and successes achieved in addressing systemic issues. Existing structures and processes can be used to provide updates.

- **Board of education reports and accountability committee reports:** Provide updates through official channels to ensure transparency and accountability at the governance level.
- **Engagement with PTOs and PTAs:** Share updates with parent-teacher organizations to involve parents in the progress and gather feedback from the community.
- **Reports to community organizations:** Communicate progress with community organizations like Rotary Clubs, homeowners' associations, and the city council to foster community involvement, support, and goodwill.
- **District and school communication channels:** Use electronic newsletters, special video productions, and online platforms to reach a broader audience within the district and school communities, ensuring accessibility and engagement.

11. Craft the Shared Vision, Mission, and Values

With the initial phase of implementation underway, assemble a representative group of supportive individuals to initiate the drafting process for the written shared vision, shared mission, and organizational values. This group should establish and communicate an iterative process for gathering feedback from all stakeholders and refine the language until there is widespread support. The final language should be recommended to the board of education for adoption, which emphasizes its significance as the school district's new North Star.

12. Reinforce and Sustain the Shared Vision

To strengthen and sustain the shared vision as the implementation of the PCBS progresses—particularly during the initial years, until it becomes totally embedded within the organization—consistent and intentional reinforcement is crucial. This can be accomplished by doing the following.

- Begin all leader and staff meetings with participants sharing real-life examples of the shared vision in practice within their schools or classrooms.
- Ensure high visibility of the shared vision on the school district's website and in all published district materials and newsletters distributed to stakeholders, such as the annual budget book, planning documents, grant applications, event notices, and hiring materials.

- Establish a periodic review process to refresh and reinvigorate the shared vision throughout the school year.
- Conclude regularly scheduled board meetings by reciting the shared vision.
- Invite stakeholders into the school district to witness the implementation firsthand by organizing school visits where they can interact with students, teachers, and school leaders.
- Encourage and support students, teachers, and leaders, including board of education members, to share their experiences and tell their stories at conferences, symposia, conventions, and similar events.

Creation of the WPS Shared Vision

Transforming a traditional school district to a PCBS does not start with concrete action steps. It starts with the leaders of the district having shared experiences that convince them of the need to make such a transformation and provide firsthand interactions with schools and districts that have already undergone this transformation. To this end, WPS spent considerable time and energy seeking out relevant common experiences. We recommend that all districts and schools undertake a similar journey.

As mentioned earlier in the chapter, several WPS leaders attended a conference showcasing Chugach School District's successful transformation to CBE in December 2006. Returning to WPS, the board of education secretary, a former high school mathematics teacher, briefed district leadership on her reflections and urged a deeper exploration of systemic standards-based concepts. The team unanimously agreed to delve further into the information shared and discussed potential next steps. The decision to move forward with exploration was driven by two primary factors: (1) the sudden, substantial increase in accountability expectations in Colorado, coupled with severe sanctions for failure, and (2) the district's groundwork from the prior decade, including the development of more coherent, robust standards; aligned assessments measuring growth; and the integration of technological tools for monitoring student progress. The valuable lessons from the previous decade were deemed crucial for informed decision making as the district moved forward.

Proactive Approach to Accountability

In anticipation of the increased accountability challenges due to a continued decline in state-level student scores, district leadership proactively sought a systems appraisal audit to address persistent performance issues. Acknowledging the need for genuine reform through critical system evaluation, the district collaborated with the Colorado Department of Education, and in December 2006, a team of state-approved educational leaders specializing in curriculum and instruction, assessment, systems design, and leadership conducted a thorough six-day Comprehensive Appraisal for District Improvement audit.

In early spring 2007, guided by the thematic findings of the CADI audit and the new state requirements, district leaders initiated a strategic planning process involving all stakeholders using an outside consultant as a facilitator. The aim was to fulfill the commitment of ensuring every student possesses the skills and knowledge essential for success as a 21st century citizen. Four key goals, along with associated strategies and actions, were formulated to address the moral imperative of preparing students as 21st century learners and citizens ready to contribute to the community workforce. The overarching strategic plan goals were as follows.

1. Implement effective academic programs to raise student performance to the highest levels in the state.
2. Foster school-community and business partnerships that embrace the community's diversity and nurture student success.
3. Operate with fiscal responsibility to maximize resource effectiveness and efficiency.
4. Provide safe, secure, and adequate school facilities.

Implementation of the strategic goals commenced in the fall of 2007, coinciding with the initial stages of planning for the development of a PCBS, then referred to as the standards-based system. As the shared vision for a PCBS crystallized, especially during the 2008–2009 school year, the execution of the newly adopted five-year strategic plan became more complex. The actual rollout of the PCBS was scheduled for the fall of 2009. Despite the timeline adjustments, the planning and execution of the system aligned seamlessly with the first goal identified in the strategic plan. Over time, the strategies and actions in the strategic plan were aligned with the new PCBS model for learning.

During the two-year learning phase, it became increasingly clear that a flexible, integrated, and robust learning management system (LMS) was essential for translating student learning data into actionable instructional steps. Being able to leverage the LMS to enhance student learning outcomes and to predict future performance was desired. District leadership, well aware of past technical challenges, recognized the difficulty of electronically scoring and tracking student progress in real time. The envisioned LMS needed to be student- or standard-centric and capable of efficiently processing a substantial volume of on-demand data, spanning multiple years, and accommodating simultaneous use by teachers and students. Such an LMS would bolster and reinforce the four tenets of the PCBS model.

Preparation for Transformative Second-Order Change

With the heightened urgency stemming from the Academic Watch designation for the 2006–2007 school year, declining test scores, insights from the CADI audit, a new strategic plan, and a wealth of historical institutional knowledge, the environment was conducive for comprehensive second-order change. The goal was to consistently align curriculum, instruction, assessment, recording, and reporting across all schools, freeing learning from rigid time constraints. The shift away from loose site-based management, which led to a lack of a unified district focus, underutilization of expertise across sites, and a deficiency in meaningful ways to acknowledge and celebrate student and teacher success districtwide, became a moral imperative.

District leadership was fully prepared for significant holistic change, utilizing a model adapted from the Re-Inventing Schools Coalition (RISC). In the summer of 2007, a group of board members, central office leaders, school administrators, and teachers attended a summer symposium, focusing on the success story from Chugach, Alaska. Following this, RISC personnel were invited to engage with all school leaders and some teacher leaders in WPS, sharing insights from the successful transformation in the Chugach School District. This engagement generated momentum and even some consternation among school and teacher leaders, who wanted to see the Chugach model in action. In January 2007, thirty-four WPS personnel traveled to Chugach to observe their learning model in action and hear directly from teachers, students, and parents.

Following the Chugach trip, several professional learning days were dedicated to analyzing the RISC model and adapting it for a larger suburban school district while considering the negative influence of the state's accountability model that had the potential for parents and students to choose alternative schooling options. Despite professional learning opportunities, many questions lingered about how the RISC model could function in the context of WPS, as a widespread literature base for implementing CBE was severely lacking in 2007. While overall parental support was strong in moving forward, especially given the flexibility in the innovative approach for their students, some high school parents had reservations and expressed concerns about their child's grade point average and potential impacts on college entry. Consequently, some parents chose to leave the district, favoring the perceived clarity of college success garnered from the traditional model.

Teacher support for the new learning approach varied initially, with stronger backing from high school teachers and much less from K–2 primary educators. While teachers appreciated the model's principles, concerns surfaced about implementation logistics and the requisite tools and skills. Prior to the final decision to embark on the PCBS journey, teachers were given the opportunity to vote based on their support for moving forward with implementation beginning in fall 2009. Recognizing the need for a majority coalition for successful second-order change, WPS set an 80 percent threshold for teacher and instructional staff support, as they were most directly affected. A collective vote took place in the high school auditorium, which garnered only 75 percent of instructional staff in favor of the proposed change, falling short of the district's required threshold, prompting a hold on implementation plans. While some staff were relieved, the majority expressed visible disappointment.

Principals were tasked with identifying the specific needs of their schools to achieve or surpass the 80 percent support threshold. Several schools were already at the 100 percent support level, but others were still wary and required more details on how the innovative approach could be implemented effectively as well as permission to experiment and learn from mistakes. During targeted school visits, district leadership encountered varied levels of support. Acknowledging that shifts of this magnitude often result in an implementation dip in student achievement, district leadership emphasized patience, tolerance for ambiguity, and a mindset of continuous improvement—comparing the process to building an airplane while flying it.

After these efforts, a second vote was held, this time at the school level, and when aggregated to the district level, the results exceeded the 80 percent threshold. At Metz Elementary School (now the Metropolitan Arts Academy), staff were particularly inspired by the innovative approach and volunteered to pilot elements of the new model during the 2008–2009 school year. Their focus was on the competency-based design component of the WPS learning model, specifically in the areas of standards and assessments. This pilot provided an early example of how attending to the five key components of the WPS learning model could guide schools toward a successful transition to PCBS.

Curriculum and Instructional Frameworks

Building on the progress made in the mid-2000s with information-based educational practices to clarify learning and drawing on insights from Robert J. Marzano and John S. Kendall's (1998) report *Awash in a Sea of Standards*, it soon became evident that the district needed to streamline the number of required learning outcomes for all students. In fall 2007, the district, working with Marzano, created measurement topics and aligned assessments for ten content areas. This was a critical step toward establishing a guaranteed and viable curriculum. Each content area was assigned ten teachers, forming the WPS "Marzano 100" group. Work commenced in January 2008, focusing on drafting standards and measurement topics for all ten content areas: (1) literacy, (2) mathematics, (3) science, (4) social studies, (5) physical education, (6) performing arts, (7) visual arts, (8) personal social, (9) technology, and (10) world languages.

Figure 1.1 depicts an early example of the measurement topic for level 1 (first-grade mathematics) created from that joint effort. Note that chapter 3 (page 53) addresses the format of measurement topics like this in detail.

Strand: Numbers and Operations	
Topic: Addition and Subtraction	
Level 1	
Score 4.0	In addition to score 3.0, in-depth inferences and applications that go beyond what was taught such as: • Using addition and subtraction with simple numbers
Score 3.5	In addition to score 3.0 performance, in-depth inferences and applications with partial success.
Score 3.0	While engaged in tasks regarding whole numbers, the student: • Manipulates sets to simulate addition and subtraction with simple numbers
Score 2.5	No major errors or omissions regarding the simpler details and process and partial knowledge of the more complex ideas and procedures.
Score 2.0	There are no major errors or omissions regarding the simpler details and processes as the student: • Recognizes or recalls specific terminology such as + Addition or subtraction • Performs basic tasks such as: + Explaining addition and subtraction (symbols) However, the student exhibits major errors or omissions regarding the more complex ideas or processes.
Score 1.5	Partial knowledge of the simpler details and processes but major errors or omissions regarding the more complex ideas and procedures.
Score 1.0	With help, a partial understanding of some of the simpler details and processes and some of the more complex ideas and processes.
Score 0.5	With help, a partial understanding of some of the simpler details and processes but not the more complex ideas and processes.
Score 0.0	Even with help, no understanding or skill demonstrated.

Source: © 2024 by Westminster Public Schools. Used with permission.

FIGURE 1.1: Westminster Public Schools measurement topic.

Primary curricular resources that existed at that time, such as Everyday Mathematics (University of Chicago School Mathematics Project, 2007) and Open Court (McGraw-Hill Education, 2005) at the elementary level, were aligned and integrated with the measurement topics. As a side benefit, this process made clear that measurement topics were the driving force for instruction and not the textbook. Upon completion of all the measurement topics for all content areas, the Marzano 100 was reduced to the Marzano 40. This group was then assigned the task of creating aligned sample tasks amenable to electronic scoring via Scantron scanners.

Cultural Shift and Professional Development

The initial development of measurement topics and sample tasks illustrates how this hands-on work became a tangible representation of the district's shared vision in action. It signaled a concrete, practical manifestation of the second-order transformative change that was underway. The work also provided impetus for new teacher training that would lead to more coherent and consistent classroom practices across the school district. This, in turn, assisted teachers in visualizing and embracing the new competency-based learning paradigm. The WPS shared vision was also reinforced in routine meetings and training with principals and teachers. Illustrations of optical illusions were often used to emphasize the individual "mind shift" required to visualize the new learning paradigm. The key message conveyed was that one could not perceive or actualize the new learning paradigm without being willing to let go of the old one. District leadership humorously exemplified this concept using the well-known optical illusion that originated as a German postcard in 1888 but gained popularity through British cartoonist William Ely Hill (1915), who named it "My Wife and My Mother-in-Law"; see figure 1.2.

When observing the image, one can perceive either an old woman or a young woman, but not both simultaneously. This illustrated to WPS educators the necessary shift in beliefs, assumptions, actions, and interactions required for each teacher and leader to wholeheartedly embrace the second-order transformative change for implementing a PCBS. The transition to CBE necessitates a complete paradigm shift. It is an all-or-nothing proposition.

WPS district administrators also recognized the school leaders must expand and hone their skills for guiding second-order change with their teachers, students, and parents amid often stressful and dynamic circumstances. To expand leadership skills among administrators, WPS used Robert J. Marzano, Timothy Waters, and Brian A. McNulty's (2005) *School Leadership That Works*, as well as the Westminster Leadership Toolbox, which provided several mental models for navigating change with expertise.

Source: Hill, 1915.

FIGURE 1.2: My Wife and My Mother-in-Law.

Continuous Reflection and Evolution

As the WPS PCBS implementation progressed, continuous reflections occurred, leading to updates, revisions, and revitalization of the district's shared vision. Initially, there were often misunderstandings regarding the difference between the vision and the mission. To clarify, WPS defined its vision as aspirational, like John F. Kennedy's declaration to put a man on the moon by the end of the 1960s, while its mission outlined the operational details, as seen in NASA's undertaking of that goal. It is essential to help all stakeholders understand that a vision is inspirational, whereas a mission is practical and action oriented.

In WPS, the shared vision encompasses the shared mission, leadership values, and operating principles (see figure 1.3, page 28). While this integrated approach worked well for WPS, every district must consider their particular context, priorities, and stakeholder needs to determine whether this model is the best fit for their PCBS efforts. Adapting the framework to the specific circumstances of your district is necessary to ensure its effectiveness. The values and operating principles of leadership emerged later, in response to implementation challenges encountered in the field, which were primarily due to a lack of clarity. These agreements also proved beneficial for new personnel who joined WPS after the initial creation and deployment of the PCBS.

Westminster Public Schools
Where Education Is Personal

Vision

Preparing future leaders, learners, and thinkers for a global community.

Mission

Westminster Public Schools will create opportunities to develop competent, agile learners who will contribute to their community and achieve personal success.

Our Values and Operating Principles of Leadership

1. **We Agree** to prepare students for the day after graduation and promote entrepreneurial thinking, college and workforce readiness.
2. **We Agree** to respect our community through culturally responsive instructional and communicative practices.
3. **We Agree** to create and maintain a positive district culture through clear communication and a demonstration of competency, self-accountability, mutual respect, and collective effort.
4. **We Agree** to customize and demonstrate a balance of best instructional practices as outlined in the Westminster Public Schools Learner-Centered, Competency-Based Instructional Model.
5. **We Agree** to promote positive and trusting relationships with all stakeholders, through honesty and transparency, where people come first.
6. **We Agree** to expect our students and adults to be challenged through deep and critical thinking and problem-based learning opportunities at or above current levels of competency.
7. **We Agree** to develop personalized learning pathways for students through collaboration, student ownership, goal setting, and tracking performance.
8. **We Agree** that we will better our craft through personal and professional development, collaboration and continuous improvement with specific professional goal setting aligned to the evaluation tool, using data, and the instructional model.
9. **We Agree** to embrace technology as a tool to enhance highly engaged teaching and learning.
10. **We Agree** that adults will provide aligned and targeted learning opportunities for students to read, write, speak, actively listen and think critically every day.

Created by the District Leadership Team 2014 with input from Teachers, Staff, and the Community

Source: © 2024 by Westminster Public Schools. Used with permission.

FIGURE 1.3: Westminster Public Schools vision, mission, and leadership values and operating principles.

Ways to Sustain the Shared Vision

To guarantee the ongoing success of the PCBS and drive continual improvement, it is crucial to establish regular rituals and practices in reinforcing the shared vision. These rituals serve as signals to both internal and external stakeholders that the new learning approach is not a passing phase. In education, many innovative practices have suffered and withered away because they were not deeply integrated into classroom practice or were unfortunately perceived as the sole creation of one person who had not garnered extended ownership and leadership. For long-term success, it is essential to avoid the mentality of "this too shall pass" by establishing and continuing to strengthen the moral imperative for improving outcomes for students and teachers.

While these actions proved effective in sustaining WPS's shared vision, districts should not merely adopt but instead adapt them to fit their unique needs. Even with adaptation, the underlying principle remains the same: consistent rituals and practices keep the shared vision as the guiding force, embedding it within the district instead of leaving it an abstract ideal. By adopting and adapting these strategies, other districts can foster long-term sustainability and commitment from stakeholders to realize their own shared vision. Important rituals and practices that WPS has executed include the following.

1. **Board resolution:** Every August, the WPS Board of Education signals its collective support for the ongoing implementation of the PCBS to staff, parents, and the community. This is achieved by adopting and disseminating an updated resolution that includes the latest expectations for system improvement and evolution.
2. **Measurable progress:** WPS has established mechanisms to demonstrate the positive impact of the innovative approach to learning. Specifically, WPS developed an illustrative display to depict the aggregate annual progression of student achievement in schools. What became known as the color chart utilizes the state's accreditation designations for each school and the district to highlight the overall academic improvement from year to year. The charts list each school's school performance framework score measured by performance on the spring state assessments, with one of four colors denoting the school's state designation category based on its score: red and orange are considered "on watch," while yellow and green are considered "performing." A context-specific example appears in chapter 5 (page 143) as it relates to continuous improvement.
3. **Progress monitoring:** During the initial implementation phase, WPS regularly monitored the progress of all five components of a PCBS each semester (December and May) using a self-assessment rubric; see figure 1.4 (page 30). The rubric aimed to facilitate reflection on the status of implementation practices and strategically plan next steps. Staff individually indicated their perceived stage of implementation (basic, partially proficient, proficient, accomplished, or exemplary). These individual results were then aggregated to provide an overall school picture and then discussed in a subsequent staff meeting. The results from schools were further aggregated to the district level.

Shared Vision				
The shared vision establishes the collective purpose of an organization. It is derived from the commonly held beliefs and values of all the stakeholders involved with the organization and drives the daily work toward continued improvement.				
Traits include: • Voices of all staff, all students, administrators, and parents to create a preferred future for all learners • Actions that support the creation and deployment of the shared vision and code of cooperation with and for all learners • Aligned goals, action plans, timelines, key performance indicators that drive the Unified Improvement Plan (UIP)				
Basic	**Partially Proficient**	**Proficient**	**Accomplished**	**Exemplary**
Shared vision (vision, mission, code of cooperation, values, beliefs, and goals) is:				
Displayed in all classrooms	Part of all routine school communications with staff and other stakeholders	Focused on student achievement	Parents know the shared vision, can explain and support it	Staff and parents collaboratively implement strategies to address the school's shared vision
Displayed and explained on the school website	Integrated into school programs	Classroom shared vision processes and expectations mirror that of the school	Staff identify and address barriers to achieving the shared vision	Staff and parents assume leadership roles in updating the school's shared vision
Familiar to all stakeholders	Fosters a healthy professional learning community	Students know the shared vision, its purpose, and how it drives their work	Students lead the revision and reinvigoration process	School shared vision processes are used as exemplars
Developed through a collaborative process including staff and other stakeholder groups		Students are able to explain their contribution in its creation	Each iteration of the shared vision goes deeper and builds on the previous version	
Aligned with distinct priorities				
Routinely updated				

Source: © 2024 by Westminster Public Schools. Used with permission.

FIGURE 1.4: Rubric for the shared vision component of the PCBS.

Over the years, the WPS progress-monitoring process has undergone multiple iterations. In addition to the semester self-assessment check and prompted by feedback from our accountability partner Cognia, monthly learning walks were introduced. These were conducted by representative teams using the Effective Learning Environments Observation Tool (eleot®) to gather systems-level data on seven elements: (1) equitable learning environment, (2) high expectations environment, (3) supportive learning environment, (4) active learning environment, (5) progress monitoring and feedback environment, (6) well-managed learning environment, and (7) digital learning environment. This tool prompted users to observe and record what students were doing rather than teachers. While the eleot provided valuable systems-level data for accountability, it proved less specific for instructional purposes. This highlighted the necessity of aligning the observation process with the Westminster Instructional Model (WIM) to collect more detailed data on embedded instructional practices while focusing on student learning behaviors, leading to the further evolution of the learning walk process.

As of 2023, WPS transitioned its progress-monitoring method to fully integrate with the district's High Reliability Schools process, based on the work of Robert J. Marzano, Phil Warrick, and Julia A. Simms (2014). This comprehensive HRS approach, which WPS adapted and personalized to meet its unique needs, encompassed all components and tenets of authentic personalized competency-based systems while addressing both accountability and instructional outcomes within the shared vision. The following practices, established prior to the district's adoption of the HRS framework, now serve as examples of how the tenets provided a robust mechanism to sustain and deepen the shared district vision. These practices align with the systemic, interconnected nature of PCBE and illustrate how WPS operationalized its commitment to continuous improvement. The transition to HRS is explored in greater detail later in chapter 6 (page 171).

1. **School and classroom shared visions:** Every school in WPS develops its unique shared vision and mission that reflects the distinctiveness of the school and its community in a process like the one already outlined. Likewise, each classroom establishes its own shared vision and code of cooperation that mirror the values and aspirations of the students. More detailed information about the classroom shared vision can be found in chapter 4 (page 119). Typically, the creation of the shared vision at the school and classroom levels extends and sustains ownership and leadership of the district shared vision.
2. **School visits:** WPS consistently provides both virtual and in-person opportunities for teachers, school and district leaders, and other individuals interested in learning about and visiting WPS schools. These experiences

offer a firsthand look at personalized competency-based education in action. The visits reinforce and strengthen the underlying beliefs and importance of the shared vision among all leaders, including board of education members, teachers, and students, while simultaneously recognizing and acknowledging their dedicated efforts in moving the system forward. All board members, leaders, and staff participate in sharing their knowledge and expertise during these visits, and this furthers broad embeddedness and sustainability.

3. **CBE summits:** WPS also hosts a three-day CBE summit biennially to provide attendees a firsthand glimpse at personalized learning in action, which includes school visits to classrooms, tailored CBE sessions, and keynote addresses from influential speakers. These rituals and processes not only strengthen and embed the shared vision but also highlight the dynamic interconnectedness of all system components and tenets. It is impractical to entirely separate any single component from the others, and that's precisely why WPS incorporates the word "system" in the title of the PCBS.

Final Thoughts

The journey to implement a PCBS is one of profound transformation, requiring a deep commitment to systemic change and a willingness to embrace new paradigms of learning and leadership. As this chapter has outlined, the creation of a shared vision is not merely a preliminary step but a sustaining force that drives and unites all efforts toward achieving the desired future state. By ensuring this vision is collaboratively developed, clearly articulated, and consistently reinforced, school districts can build the collective efficacy necessary to navigate the challenges of second-order change. The success of such a transformation lies in the shared commitment of all stakeholders to a common purpose, a commitment that must be nurtured and maintained throughout the entire journey. In the end, the shared vision becomes the living embodiment of the district's aspirations, guiding its path forward and ensuring that every decision and action contribute to the overarching goal of creating a more equitable, student-centered learning environment.

CHAPTER 2

Leadership at All Levels

Leading a school district through second-order change requires a multifaceted array of strategies and skills that go beyond conventional top-down or bottom-up management approaches. This complexity is starkly evident in WPS's implementation of its PCBS. This process can be compared to the rhythmic ebb and flow of tides along a shoreline, symbolizing the fluid interaction of leadership at various levels within the organization. Just as a shoreline's character is shaped by both the ebb and the flow, effective organizational transformation depends on the balance of top-down and bottom-up leadership. Top-down leadership provides clear vision and structure, while bottom-up leadership ensures stakeholder engagement and practical insights. Neither alone will suffice; together, however, they create the exact synergy required to ensure sustainable change. The absence of either leads to stagnation rather than progress. In this chapter, we will explore leading a district through second-order change, using leadership frameworks to guide leaders at all levels, understanding and implementing systemic change, empowering voices, creating leadership cabinets, ensuring effective messaging with parents and the community, navigating board dynamics and policy implementation, and sustaining leadership at all levels.

Leading a School District Through Second-Order Change

When a school district chooses to implement a PCBS, it is also choosing to lead its people through second-order change—discussed in chapter 1 (page 11) as new systemic changes to which individuals in an organization must adapt and indeed commit (Fullan, 2001). To achieve this, school and district administrators must cultivate a sense of ownership in the change initiative, which necessitates a distributive leadership approach. WPS refers to this approach as "leadership at all levels." This is not just a slogan but a strategic and intentional leadership design that fosters commitment to the PCBS at every level of the district—even in roles that do not hold formal leadership titles.

The journey toward implementing a PCBS in WPS began with developing a compelling shared vision. This transformative process affected not just the faculty and staff but also students, parents, and the broader community. The district needed to answer a critical question: Why us, and why now? As discussed in chapter 1, this dialogue was crucial in acknowledging that the traditional educational system was effectively serving only a fraction of its students. Recognizing this reality brought many members of the community together around the urgent need for change, and this collective realization became the driving force behind a more inclusive and effective educational approach.

With a shared vision established, the next step for district leadership was to cultivate a culture of genuine collaboration. Creating leadership at all levels necessitated ensuring every individual felt their perspectives were valued and seriously considered. While this might seem intuitive, research shows the approach leaders take to solicit and respond to input impacts the trust and collaboration they can expect. Harvard Business School professor of leadership Amy Edmondson (2019) highlighted that genuine collaboration requires psychological safety. Individuals must believe their input is not only welcomed but also acted on. Leaders who fail to demonstrate authenticity in seeking input risk fostering mistrust, as staff can quickly recognize disingenuous efforts. Such mistrust can undermine organizational culture and hinder progress toward shared goals.

WPS was aware of this and understood that any structure designed to foster leadership at all levels must include actionable ways for district and school leaders to thoughtfully consider and implement suggestions and feedback from all stakeholders. To facilitate this, WPS established the superintendent's cabinets—a series of working groups composed of diverse stakeholders from across the district. These cabinets collaborated directly with the superintendent and her team to help find and lead the best path forward (these cabinets will be discussed in more detail later in this chapter).

Using Leadership Frameworks to Guide Leaders at All Levels

With formalized structures in place to support leadership at all levels, the next step for district leadership was to equip these leaders with the necessary tools and support to effectively guide their spheres of influence through the second-order change. For instance, how should a teacher selected to serve on the superintendent's teacher leadership cabinet approach the task of explaining the benefits of performance-based grouping or the lesson planning adjustments that come with a new instructional model to their colleagues back at school? Similarly, how should a school front office manager communicate changes in enrollment practices discussed at the superintendent's support staff cabinet meeting?

Recognizing that many of these leaders were not formally trained in leadership and did not hold official titles of authority, it was crucial for the district to provide them with effective leadership strategies. Over the years, WPS developed a comprehensive set of frameworks designed to guide strategic thinking and decision making for individuals leading in various capacities across the district. These frameworks, known internally as the WPS Leadership Toolbox, became essential to ensuring effective leadership at all levels, including formal leaders such as school principals and district-level directors.

The WPS Leadership Toolbox evolved to include over fifty different frameworks, each tailored to address specific aspects of leadership and change management. This toolbox gave WPS leaders a range of options to reference, depending on the challenge or change initiative they were tasked with leading. While the WPS Leadership Toolbox comprises a wide variety of frameworks all designed for different leadership purposes, this chapter focuses specifically on John Kotter's change management model. This model was selected due to its applicability in guiding significant second-order change, such as the transition to a PCBS. Although the other frameworks are not detailed here, they remain critical components of the WPS Leadership Toolbox and contribute to the district's ongoing leadership development. Let us explore how WPS utilized Kotter's model during the district's initial transition to a PCBS.

Understanding and Implementing Systemic Change

The topic of organizational change is widely discussed in the literature, with many experts, including John P. Kotter (1996), offering detailed explanations of its concepts. Later works, such as Ronald Heifetz, Alexander Grashow, and Marty Linsky (2009); Edmondson (2019); and Michael Fullan and Joanne Quinn (2016), highlight the interplay between the theoretical understanding of change and the practical skills needed to navigate it effectively. Familiar with this, WPS took a distinctive approach, emphasizing that the true essence of leading second-order change lies in understanding not merely the theoretical process of change, as shown in figure 2.1, but how leaders guide and implement it. In other words, both the what of change and the how to implement it are critical in driving systemic change.

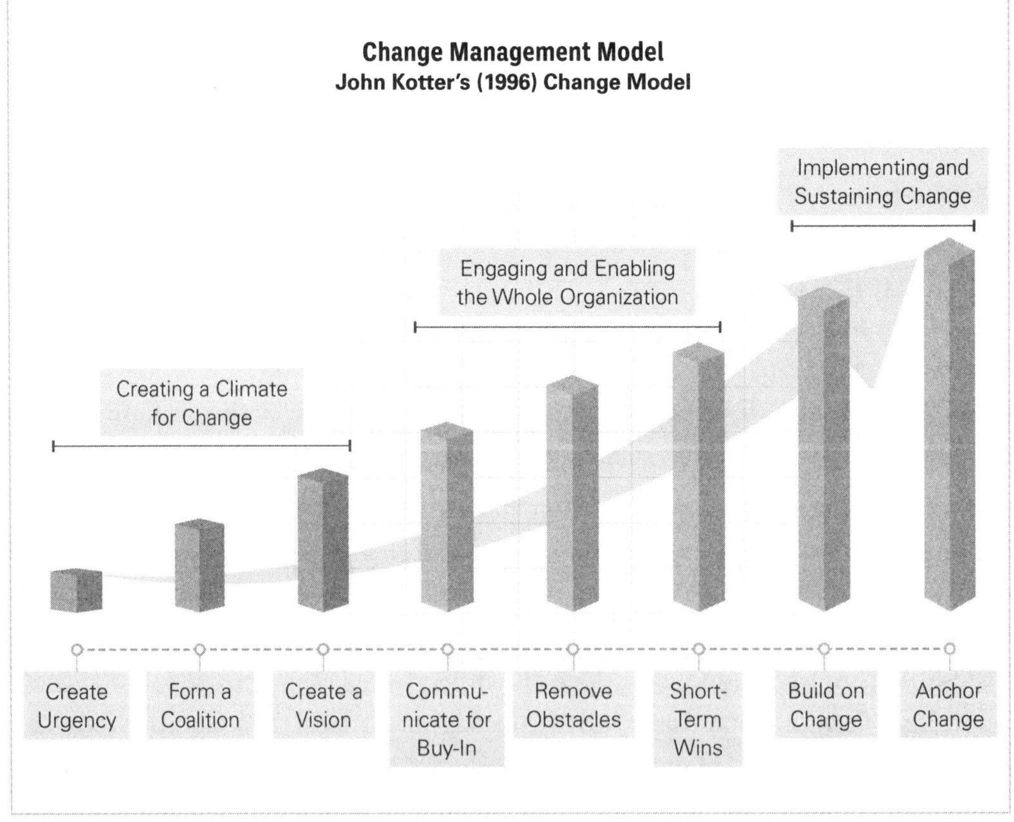

Source: © 1996 by John Kotter. Adapted with permission.

FIGURE 2.1: Kotter's change management model.

Leading systemic change, such as adopting a PCBS within a school district, is not a static process; it is fluid and requires the ability to adapt quickly to evolving circumstances. This type of change involves making deep, systemic modifications to the organization's structure, culture, and processes. As second-order change is implemented, leaders often encounter resistance, which is a natural part of the change process. It can be tempting for leaders to focus on the immediate symptoms of this resistance—such as pushback from staff and disruptions in workflow—without addressing the underlying causes.

This is where leadership frameworks that focus on root cause identification become essential. These frameworks guide leaders in diagnosing the true source of resistance rather than merely treating the symptoms. By identifying and addressing the root causes, leaders can tackle the genuine issues that are hindering progress, thereby fostering sustained forward momentum and ensuring the change takes hold across the organization. This approach not only helps in overcoming resistance but also strengthens the overall implementation of the change initiative, leading to more effective and lasting outcomes.

WPS recognized that while understanding leadership frameworks like Kotter's (1996) change management model protocol is essential, the challenge lies in applying this framework effectively. It is not just about knowing the steps in a model or protocol; the true difficulty is in guiding people successfully through those steps to achieve the intended outcomes.

In practice, this means going beyond theoretical models and equipping leaders at all levels with practical strategies for implementation tailored to their unique contexts within the school district. These strategies needed to be adaptable, enabling leaders to respond in real time to the challenges inherent in second-order change. District leadership emphasizes the importance of context, recognizing that while the principles of change management are universal, the strategies for applying them must be customized to meet the specific needs of each school or department within the district.

Empowering Leadership Voices From the Ground Up

Over time, district leaders in WPS recognized the importance of managing the velocity of change when pursuing full systemic transformation. While there are moments when accelerating progress is necessary, there are also times when it is crucial to tap the brakes. The goal is to maintain consistent progress without overwhelming the system. For those leading the change, the need to slow down can be frustrating, but it is essential to understand that nurturing the internal culture requires ongoing, almost daily attention.

A key component of WPS's strategy was fostering a strong, collaborative relationship with the district's union leadership. This partnership was critical in advancing the implementation of the PCBS. Early on, it became evident that the new system would demand more from instructional staff, particularly in areas like recording and reporting student progress. Initially, the process of problem solving and maintaining clear, collaborative communication between the union and the district was challenging. However, as the relationship matured, this collaborative approach became the standard operating procedure (SOP), allowing both parties to work together effectively in navigating the complexities of systemic change.

One significant outcome was the development of a new type of salary schedule for licensed staff, which became a win-win solution for both the district and its educators. The traditional salary schedule, with its numerous vertical steps based solely on teacher tenure, was redesigned into a more streamlined system. Offering higher salaries allows educators to feel valued and supported, encouraging them to focus on professional growth, collaboration, and innovation. When this occurs, it creates the environment necessary for leadership to emerge naturally at all levels, as faculty and staff alike are more likely to take initiative, share expertise, and assume ownership toward the collective success of their schools and the district.

This new compensation structure features fewer steps based on experience and places a greater emphasis on incentivizing educators to enhance their professional competencies. The compressed salary table has become a model for rewarding professionals in a manner that aligns with their personal growth and expertise. As of 2024, WPS's licensed salary schedule offers the highest salaries in Colorado and has gained national attention for its innovative approach. Although each district's budget reality is unique, a high salary scale can become feasible if the district is willing to prioritize competitive compensation as a foundation for building a collaborative, growth-oriented culture that encourages leadership development and professional excellence.

While instructional staff often serve as the focal point during systemic organizational changes, it is equally important to engage noninstructional staff as leaders within the community. Often, as was the case in WPS, these employees make up the largest segment of the workforce within a school district. During the initial stages of piloting and implementing the PCBS, noninstructional support staff were actively involved in understanding the rationale behind the system and received professional development to support its adoption. Their ownership, input, and impact made significant contributions to the initiative's success. To parallel the salary schedule provided to licensed staff, the district developed a highly competitive compensation package for all noninstructional support staff, rivaling those offered in the private sector. This initiative fostered an environment where all employees felt valued, significantly enhancing the district's culture.

District leaders also established a leadership cabinet specifically for nonlicensed support staff within the school district, which further cultivated ambassadors for the PCBS, both internally and externally. This initiative ensured support staff were not only included in the transformation process but also empowered to advocate for the system, enhancing its acceptance and implementation across the entire district.

Creating Leadership Cabinets

The superintendent leadership cabinets were established as a strategic method to elicit collaborative decision making across the district. Composed of various stakeholder groups, these cabinets—ranging from students and parents to teachers, support staff, and administrators—served as avenues for gathering needed perspectives and providing open communication to help inform the district on the best way to move the PCBS forward. By empowering leaders at all levels of the organization to participate in shaping policies and practices, the leadership cabinets play a critical role in cultivating a unified vision and maintaining the momentum of systemic change across the district.

In hindsight, the management team structure with the executive leadership, superintendent, and school board as members became the first of several leadership cabinets. These cabinets provided information that promoted a healthy organizational culture and made decisions related to the systemic changes in the competency-based framework.

- **Student leadership cabinet:** Composed of ten to fifteen high school students, this cabinet focuses on providing student perspectives on district initiatives and the impact of PCBS in classrooms. Meeting monthly, the group often addresses issues such as grading practices, learning environments, and student life.
- **Parent leadership cabinet:** With fifteen to twenty members, this cabinet consists of parents representing every school across the district. Meeting monthly, the cabinet provides input on school accountability, district budget priorities, and how district decisions and PCBS implementation affect families, ensuring the community's voice influences district policies and practices.
- **Support professionals cabinet:** This group consists of fifteen to twenty members representing roles such as paraprofessionals, custodial staff, and office personnel. The cabinet meets quarterly to discuss how PCBS impacts operational and logistic areas of the district. It also discusses noninstructional considerations as they relate to wider district operational decision making.

- **Teacher leadership cabinet:** With one representative from each school, this cabinet includes educators who meet monthly to address instructional challenges, propose solutions, and offer feedback on the implementation of PCBS. The cabinet acts as a bridge between teachers and district leadership, ensuring classroom-level concerns are addressed systematically.
- **Instructional cabinet:** Consisting of ten to fifteen district and school instructional leaders, including instructional coaches and curriculum specialists, teachers, principals, and learning services directors, this cabinet meets monthly to align the PCBS framework with instructional strategies. Their focus is on integrating proficiency scales, assessments, and resources across schools to maintain consistency and quality in teaching and learning.
- **Principal advisory cabinet:** This group of school principals meets monthly to collaborate on school-level implementation of PCBS, sharing best practices and discussing common barriers. The purpose is to ensure alignment between district initiatives and the unique needs of individual schools, as well as providing a framework for the district to better understand the challenges experienced at the school level.
- **Administrative cabinet:** Including fifteen to twenty district-level administrators from departments such as human resources, finance, operations, and learning services as well as school-level administrators from select schools to ensure preK–12 representation, this cabinet meets monthly to discuss the operational and systemic changes required to support PCBS. Their purpose is to ensure the district's infrastructure aligns with the instructional goals of the framework.
- **Senior leadership cabinet:** Composed of the superintendent and the district's executive team (eight to ten members), this cabinet meets weekly to guide high-level decision making. They focus on setting priorities, allocating resources, and maintaining accountability for PCBS implementation across all levels of the district.

Each cabinet was a valuable tool for the ambassadors, enabling them to gather feedback from their constituents, propose agenda items, and actively participate in the decision-making process for implementing necessary system adjustments. For example, when the teacher leadership cabinet began prioritizing issues within the PCBS and collaborating on potential solutions, the superintendent often scheduled a principals' meeting soon thereafter to discuss the details. In addition to keeping school leaders up to date with the teacher leadership cabinet's proposed suggestions, these follow-up meetings gave principals time to review and provide feedback before the district made any significant changes to the system.

Another advantage of this approach was that it fostered leadership and a sense of ownership in the success of the adjustments made at all levels of the organization. To ensure these cabinet discussions provided honest feedback, district leadership created an environment where meetings were perceived as safe spaces. Ground rules were established to alleviate concerns, ensuring any feedback provided—especially if it contradicted supervisors—would be held in confidence. The district recognized these groups as an integral part of the continuous improvement process, which was well understood and valued across the organization.

In addition to job classification cabinets, the district also established a student leadership cabinet, which was systematically involved in shaping district policy. For example, after a Colorado snowstorm, district leadership decided to take an unconventional approach to the situation. Since WPS was a one-to-one technology district, instead of calling for a traditional snow day, they opted to declare a remote learning day. This decision was informed by feedback from the student leadership cabinet, illustrating the cabinet's influence on district decisions and its role in the broader educational process.

During a subsequent student leadership cabinet meeting, the student-elected ambassadors initiated a discussion that led to a well-thought-out negotiation regarding remote learning. While students acknowledged the necessity of remote learning during inclement weather, they wondered if the district administration would consider a compromise. They proposed the district call traditional snow days for the first two instances of inclement weather each year, after which remote learning would resume. This compromise was also supported by parents who were experiencing postpandemic remote learning fatigue. Thanks to this thoughtful dialogue, the superintendent accepted the compromise as the new standard practice.

This example underscores a critical truth about leadership: establishing leadership cabinets is not only about hearing diverse voices but also about being committed to empowering those voices and taking meaningful action based on the feedback provided. Engaging with the unfiltered perspectives of various stakeholders can be challenging and sometimes uncomfortable for district leadership, but it ensures crucial viewpoints are considered in the decision-making process. This process illustrates how the superintendent and her leadership team prioritized genuine continuous improvement, recognizing that multidimensional communication is essential for advancing organizational change. To support this approach, they developed a model for effectively communicating and implementing change, depicted in figure 2.2 (page 44).

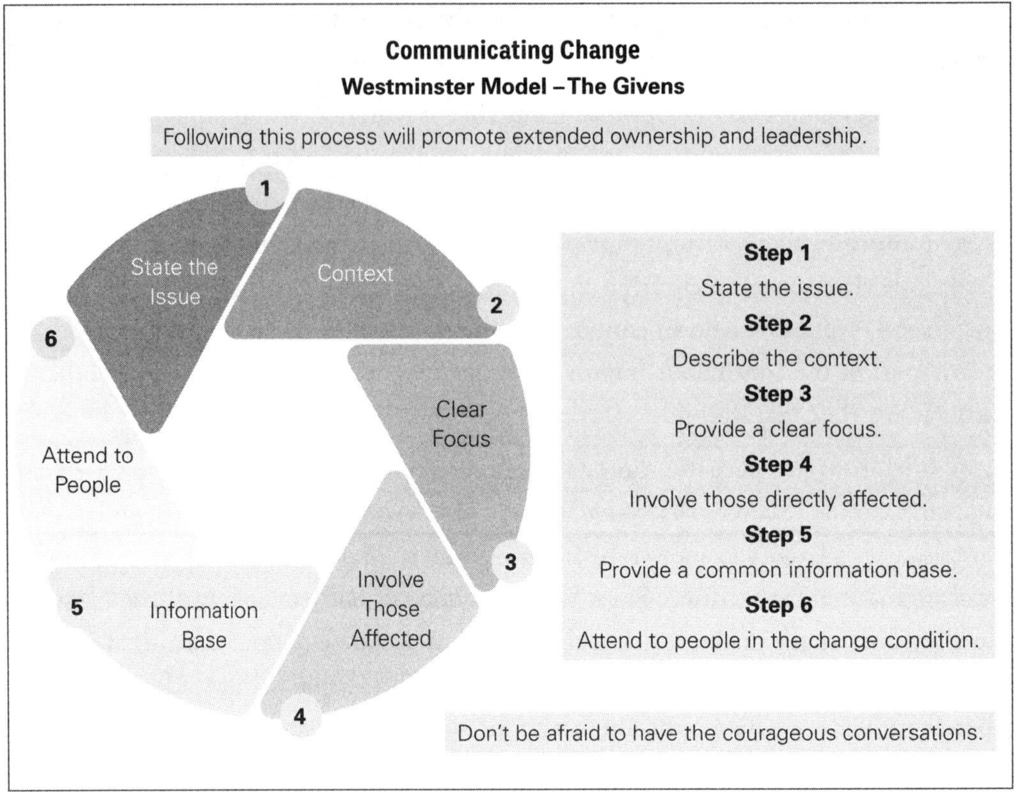

Source: © 2024 by Westminster Public Schools. Used with permission.

FIGURE 2.2: Communicating change model referred to as the "Givens."

The communicating change model, depicted in figure 2.2, illustrates a step-by-step framework for effectively guiding transformative change while ensuring collaboration and ownership among stakeholders. This model highlights the importance of clear communication and intentionally involving those most directly affected by the change, creating transparency and shared accountability. By following this six-step process, district leaders can foster an environment where feedback is valued and actionable.

1. **State the issue:** Clearly articulate the problem or challenge that needs to be addressed. This step ensures all stakeholders begin with a shared understanding of the issue at hand.
2. **Describe the context:** Provide any background information and explanation for why the issue is relevant or urgent. Context allows stakeholders to see the bigger picture and the call for action.
3. **Provide a clear focus:** Narrow the conversation to specific goals or outcomes. A clear focus prevents mission creep and aligns all efforts toward attainable objectives.

4. **Involve those directly affected:** Engage all stakeholders who are most impacted by the change. Their involvement is critical to identifying practical solutions and ensuring buy-in.
5. **Provide a common information base:** Ensure all stakeholders have access to consistent and accurate information. This ensures decisions are informed and that everyone operates from a shared foundation of knowledge.
6. **Attend to people in the change condition:** Recognize that change is hard and can create emotional and psychological impacts on stakeholders. Providing support by addressing concerns builds trust and commitment.

The note at the bottom of the model about courageous conversations highlights the importance of engaging in difficult discussions with honesty and empathy. These conversations may be, and often are, challenging, but they are essential for achieving sustained progress. The iterative nature of this model allows for ongoing reflection and adjustment, making it well-suited for second-order change initiatives like the implementation of PCBS.

This model serves as more than a communication tool; it is a practical guide for advancing transformational change while promoting extended leadership at all levels. By referencing this framework, district leadership can navigate the complexities of second-order change, address resistance constructively, and ensure alignment across all levels of the organization. Districts can adapt this model to their unique contexts, but its principles remain universally applicable for fostering collaboration, addressing challenges, and sustaining momentum for change.

Ensuring Effective Messaging and Engagement With Parents and Community

In relation to leadership at all levels, WPS believes its parent community is more than just a partner in their children's education—they can also become influential community leaders for district initiatives. This belief was particularly important in the initial stages of implementing PCBS. District leadership strategically focused their communication efforts on the parent community, delivering a unified message about the intended benefits personalized competency-based education would offer students. Leaders conveyed to parents how the personalized nature of PCBS would benefit students and how their children would progress based on their mastery of skills rather than their age or grade level. They highlighted proficiency scales and how they would provide clear, actionable feedback on students' learning. They emphasized how PCBS aimed to better prepare their child for the day after graduation by ensuring mastery of essential skills.

At times, these meetings were intimate, sometimes with just one or two parents. In every interaction, however, district leadership ensured WPS families were well informed about how the new system would enhance their children's educational experience. Many of these meetings were held during parent-teacher conferences. In the case of the first round of parent-teacher conferences to share the students' initial level placements in the content areas of mathematics, literacy, science, and social studies, district leadership collectively cleared their schedules the following day, anticipating a surge of inquiries from parents. To their surprise, no calls came through. This unexpected outcome underscored the power of early communication and transparent messaging. Parents felt reassured because they were well informed and had opportunities to ask questions in a personalized setting before the rollout. Parents also noted how they appreciated the district's acknowledgment of their children's true learning levels, whether above or below grade expectations, and they valued the tailored supports provided in response.

This experience highlighted the importance of leaders truly listening to all voices during organizational change and reinforced the value of clear, proactive communication. It became a crucial lesson, leading to ongoing reflection and continued progress in engaging the parent community as active leaders in the district's transformation efforts. By providing consistent and empathetic communication, WPS leadership earned parents' trust and fostered a sense of shared responsibility for the success of the district's students.

Navigating Board Dynamics and Policy Implementation

From the outset of WPS's personalized competency-based journey, a systemwide approach was essential. The management team concept, which emphasized collaboration among the superintendent, her team, and the board of education, proved highly effective for WPS. While the elected governing body plays a key role in policymaking and hiring the superintendent, the strong partnership between executive leadership and the board exemplifies systemic leadership both within the organization and in its external relationships.

In 2012, the WPS Board of Education faced significant challenges in maintaining cohesiveness. Frequent disagreements, power struggles, and personality conflicts created considerable distractions for the organization. However, amid these challenges, the entire board found common ground in the concept of implementing personalized competency-based education at a systemic level. A pivotal strategy that helped the board move forward was the adoption of the initial CBE resolution (see figure 2.3). This resolution, approved by the board, has since become an annual item, reaffirming the operational framework of their educational system to both the district and the broader community.

Resolution to Rename the District 50 Educational Model from Standards-Based System (SBS) to Competency-Based System (CBS)

WHEREAS in 2009 the Adams County School District 50 implemented a new learning model known as a Standards-Based System (SBS) to ensure that the focus on learning requires that all students show competency in core learning topics; and

WHEREAS District 50 is committed to ensure that all District 50 students receive a quality education based on the belief that students should attain a level of competency at one level of core content before moving on to the next level in their education; and

WHEREAS District 50 is committed to ending "social promotion" of students by placing an emphasis on measurable learning rather than advancement by seat time; and

WHEREAS now that the educational model is in the second full year of districtwide implementation, sufficient data now exists that can be used to strengthen and to streamline the educational model; and

WHEREAS extensive work with administrators, principals, teachers, support staff, the board of education, parents and students has revealed that the educational model needs adjustment to promote better understanding among parents, students, staff and the community of District 50's mission to educate every child; and

WHEREAS two of the three main focus areas of District 50 centers on the educational system and community connectedness, renaming the District 50 Educational Model to Competency-Based System focuses the district on those two areas while aligning the model better with federal "Race To the Top" policy which uses the term "competency-based learning;" and

WHEREAS District 50 has the ongoing goal of achieving proficiency as a school district to ensure Postsecondary and Workforce Readiness for all district students; now,

BE IT RESOLVED that from this date forward, based on the foregoing and to promote the mission of District 50, the Adams County School District 50 Educational Model shall be renamed and known as Competency-Based System (CBS).

DATED AND SIGNED by the Directors of the Adams County School District 50 Board of Education this 10th day of April, 2012

Source: © 2024 by Westminster Public Schools. Used with permission.

FIGURE 2.3: 2012 board-approved competency-based resolution.

Over the years, this resolution has evolved, gaining greater depth and substance with each iteration. This growth reflects the board's continued commitment to CBE, regardless of the changes in its composition. Notably, the resolution passed in January 2024 (see figure 2.4, page 48) highlights the ongoing commitment to this educational framework.

Once Westminster established a governance board that was deeply familiar with the tenets of the district's PCBS, a cultural norm began to emerge. Board members started to intuitively recruit and vet potential candidates based on their understanding and support of Westminster's educational framework. In Colorado, boards of education members are limited to two four-year terms, making this recruitment practice crucial for maintaining continuity. This proactive approach not only unified the governing board in their commitment to sustaining effective leadership but also reinforced each member's dedication to WPS's PCBS, ensuring its longevity and consistency over time.

Westminster Public Schools
Where Education Is Personal

Resolution to Continually Improve the Westminster Public Schools Competency-Based System
Resolution 2024-01-09

WHEREAS Westminster Public Schools continues its steadfast commitment to ensuring that all students receive a quality and equitable education every day based on the belief that all students shall attain competency to successfully advance to the next level; and

WHEREAS Westminster Public Schools Competency-Based System is the most effective educational model to provide flexible Anywhere Anytime learning, to address lost learning opportunities, to equip students for the skills necessary to succeed in the competitive global economy; and to meet the needs of our business community especially in response to large-scale disruptions like a Pandemic; and

WHEREAS Westminster Public Schools has high expectations for all students and staff, and "Where Education is Personal" reflects the commitment to students, staff and the community for improving educational outcomes for all; and

WHEREAS Westminster Public Schools believes every student is capable and must be a participant in their education, making choices that align with their personal interests, strengths, and aspirations, while provided opportunities to develop and exercise their agency in and out of the classroom; and

WHEREAS Westminster Public Schools recognizes the fundamental importance of fostering an inclusive and empowering educational environment for all students, regardless of their background, identity, or circumstance; and

WHEREAS Westminster Public Schools firmly commits to maintaining its position as a state leader in students obtaining industry credentials and will continue to expand on our CTE/STEM pathways for their academic and career growth. WPS actively monitors each student's academic progress, striving for 1.5 years of growth in academic areas, while also supporting their Individual Career Academic Plan (ICAP) and graduation expectations to ensure a successful "day after graduation" for all; and

WHEREAS Westminster Public Schools is committed to ending "social promotion" by ensuring honest and accurate conversations with students and parents about current academic performance and by placing greater focus and emphasis on measurable learning over time inclusive of intentional planning rather than advancement by seat time or age-based cohorts.

Source: © 2024 by Westminster Public Schools. Used with permission.

FIGURE 2.4: 2024 board-approved competency-based resolution.

Sustaining Leadership at All Levels

One of the significant challenges faced during the journey of systemic transformation in WPS was ensuring sustained leadership at all levels of the school district through effective organizational mechanisms. A strategic decision was made a few years into implementing WPS's PCBS to exclusively hire central office leaders and school principals from internal candidate pools. This decision stemmed from the belief that effective leadership requires a profound understanding of the system being supervised. PCBS poses unique challenges that require a nuanced knowledge of the district's approach, such as reporting and recording student progress, aligning policies, enabling flexible student progression, and reimagining awards and celebratory events.

To meet the demand for competent leaders, WPS established an Aspiring Leaders program aimed at recruiting and developing internal candidates for administrative roles. This two-year program provided essential professional growth, equipping future leaders with a comprehensive understanding of WPS's PCBS and strategies for implementation and sustainability. The program's success led to an expansion of leadership support initiatives, including the creation of a dean and assistant principal academy, which further nurtured new WPS leaders during their early years in these roles.

WPS also recognized that classroom teachers are leaders, responsible for guiding students within the classroom. New teachers required tailored professional learning specific to the WPS PCBS. To address this, the human resources and learning services departments designed and implemented a five-day new teacher orientation before the start of each academic year. This orientation provided foundational knowledge of the district's system, followed by ongoing professional learning and individualized attention throughout their first year. Additionally, each new teacher was paired with a trained mentor—a veteran WPS teacher designated in each school—who provided formal and informal support. These mentors helped new teachers navigate instructional resources and served as collaborative partners. What follows is a vignette further describing WPS's new teacher orientation program and its impact on supporting teachers in their transition to the district's system.

Practitioner Perspective

Enhancing New Teacher Onboarding in a Competency-Based Education District

By Mike Lynch, Executive Director of Learning Services, Westminster Public Schools

WPS district leadership recognizes that effectively onboarding new teachers into a PCBS requires a strategic and intentional approach. To ensure new educators understand the foundational concepts and possess the necessary skills to implement the system, a comprehensive five-day New Teacher Orientation and Training (NTOT) was developed. This initiative proved crucial in equipping teachers to provide personalized competency-based instruction. However, like many aspects of WPS's PCBS journey, the NTOT program has undergone significant changes over the years to better serve the needs of new educators.

Through surveys and feedback from new teachers, it became clear that retaining the intensive five-day NTOT learning format was overwhelming. In response, WPS streamlined the content, eliminating nonessential presentations and breakout sessions and focusing instead on what teachers needed to succeed in the first days and months of school. This approach shifted the NTOT from a concentrated five-day event to a more gradual process that spans the first five months of the school year.

Key aspects of NTOT are now embedded into monthly meetings and support groups, such as teacher mentors, literacy and mathematics leads, data and assessment facilitators, and learning management system facilitators. This enables new teachers to absorb critical information about the PCBS in manageable, bite-sized chunks over time, reinforcing learning and allowing for more effective implementation.

To help new teachers visualize how the PCBS functions in practice, WPS introduced the concept of "model classrooms." Each principal coordinates with a teacher to set up a classroom before NTOT begins. On the first day of orientation, new teachers tour this model classroom, allowing them to see firsthand the tools they will use, such as focus boards and student-friendly proficiency scales. This immersive experience, combined with a district-provided lunch with the principal, helps new teachers feel welcomed and provides a clear, practical understanding of what their own classrooms should look like.

A central tenet of NTOT is ensuring the professional learning new teachers experience mirrors the learning environment that WPS aims to create for students. All NTOT sessions model instructional practices that new teachers are expected to use in their classrooms. The WPS New Teacher Playbook—a comprehensive guide aligned with WPS learning targets and teacher proficiency scales—helps new teachers experience personalized learning themselves. This hands-on approach ensures they are equipped to provide the same learning environment for their students when the school year begins.

In keeping with the district's commitment to continuous improvement, feedback is gathered annually from new teachers, mentors, and school leaders to assess and refine the orientation experience. District administrators also conduct follow-up interviews with new teachers throughout the year to gauge how their experiences align with the information and training they received during NTOT. This continuous feedback loop ensures WPS remains responsive to the needs of new educators while reinforcing the key principles of the PCBS.

By adopting a five-month orientation process, WPS has personalized the learning experience for new teachers. Key personalized competency-based skills and checks for understanding are distributed across different targeted support groups, with learning targets aligning with the New Teacher Playbook's proficiency scales. This approach helps new teachers gradually adapt to WPS's PCBS and provides ongoing support throughout their first year.

The district's deliberate focus on modeling classroom practices during NTOT has further refined the program. For instance, the introduction of model classroom tours allowed new teachers to immerse themselves in a fully operational personalized competency-based classroom, helping them better understand how to replicate that environment in their own teaching. Additionally, by maintaining continuous data collection—through surveys, student growth comparisons, and retention analysis—WPS has continually refined its NTOT program to align with the district's personalized competency-based goals and ensure long-term success for its educators.

Reflective Leadership on Second-Order Change

Often attributed to former first lady Rosalynn Carter, the saying "A leader takes people where they want to go. A great leader takes people where they do not necessarily want to go, but where they ought to be" perfectly encapsulates the kind of transformative leadership needed to drive second-order change. When WPS embarked on its PCBS journey, district leadership fully embraced this philosophy. Reflecting on the district's historical efforts to lead systemic change, WPS leadership saw their role as one that went beyond simply unlocking the potential of each student. They also sought to liberate each employee from the traditional constraints and comfort zones that often hinder innovation.

This journey required every stakeholder to confront long-standing beliefs and practices, creating an environment where innovation and risk taking were not only encouraged but necessary. Leading people to where they "ought to be" often means guiding them through uncertainty and discomfort, a process typically met with resistance. Yet as WPS pushed through these challenges, enduring the growing pains of change, the district witnessed a true transformation. This systemic shift empowered students, teachers, and administrators alike to reach new heights, achieving levels of success previously thought unattainable.

Final Thoughts

Leading a school district through second-order change to implement a PCBS requires a commitment that goes beyond conventional leadership models. WPS provides a powerful example of how transforming systems to a better way is achieved by aligning all stakeholders with a clear purpose, maintaining a strategic vision, and fostering leadership at all levels.

WPS's journey underscores the significance of understanding the why behind systemic change. The district invested in continuous professional development and established leadership cabinets that facilitated broad ownership of the transformation. By cultivating an environment that embraces innovation, WPS created a culture of continuous improvement where all individuals were encouraged and supported to contribute meaningfully.

Organizational transformation is not merely about introducing new systems—it is about fostering a culture where both students and staff can fully realize their potential. WPS's experience demonstrates that when leaders take their organization beyond the comfort zone of the familiar, meaningful and enduring change is not only possible but inevitable.

CHAPTER 3

Competency-Based Design

This chapter explores the competency-based design component of the Westminster learning model, which is integral to the district's mission of providing a PCBE for every student. By focusing on well-defined standards organized into proficiency scales, aligning classroom assessments, developing and observing pedagogy through a dynamic instructional model, and using innovative recording, reporting, and scheduling practices, WPS has developed a PCBE system that not only supports academic achievement but also fosters lifelong learning and adaptability.

This chapter guides you through the critical elements that make up WPS's PCBS, detailing the adoption of proficiency scales, key considerations and tools for developing scales, aligned assessments, the Westminster Instructional Model, recording and reporting, scoring on proficiency scales, progress reporting and transcripts, and scheduling for performance-based groups.

Delving into WPS's unique approach, this model shifts the focus from traditional, one-size-fits-all education to a more personalized, student-centered experience. The insights and strategies presented in this chapter offer valuable lessons learned and suggested pathways for any district or school seeking to embark on its own PCBE journey. More importantly, by careful design and a commitment to continuous improvement, this chapter shows how it is possible to create an educational system that truly serves every student.

Adoption of Proficiency Scales

To begin, proficiency scales are fundamental in a competency-based system, serving as the backbone that drives all aspects of instruction. These scales illustrate the relationship among standards, aligned assessments, and the recording of student progress, displaying related learning targets and goals and offering progressive steps for scaffolded learning. They demonstrate progression within content domains and across performance levels, creating a structured method to track evidence of student progress. By design, a proficiency scale is a continuum tool that articulates levels of knowledge and skills around a specific topic, ranging from simple to complex. Developed with increasing rigor, scale values range from 0.0 to 4.0, with 3.0 identified as the required proficiency level for progression. This approach is crucial for providing consistent focus and rigor in instruction and learning throughout the district, thus enabling the practicality of CBE.

Since 2009, Westminster has developed six versions of proficiency scales in response to both external demands and internal learnings. This process can be viewed as a progression of phases that reflect the district's evolution in understanding and refining its approach. Early on, district leadership recognized the importance of developing a procedure and timeline for refreshing the proficiency scales to stabilize the system. With proficiency scales being a crucial component of instructional planning, any shift in the format or content of the scales could potentially negate the prior work done by instructional staff.

From 2009 to 2013, WPS significantly revamped the scales every year because of the changes to standards at the state level. While necessary to align to the ever-evolving state standards, this constant flux was damaging to staff morale and willingness to continue with the system. Teachers expressed frustration with the scales being changed so often, which hindered their use in relation to instructional planning and aligning assessments. In response to this, district leadership sought to ensure more stability in the rate and frequency of proficiency scale modifications.

By 2014, WPS synthesized these learnings and developed a model that supported planning and addressed the data burden teachers reported experiencing in the system. This revised model created a systematic approach to updating scales, specifically a commitment to adhere to a built-in timeline for proficiency scale review and refinement. This provided more stability for instructional staff and ultimately allowed for better buy-in and deeper implementation.

At different points in the implementation, WPS transitioned from unidimensional scoring guides to individual state standards statements and finally to the current 4.0 proficiency scale based on a coherence model. Shifting from a 4.0 scoring guide back to basic state standards language, because of the state overhauling the Colorado Academic Standards, underscored the necessity of scales for guiding teachers in the progression of teaching a standard from basic skills and processes to complex ideas and processes. The system was overwhelmed by the sheer number of individual standards teachers were required to plan for and record. Grouping standards based on the concept of "things that are taught together and assessed together" under a common theme provided a certain level of efficiency for teachers. To better understand how this refinement process shaped the WPS PCBE, the following sections will delve into key areas of proficiency scale adoption, beginning with the concept of a guaranteed and viable curriculum.

Guaranteed and Viable Curriculum

In many districts and schools, the curriculum was often limited to just the objectives listed on the first page of each chapter in a textbook, giving publishers significant control over daily classroom content. In effect, the publisher determined the recommended pace, scope, and sequence, regardless of the needs and values of individual school communities. Claiming WPS had a "guaranteed and viable curriculum" at that time would have been an overstatement. However, WPS recognized a more learner-centered approach that was tailored to its student population and aligned with state expectations was necessary. Considering the unique makeup of the student body, their lived experiences, individual starting points, and the specific expectations of the state assessment system, WPS recognized the need for a different approach. Debates abounded over what constitutes a curriculum versus a curriculum resource. In WPS, the curriculum is defined by the proficiency scales, supported by corresponding resources to aid instruction and proficiency attainment. Textbooks and instructional materials are not considered the district's adopted curriculum.

As described previously, the journey to define the curriculum began in 2007. WPS embarked on developing a set of scoring guides across ten content areas: (1) mathematics, (2) literacy, (3) science, (4) social studies, (5) physical education, (6) personal social, (7) performing arts, (8) visual arts, (9) world languages, and (10) technology. These unidimensional scoring guides were built on a four-point scale with 0.5 increments. Standardized language defined each score on the scale, with specific content language for scores 2.0, 3.0, and 4.0. The fundamental concepts of these scoring guides have been retained in all subsequent iterations with a few minor modifications that will be discussed later. The content for the scales was derived from state and national standards documents, including the Common Core State Standards (CCSS; National Governors Association Center for Best Practices & Council of Chief State School Officers, 2010a, 2010b), Next Generation Science Standards (NGSS Lead States, 2013), National Career Clusters Framework (Advance CTE, n.d.), the Colorado Academic Standards (Colorado Department of Education, 2025a), and the Marzano Critical Concepts (Marzano Resources, n.d.a). See figure 3.1.

Strand Numbers and Operations Measurement Topic: Number Sense and Number Systems (.01) MA.02.01.03.01	
Score 4.0	In addition to score 3.0, in-depth inferences and applications that go above and beyond what was taught such as . . . • Writing a number from the given place values to 10,000 (i.e., between 1,274 and 1,300)
Score 3.5	In addition to score 3.0 performance, in-depth inferences and applications with partial success
Score 3.0	While engaged in tasks regarding whole numbers and/or ordinary numbers, the learner . . . • Identifies place value of whole numbers to 10,000 The student exhibits no major errors or omissions
Score 2.5	No major errors or omissions regarding the simpler details and process and partial knowledge of the more complex ideas and processes
Score 2.0	While engaged in tasks regarding whole numbers and/or ordinal numbers, the learner . . . • Identifies place value of whole numbers to 1,000
Score 1.5	Partial knowledge of the simpler details and processes but major errors or omissions regarding the more complex ideas and processes
Score 1.0	With help, a partial understanding of some of the simpler details and processes and some of the more complex ideas and processes
Score 0.5	With help, a partial understanding of some of the simpler details and processes but not the more complex ideas and processes
Score 0.0	Even with help, no understanding or skill demonstrated

Source: © 2024 by Westminster Public Schools. Used with permission.

FIGURE 3.1: The first iteration of scales in Westminster, known as scoring guides, developed by the Marzano 100.

WPS has navigated shifts in state standards and explored the relationships among competencies, standards, and units. The competency-based approach, distinct from the standards and unit-based approaches, necessitated careful determination of content areas.

Initially starting with ten content areas, WPS has expanded to include STEM (science, technology, engineering, and mathematics), dance, English language development, career and technical education (CTE), personal relational competencies, and leadership. While we were often at the forefront of scale development, where possible, we began with a base set of scales received from either a competency-based organization or a consultation with a content expert. The Marzano Resources Critical Concepts (a set of proficiency scales for essential K–12 content knowledge developed by analysts at Marzano Resources; Marzano Resources, n.d.a) were used as a starting point for this work, but it is vital to avoid the temptation of adopting scales wholesale from any external group. Ensuring that local staff can tailor these scales to their specific context is critical. This will provide the necessary buy-in for staff to accept the proficiency scales as specific to their local needs.

Performance Levels Versus Grade Levels

The WPS system initially featured ten *performance* levels, intentionally diverging from the traditional structure to challenge preconceived notions associated with the K–12 education system. Recognizing that students, parents, and educators often have set expectations, whether positive or negative, about grade levels, WPS leadership felt performance levels were crucial to a competency-based system. This system was designed to allow individuals to progress at their own pace, challenging the traditional belief that all students are ready to advance to the next grade level on that magical last day of the school year.

In the first year, WPS leadership observed that parents and students desired more frequent opportunities for transition and celebration. One district leader related an incident she had observed where an ecstatic elementary student, thrilled about advancing in mathematics, excitedly stopped a group of visitors passing by in the lunch line to share his good news the day of a level-up ceremony in November. Originally, the system of ten levels had compressed various content levels, such as kindergarten and first-grade content, into a single level. This caused confusion among parents regarding their child's progression. To address this issue, WPS expanded the system to sixteen performance levels, thereby increasing opportunities for recognizing and celebrating student progress.

This expansion allowed more frequent celebrations of students' achievements. Schools developed various systems and methods for these celebrations, including monthly or quarterly events, with milestones marked by level-up certificates, dog tags, badges, and bracelets. However, this change introduced a challenge in translating levels to indicate whether a student was on track. Despite efforts to clarify this issue, there remained a misconception that, for example, a ninth-grade student at mathematics level 11 was ahead rather than on pace.

In 2012–2013, WPS transitioned to fourteen performance levels, aligning them directly with traditional preK–12 grade levels. WPS avoided referencing grade levels, instead using language like *mathematics level 04*, *literacy level 06*, and *social studies level 05*. For high school levels, WPS used NCAA-compliant course-based language to ensure it did not create barriers for student entry into college. This final iteration has been successful, but it requires careful goal setting to ensure all stakeholders understand the need for more than one level of growth for students who are behind pace.

Over six versions of proficiency scales, WPS noted significant variations in the number of scales per level, ranging from as many as 108 to as few as four. This discrepancy highlighted the need for a balanced approach, with twelve to twenty scales per level emerging as a practical standard. The variation in scale counts across different content areas reflects the unique needs and complexities of each subject. The overall goal is to provide enough scales for quality planning while enabling effective goal setting and progress monitoring for students. See figure 3.2.

Proficiency Scale Refresh Counts

Mathematics				
Level	**2011 PS Count**	**2015 PS Count**	**2019 PS Count**	**+/-**
PreK		5	11	6
0	31	9	11	2
1	28	10	13	3
2	32	10	13	3
3	19	15	15	0
4	30	18	18	-2
5	46	13	14	1
6	19	13	17	4
7	31	15	17	2
8	54	14	14	0
AlGeo I	50	18	14	-4
AlGeo II	34	21	14	-7
AlGeo III	54	17	13	-4
Total	428	178	182	4

Literacy				
Level	**2011 PS Count**	**2015 PS Count**	**2019 PS Count**	**+/-**
PreK		10	7	-3
0	22	34	18	-16

Level	2011 PS Count	2015 PS Count	2019 PS Count	+/-
1	17	34	22	-12
2	79	34	21	-13
3	88	35	19	-16
4	92	35	18	-17
5	105	35	15	-20
6	104	33	15	-18
7	96	33	14	-19
8	102	33	15	-18
Eng/Lang 1	100	29	14	-15
Eng/Lang 2	108	30	14	-16
Eng/Lang 3	63	30	13	-17
Eng/Lang 4	73	18	11	-7
Total	976	423	216	-207

Science				
Level	2011 PS Count	2015 PS Count	2019 PS Count	+/-
PreK		7	8	1
0	7	11	7	-4
1	9	11	9	-2
2	13	12	10	-2
3	6	14	13	-1
4	9	16	14	-2
5	9	15	14	-1
6	7	16	16	0
7	4	17	12	-5
8	13	13	9	-4
Physics	8	12	8	-4
Chemistry	5	8	9	1
Biology	4	12	13	1
Earth Science	10		13	13
Total	94	164	155	-9

Terms PreK–12	Math	ELA	Science
Total Terms	2811	2940	2612
Unique Terms	989	907	1418

Source: © 2024 by Westminster Public Schools. Used with permission.

FIGURE 3.2: Breakdown of the proficiency scales at various stages of the Westminster implementation.

Development of Proficiency Scales

While WPS went through numerous iterations of its proficiency scales, it is important to note that districts or schools developing proficiency scales do not have to undergo similar trials and tribulations if they learn from the trials and tribulations of others like WPS. This section focuses on the process WPS used for the final iteration of its proficiency scales.

This process engaged teams of Westminster teachers, supplemented by a few coaches and administrators. WPS formed content-based proficiency scale task forces for mathematics and literacy across four grade spans (preK–2, 3–5, 6–8, and 9–12). Task force members attended a mandatory full-day training to learn about proficiency scale design, understand how to group state standards, and launch the work sessions.

As work on these scales progressed, teachers quickly recognized the value proficiency scales provide as guides for planning and scoring. The work on mathematics and literacy scales began in November, and by February, teachers from science and social studies were requesting the opportunity to engage in the work, so additional teams were formed. In April, elective teachers rose up and said, "What about us?"—a testament to the value teachers found in designing proficiency scales.

The time required for this process varied based on the structure used. For the four core areas, teams met weekly from 2:30 to 6:30 p.m. at the close of the school day. This posed challenges: Teachers were fatigued after a full day, and time was needed at the start of each session for reengagement. The mathematics and literacy teams met every Monday from November to May, while the science and social studies teams, starting in February, also completed their work by May. In contrast, elective teams participated outside the school year, dedicating a week to the process, including one day of training and four days of focused work. All elective groups completed their work in the allocated time, with the visual arts team finishing in just three days. Each session was co-facilitated by a WPS learning services director and a partner from a local university, which ensured both district and industry expertise.

Task force members received a nominal payment of $1,000 for their participation. Although this did not fully compensate for their time, teachers returned each week, citing it as the best professional development they had ever received. This feedback reflects the deep understanding teachers gained about the content they teach daily. The process of deconstructing each standard provided deep insights into instructional planning and assessment, a rare experience for most teachers. An example of this was highlighted by a high school teacher who, after the first night of the 2020 refresh, changed her teaching approach the very next day because of her newfound understanding of the content.

The composition of each content area task force was strategically composed to ensure both horizontal and vertical alignment within the proficiency scales. Careful attention was paid to maintaining core concepts across all performance levels and content areas, considering elementary staff interact with multiple contents daily. Similarly, middle school teachers might need to reference elementary scales, making consistent design crucial.

A challenge arose from the Common Core State Standards, where elementary and secondary standards were based on separate constructs, complicating the transition between elementary and secondary content when addressing student needs. To facilitate this, the entire preK–12 group met weekly in the high school library. If a primary team considered changing a proficiency scale theme, they could quickly convene representatives from all levels to gain consensus before making adjustments that might impact alignment.

The structure of the scale development depended on the resources available to each content team. For some content areas, base proficiency scales were available, while others had to rely solely on state or national standards. Each approach had its challenges, but neither was significantly harder than the other. In cases like social studies and career and technical education, where teams started with standards or outcomes documents, teams literally cut the standards into strips to help teachers group them into themes and arrange skills from basic to more complex. Teachers engaged in negotiations over various groupings, sometimes extending over multiple weeks as they sought feedback from larger groups of teachers back at their school sites. These discussions were insightful and productive while creating another way of involving more teachers in the process.

In areas like mathematics and literacy, teams benefited from using the Marzano Critical Concepts (Marzano Resources, n.d.a), as shown in figure 3.3 (page 62). These scales provided a strong starting point but still required negotiations about whether the suggested groupings were appropriate for teaching and assessment in WPS classrooms or if a scale needed to be divided into two different topics. There were even more intense debates about which content in the Critical Concepts score 2.0s was most relevant to WPS context. Teams understood that simply adopting the Critical Concept scales would overwhelm teachers with the breadth of content included and would not garner sufficient buy-in.

	Generating Claims, Evidence, and Reasoning (3 ELA)
4.0	**The student will:** • Generate an opinion about a text and use details from the text to support the opinion (for example, decide whether Odysseus is or is not a hero; use details from the text *The One-Eyed Giant* by Mary Pope Osborne to support the opinion).
3.5	In addition to score 3.0 performance, partial success at score 4.0 content
3.0	**The student will:** **GCER1-**State an opinion supported by multiple reasons (for example, state an opinion about whether being a park ranger is a good or bad job and give reasons for the opinion). **GCER2-**Identify facts and information related to an opinion (for example, highlight details from Ann Posegate's "What It's Like to Be a National Park Ranger" from KidsPost at washingtonpost.com that explain what national park rangers do and why their job is important).
2.5	No major errors or omissions regarding score 2.0 content, and partial success at score 3.0 content
2.0	**GCER1-**The student will recognize or recall specific vocabulary (for example, *belief, detail, distinct, fact, feeling, opinion, prove, reason, specific, statement, support*) and perform basic processes such as: • Explain the difference between a fact and an opinion. • Identify opinions and facts in a set of sample sentences. • Write an opinion sentence. • Identify a fact that supports a particular opinion the student has. • State that a good opinion statement should be specific, it should be something someone could agree or disagree with, and it should have reasons that support it. • List reasons for an opinion. • State that a strong reason should be clear, it should be supported by details, and should be distinct from other reasons. **GCER2-**The student will recognize or recall specific vocabulary (for example, *concept, definition, detail, example, experience, explanation, fact, reason, relate, support, topic, vocabulary*) and perform basic processes such as: • List personal experiences that support an idea or reason. • Identity sections in a text that relate to a particular topic, reason, or concept. • Identify facts in a text that relate to a specific topic, reason, or concept. • Identify examples in a text that relate to a specific topic, reason, or concept. • Identify important new vocabulary from a text that relates to a specific topic, reason, or concept. • Describe details in a text that relate to a specific topic, reason, or concept. • Explain how a particular detail supports an opinion about a topic. • Write a sentence expressing a specific detail in one's own words. • Choose which details to include in an explanatory or persuasive text on a specific topic.
1.5	Partial success at score 2.0 content, and major errors or omissions regarding score 3.0 content
1.0	With help, partial success at score 2.0 content and score 3.0 content
0.5	With help, partial success at score 2.0 content but not at score 3.0 content
0.0	Even with help, no success

Source: © 2017 by Marzano Resources. Used with permission.

FIGURE 3.3: Third-grade generating claims, evidence, and reasoning scale.

Another testament to the effectiveness of proficiency scales in making PCBSs feasible is the feedback from high school International Baccalaureate (IB), Advanced Placement (AP), and career and technical education teachers. Initially, the development process was focused on the required K–12 courses for high school graduation. However, after witnessing the benefits of the scales for planning and recording, these teachers sought the opportunity to develop scales for their respective courses. This was achieved by adapting each course's prescribed outcomes to the proficiency scale framework; it proved to be a very adaptable approach. On the other end of the educational spectrum, preschool teachers also expressed interest in leveraging this approach's benefits. WPS educators achieved a comprehensive implementation of proficiency scales from preschool through high school across every content area offered in the district.

2020 Proficiency Scale Refresh

The final refresh of the WPS proficiency scales started in 2020. It was structured in three phases, beginning with a listening tour to understand what worked well in the 2014 version and what adjustments were necessary. Teachers who volunteered for this refresh were compensated and viewed the process as invaluable professional development. The phases involved updating academic vocabulary, adding score 4.0s, revising instructional progressions, and validating the final scales. The process included training with Marzano and the University of Colorado Denver's Center for Transforming Learning and Teaching on determining Depth of Knowledge (DOK) and cognitive processes and aligning sample tasks with these frameworks. Key tools in the development process were the Marzano Critical Concepts (Marzano Resources, n.d.a), Bloom's taxonomy revised (Anderson & Krathwohl, 2001), Norman Webb's (2002) DOK, and the Hess Cognitive Rigor Matrices (Hess, 2025; see www.karin-hess.com/cognitive-rigor-and-dok to download these matrices). In the 2020 refresh, WPS educators identified scores 3.0 (at the learning goal), 2.0 (below the learning goal), and 4.0 (beyond the learning goal); see figure 3.4 (page 64).

The 2020 refresh also clarified the fact that score 2.0 focused on content requiring direct teaching, while score 3.0 allowed for teaching and assessing multiple standards together. Grouping standards based on the concept of "things that are taught and assessed together" under a common theme provides efficiency for teachers. Score 4.0 integrated and applied the entire scale's content, emphasizing both declarative and procedural knowledge.

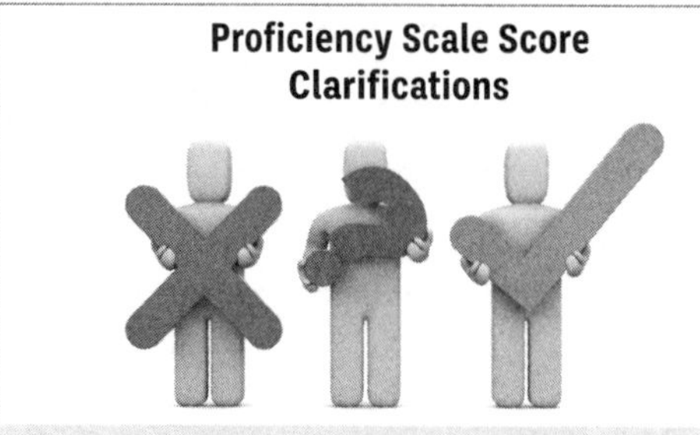

Score 4.0

Only one 4.0 statement regardless of the number of 3.0s as the goal is to integrate and apply contents of the entire scale.

Declarative: involves inferences and applications beyond what was taught

Procedural: execute with constraints or limiting conditions

Score 3.0

Two criteria to determine whether multiple standards can be included (covariance):

1. They can be taught together
2. They can and should be measured together

Covary: an increase in a student's ability relative to one target predicts an increase in their ability relative to the others

Score 2.0

Should not include all the knowledge and skills necessary to accomplish the Score 3.0, but rather the content that must be directly taught.

Include only vocabulary terms that will be directly taught.

Source: © 2024 by Westminster Public Schools. Used with permission.

FIGURE 3.4: 2020 proficiency scale refresh training with clarifications on content for each score.

Key Considerations and Tools in the Development Process

WPS proficiency scales were developed with key components in mind, including the theme, numbering system, scoring scale, content, and boilerplate language. The involvement of teachers in the development process was a crucial element, fostering buy-in and ensuring the content was tailored to the unique needs of WPS students. The development process involved ensuring alignment of each learning target or indicator with appropriate DOK levels and cognitive processes. Instructional learning progressions were developed, enabling teachers to plan effectively within and across performance levels. This also included developing vertical, instructional, and detailed learning progressions within a scale.

Figure 3.5 illustrates an example of a WPS proficiency scale for the mathematical concept of area. This proficiency scale aligns with the Colorado Academic Standards (Strand: Data, Statistics, and Probability) and the Common Core State Standards (Domain: Measurement & Data). The scale is designed to guide both instruction and assessment by outlining clear performance expectations at each score level (0.0 to 4.0) and supporting teachers in differentiating instruction to meet the needs of all learners.

<table>
<tr><th colspan="2">WPS Proficiency Scale</th></tr>
<tr><td colspan="2">CDE Strand: Data, statistics, and probability
CCSS Strand: Statistics and probability</td></tr>
<tr><td colspan="2">Proficiency scale theme: Area</td></tr>
<tr><td colspan="2">Record Learning Target: MA.04.MD.03.05
CCSS Domain: MD.Measurement & Data</td></tr>
<tr><th colspan="2">Learning Target Breakdown</th></tr>
<tr><td>Score 4.0</td><td>In addition to exhibiting score 3.0 performance, in-depth inferences and applications that go BEYOND what was taught in class. (Score 4.0 does not equate to more work but rather a higher level of performance as articulated in this sample task.)
• Determine the maximum possible area for a rectangle with a given perimeter (for example, when given that a rectangle has a perimeter of 48, identify the greatest possible area of the rectangle as 144 by using reasoning about rectangular arrays to determine that the shape of a square maximizes the area of a rectangle with a fixed perimeter). (DOK 3, AP)</td></tr>
<tr><td>Score 3.5</td><td>In addition to score 3.0 performance, in-depth inferences and applications with partial success.</td></tr>
<tr><td>Score 3.0</td><td>The learner . . .
A1-Calculate areas and unknown side lengths of rectangles. (CAS: MA.4.MD.A.3) (CCSS: 4.MD.A.3) (DOK 2, AP)
A2- Solve real-world problems involving area formulas for rectangles. (CAS: MA.4.MD.A.3) (CCSS: 4.MD.A.3) (DOK 2, AP)
The learner exhibits no major errors or omissions regarding any of the information and processes (simple or complex) that were explicitly taught.</td></tr>
<tr><td>Score 2.5</td><td>No major errors or omissions regarding the simpler details and processes (score 2.0 content) and partial knowledge of the more complex ideas and processes (score 3.0 content).</td></tr>
<tr><td>Score 2.0</td><td>A1- The learner will recognize or recall specific vocabulary (for example, area, congruent, equation, side, width, equation, formula, variables) and perform basic processes such as:
• State the formula for the area of a rectangle. (A= Lx W). (DOK 1, RE)
• Use letters to represent unknown variables in equations. (DOK 1, UN)
A2- The learner will recognize or recall specific vocabulary (for example, numerical expression, square units) and perform basic processes such as:
• Write numerical expressions and equations to represent simple numerical relationships given in verbal descriptions and word problems. (DOK 1, UN)
• Manage units correctly when representing real-world measurements or quantities as numerical expressions or equations. (DOK 1, UN)
However, the learner exhibits major errors or omissions regarding the more complex ideas and processes.</td></tr>
<tr><td>Score 1.5</td><td>Partial knowledge of the simpler details and processes (score 2.0 content) but major errors or omissions regarding the more complex ideas and processes (score 3.0 content).</td></tr>
<tr><td>Score 1.0</td><td>With help, a partial understanding of some of the simpler details and processes (score 2.0 content) and some of the more complex ideas and processes (score 3.0 content).</td></tr>
<tr><td>Score 0.5</td><td>With help, a partial understanding of some of the simpler details and process (score 2.0 content) but not the more complex ideas and processes (score 3.0 content).</td></tr>
<tr><td>Score 0.0</td><td>Even with help, no understanding or skill demonstrated.</td></tr>
</table>

Source: © 2016 by Marzano Resources, adapted by Westminster Public Schools. Used with permission.

FIGURE 3.5: Mathematics level 04 area proficiency scale in the current Westminster format.

To interpret this proficiency scale, consider the following elements.

1. **Learning targets:** At the top of the scale, you'll find the recorded learning target (for example, MA.04.MD.03.05). This target defines the specific skill or standard being addressed, ensuring alignment with state and district expectations.
2. **Score levels:** The scale is divided into performance levels from 0.0 to 4.0.
    a. *Score 0.0*—Indicates no understanding or skill demonstrated, even with help.
    b. *Score 1.0*—Reflects a partial understanding of foundational concepts with teacher support.
    c. *Score 2.0*—Focuses on mastery of simpler ideas and processes explicitly taught.
    d. *Score 3.0*—Represents mastery of the learning target, with no major errors or omissions.
    e. *Score 4.0*—Indicates advanced understanding, including the ability to apply concepts beyond what was explicitly taught.
3. **Learning target breakdown:** Each score level includes a breakdown of expectations.
    a. *Score 2.0 and 3.0*—Provides a progression of basic to proficient understanding of explicit skills, such as calculating the area of rectangles or solving real-world problems involving area formulas
    b. *Score 4.0*—Extends learning by including applications and inferences requiring higher-order thinking, such as analyzing relationships between shapes or determining optimal dimensions for a given scenario
4. **Depth of Knowledge alignment:** Each skill or process is tagged with its corresponding DOK level and cognitive process (for example, DOK 1 for recall, DOK 2 for application, DOK 3 for strategic thinking). This helps educators ensure tasks and assessments align with the cognitive rigor required at each level.
5. **Connections across content:** By grouping related standards and concepts, the scale integrates foundational knowledge with advanced applications, helping students progress logically.

Other schools and districts that want to take a similar approach can adapt this model as follows.

- **Align with local standards:** Districts can begin by identifying their own state or local standards and mapping them to learning targets within their curriculum.
- **Customize for your students:** Adapt the learning target breakdown to reflect the unique needs, prior knowledge, and goals of your student population.
- **Collaborate with educators:** Engage teachers in the development and refinement of proficiency scales to ensure buy-in and practicality for classroom use.
- **Integrate into instruction:** Use the scales to plan lessons, assess student progress, and identify areas for intervention or enrichment.
- **Leverage cognitive rigor:** Incorporate DOK levels to design tasks and assessments that challenge students at the appropriate level of rigor.

This proficiency scale provides a structured yet flexible tool for supporting personalized competency-based education. By adapting this model, districts can create clear pathways for student learning and ensure consistent expectations across classrooms. The following sections describe key aspects of how proficiency scales are used in the PCBS.

Instructional Progressions and Planning

Once the proficiency scales are designed, effective implementation must support teachers in connecting the scales to their instructional planning. This brings us to instructional progressions—guides that organize scales in a coherent and practical sequence for teaching and learning. These progressions, or scope and sequences, help bridge the gap between scale design and classroom instruction, addressing challenges such as cross-curricular connections and curriculum resource integration.

An early lesson in the teacher onboarding process was the need to provide guidance toward organizing scales for instruction. As new teachers entered the WPS PCBS, they received a set of nineteen mathematics level 03 proficiency scales. An early assumption that proved untrue was that teacher preparation programs equipped teachers with the knowledge of how to use proficiency scales for instructional planning and delivery. Initially, teachers taught one content domain at a time without acknowledging the natural connection between domains. To remedy this, WPS added a step to the 2014 development process that included the creation of an instructional progression guide for each content performance level.

The proficiency scale development process included the creation of a variety of progression or trajectory documents to support instructional planning and student goal setting. The first progression was embedded in each proficiency scale. The skills within each scale were placed in the order in which instruction should be provided from simple to complex. Once the proficiency scales for a performance level were complete, teams then developed the associated instructional progressions by designating the order in which each proficiency scale should be taught. The first draft of the instructional progressions was based on the teacher team's instructional expertise. These progressions were then verified through various research-based sources such as EngageNY (New York State Education Department, n.d.), the University of Arizona, and the Colorado Department of Education (2016) model units. The final progression the teams developed provided a preK–12 vertical sequence within content area domains. The vertical progression was designed to support gap filling for students below grade level and acceleration for higher-performing students. After the first few months of implementation, a need arose to create an additional progression document to support multilevel planning.

The "Year at a Glance" tool was developed to address pacing and academic pressure in the classroom, allowing teachers to plan a yearlong scope and sequence based on the unique needs of their student groups. This comprehensive approach to planning and implementation underscored WPS's commitment to a nuanced education system that not only meets immediate learning objectives but also prepares students for long-term success. See figure 3.6.

Curricular Resources

Once instructional progressions are determined, a district should begin to focus on the tools and materials needed to support learning within the proficiency scale framework. WPS recognized that alignment of curricular resources with the proficiency scales was critical to ensuring consistency across performance levels, as well as minimizing disruptions to student learning from term to term, from year to year, or when a student transitions to a different school within the district. This led to a rethinking of the district's curriculum adoption process to better support personalized competency-based education.

Equipped with a guaranteed and viable curriculum via the proficiency scales in a system where content is tailored to the learner, WPS educators needed to rethink the approach to curriculum adoption. Consider a situation where a student, age appropriate for fifth grade, transitions from the elementary to the middle school building but still has ten mathematics level 05 proficiency scales below a 3.0. If that student had to switch from the elementary resource of Everyday Mathematics (University of Chicago School Mathematics Project, 2007) to the middle school resource of Saxon Math (Larson, 2004),

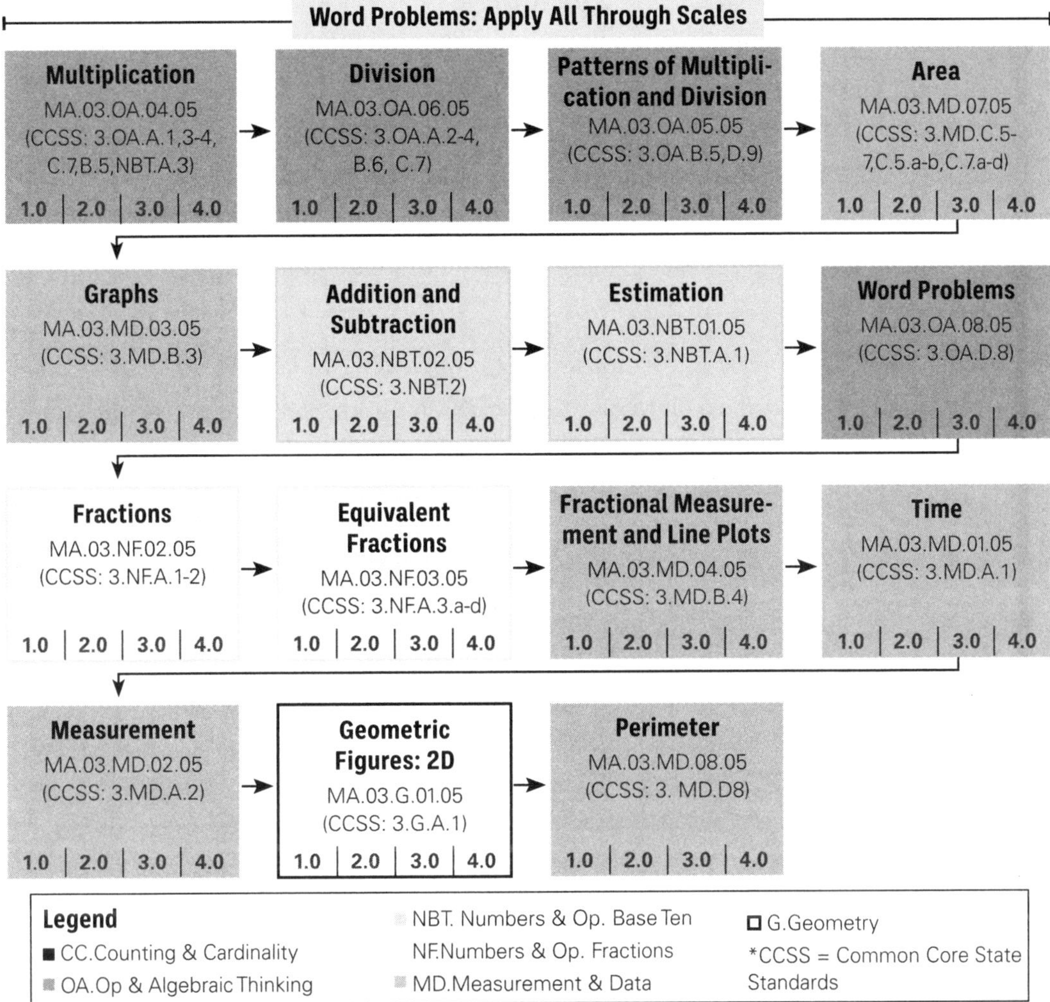

Source: © 2024 by Westminster Public Schools. Used with permission.

FIGURE 3.6: Sample instructional progression for mathematics level 03 proficiency scales.

several issues would arise. First, the adopted materials may not cover lower levels of content, requiring middle school teachers to be trained in additional curricular resources, which is a time-consuming process. The district would also need to purchase a significant surplus of resources to accommodate this overlap. Most importantly, students typically face a challenging shift in instructional approaches when transitioning from the elementary to middle level, which impedes their learning.

To address these concerns, WPS changed its textbook and material adoption process to include a focus on finding resources that were comprehensive from K–12 whenever possible. This approach was not only fiscally responsible but also most supportive of a PCBS.

With curricular resources aligned to proficiency scales, the next challenge is to ensure educators have the knowledge and tools to implement these resources effectively. Training on these skills became essential, as WPS recognized that clear, consistent professional development was necessary for guaranteeing instruction was aligned to the district's PCBS framework. This also required the creation of tools to streamline instructional planning to ensure a personalized approach to classroom instruction prevailed.

Training and Implementation

In education, the criteria for demonstrating proficiency can vary significantly from one classroom to another. To alleviate this problem, an initial step was taken when the proficiency scale task force designated the DOK for each standard on the scale, based on Norman Webb's (2002) work, as well as the Cognitive Process (Hess, 2025), based on Bloom's taxonomy (Anderson & Krathwohl, 2001). Rather than ask seven hundred individual teachers to engage in this work, WPS had the existing proficiency scale task forces complete it. To ensure all district instructional staff could utilize this component of the proficiency scales, the district launched a variety of professional development initiatives. In the fall of 2017, WPS introduced a Symposium Model, or a conference-style format, to ensure training opportunities were provided that met the needs of WPS's diverse teaching cadre. Finding this model effective, WPS extended the training multiple times throughout the school year to provide opportunities for all staff to deepen their knowledge.

The implementation phase also involved the development of instructional planning tools, such as the "Year at a Glance" and the "Multilevel Planning" spreadsheets, into the WPS-adopted LMS. Developing "Unit Overviews" for each unit in the "Year at a Glance," focusing on addressing student academic needs through instruction and assessment in small groups, enhanced the planning process further. This strategy was pivotal in moving from a one-size-fits-all teaching method to a more targeted approach based on individual student needs.

Proficiency Scales Versus Rubrics

As WPS teachers practiced implementing proficiency scales, a recurring area of confusion emerged: the difference between proficiency scales and rubrics. Many people mistakenly believed that a proficiency scale was simply another type of scoring rubric. WPS realized it needed to offer clarity on how proficiency scales can serve multiple purposes, including instructional planning and designing assessment of learning, while rubrics provide measurable criteria for evaluating the quality of a specific student performance or product. While rubrics are short-term grading tools for specific activities, proficiency scales are designed to create natural progressions of learning by thematically grouping academic standards. This makes proficiency scales more suitable for long-term use, as they are part of a course-based or instructional-level learning progression linked to standards. Professional learning sessions were provided that focused on these misconceptions and worked to establish a shared understanding of how both proficiency scales and rubrics complement the PCBS framework.

Another challenge was teachers often hesitated to score a student at 3.0 or higher, fearing it might reduce the student's motivation to apply the skill further. It was essential to discuss what proficiency meant and explore different methods for holding students accountable for demonstrating skills in which they are proficient. This was achieved through the development of rubrics for various activities linked to specific standards within a proficiency scale. For instance, a teacher would mark a grammar proficiency scale proficient when a student consistently demonstrated understanding of the purpose and use of a comma. After multiple demonstrations over time, the scale would be marked at 3.0, 3.5, or 4.0. Subsequently, the teacher would include this criterion in a rubric for any writing-related evidence.

Implementation and Monitoring

With proficiency scales informing instructional planning and assessment, and supporting tools in place, the next step for a district is to focus on monitoring the implementation to ensure fidelity and consistency across classrooms and schools. This goes beyond just tracking progress because it also requires providing actionable feedback to support teachers and students in effectively using proficiency scales.

Monitoring the deep implementation of proficiency scales was a major WPS goal. To this end, teachers and leaders used Marzano Resources tools related to providing proficiency scales, tracking student progress, and celebrating success (Marzano Resources, n.d.a) that included look-fors, rubrics, and resources to support implementation. Central to this process were specific teacher and student look-fors, which outlined key behaviors and practices aligned with the scales, such as how teachers incorporated them into instruction and how students demonstrated understanding.

One critical insight gained during this monitoring phase involved the discovery of a widespread implementation gap. A state grant enabled WPS to create measurement topic assessments for the initial 2009 scoring guides, developed by an external vendor and vetted by WPS teachers. The first administration of these assessments revealed a significant challenge. After administering a third-grade measurement topic assessment, a school principal contacted the assessment director with concerns that the test did not accurately reflect students' knowledge. During a detailed conversation centered on the associated scoring guide, it became clear that the evidence gathered at the classroom level only demonstrated a score 2.0 level of understanding.

Further investigation revealed that this issue extended across many classrooms in the district. Teachers were only instructing and assessing students at the score 2.0 level, often neglecting the score 3.0 indicators, which require deeper reasoning and understanding. For example, students could calculate a mathematics problem as required for a score 2.0 but were not taught or expected to explain the reasoning behind their answers, a clear expectation for score 3.0. This realization served as a critical call to action.

In response, the district quickly pivoted to provide school leaders and teachers with targeted professional learning and support to ensure students were being instructed and assessed at the score 3.0 level for each proficiency scale. This example underscores the necessity of continual improvement and adaptability when implementing personalized education systems, as unforeseen challenges can emerge even with the best planning. See figure 3.7.

<table>
<tr><th colspan="2">I. Proficiency Scales</th></tr>
<tr><td colspan="2">Feedback: The teacher designs and communicates proficiency scales that help students understand the progression of knowledge they are expected to master for specific domains.</td></tr>
<tr><td>Teacher Evidence for Level 2 (Developing)
The teacher is:
• Communicating the scope of domains (1a-compendium E1)
• Communicating proficiency scales for each topic (1a-compendium E1)
• Creating student-friendly proficiency scales (1a-compendium E1)
Tracking Progress:
• Helping students track their progress on specific proficiency scales (lb-compendium E2)
• Use of data notebooks (1b-compendium E2)
Celebrating:
• Celebrating students' status on specific proficiency scales (1c-compendium E3)
• Celebrating students' growth on specific proficiency scales (1c-compendium E3)
When asked, the teacher can:
• Describe the domain on which they are currently focused and how they make proficiency scales user friendly for students
• Describe how they ensure students are tracking their progress
• Describe how they celebrate students' status and growth</td><td>Student Evidence for Levels 3 (Applying) and 4 (Innovating)
Students are:
• Tracking their progress on proficiency scales
• Referencing proficiency scales to determine what they must do to progress
• Seeking or providing help regarding working through specific proficiency scales
• Celebrating their status and growth
When asked, students:
• Can identify the proficiency scale on which they are working
• Describe what they need to do to improve their status on proficiency scales
• Say they are proud of their status or growth</td></tr>
</table>

Source: © 2024 by Westminster Public Schools, adapted from Marzano & Abbott, 2022. Used with permission.

FIGURE 3.7: Tool for monitoring deep implementation of proficiency scales in the classroom.

Sustainable Proficiency Scales

To ensure the long-term viability of proficiency scale implementation, it is important to create structures that promote stability with adaptability over time. Sustaining proficiency scale use necessitates the development of processes that support consistency for teachers while allowing for periodic updates to align with evolving state standards and district needs.

Since the proficiency scales are the district's official curriculum, completing annual overhauls of scales becomes problematic for teachers. Understanding the significant impact that changing scales has on instructional practice, WPS realized the need for stability. Toward this end, the district committed to refreshing proficiency scales only every five years and has adhered to this schedule since 2015. This five-year timeline allows for the scales to be modified frequently enough to adapt to the ever-changing realities of academic standards while also providing teachers with year-to-year consistency for instructional planning and delivery.

Another common procedure that required adjustment to uphold a commitment to a guaranteed and viable curriculum through proficiency scales was the annual course proposal process. Linking proficiency scales to course development necessitated an additional step. To aid in this process, WPS created a new course proposal workflow. Now, teachers receive provisional approval for a new course, which indicates sufficient merit to warrant the development of aligned proficiency scales. While the district offers support for this step, unlike the task force members, teachers do not receive a stipend as it is considered part of the new course proposal process. Only after proficiency scales are submitted and approved by the learning services department will the course be listed into the district's course catalog. Ensuring the creation of aligned scales for all courses offered throughout the district, especially in noncore electives, helps ensure competency-based recording and reporting is in place for all classes.

Aligned Assessments

WPS's assessment system mirrors that of most other schools and districts, encompassing state, district, and local assessments, which are administered three times during the school year. WPS annually participates in the state assessments in English language arts (ELA), mathematics, and science, consistently exceeding the 95 percent participation rate required by the Colorado State Department of Education. District and school leaders believe it is crucial for the efficacy of the competency-based system not to opt out of state assessments so that they avoid narratives suggesting personalized learning is a cop-out. With that said, WPS consistently engages with state department officials and legislators about how results are inappropriately used to rank and shame schools and seeks flexibility for more effective test administration to better align with student needs.

While WPS has the flexibility to retain a student in a grade level to take an appropriate assessment at the individual's academic performance level, this approach assumes the student is performing at the same level across all content areas, which is often not the case. For example, a student may perform at a third-grade level in mathematics, fifth-grade level in English language arts, and fourth-grade level in science. For state assessment purposes, the district must choose one grade level for all content areas for this student, almost guaranteeing an inaccurate representation of the learner's knowledge. Research identifies the role of context and retrieval in accurately assessing knowledge. Michael Seddon (2019) found that students don't perform as well when assessed in contexts different from where they initially learned the material. This highlights the importance of consistent contextual cues for memory retrieval. Similarly, Mary Pyc and Katherine A. Rawson (2009) demonstrated that student retrieval efforts that were more cognitively rigorous resulted in higher rates of long-term retention than easier retrievals. These findings underscore that memory and performance are influenced not only by what is learned but also by how and where it is retrieved, making single-grade assessments a potentially misleading measure of student competencies.

If the district chose the lowest common denominator to have the hypothetical student take the third-grade assessments, it may not accurately represent the student's understanding due to the time elapsed since the individual engaged with that content. Although the technology for state assessments allows for a differentiated approach, this flexibility has not yet been embraced at the state level.

State assessments often act as an autopsy, providing results long after they can inform daily instruction. For more immediate adjustments, WPS used various benchmark assessments such as Renaissance Star (Renaissance Learning, Inc., n.d.) and DIBELS 8 (University of Oregon, n.d.), administered in August, December, and May each year. These assessments, which include progress-monitoring options, support instruction and intervention by guiding school-level data cycles aimed at ensuring all students achieve optimal growth of one to one-and-a-half years annually. An additional feature of WPS assessments is the option to administer them in Spanish, supporting both content and language objectives.

Placing Students New to the System

Since personalized competency-based education groups students into learning environments not by age but instead by academic ability levels, placing new students in the district who have no historical performance data can be challenging. WPS utilizes local benchmark assessments for initial placement until a larger body of evidence can be compiled. The Renaissance Star Early Literacy, Reading, and Math assessments are administered to all new students in traditional grades K–10. A set of cut scores were developed to outline the "minimum performance level" required on the Star Assessments to align with WPS performance levels. For preschool and kindergarten students, placement is automatic at the preschool performance levels. This does not mean all incoming kindergarten students are placed into preschool classrooms; instead, the kindergarten teacher is required to instruct and assess preschool proficiency scales as they scaffold the kindergarten instruction. Initially, kindergarten students were placed at the kindergarten level inside the WPS LMS, meaning a student's academic progression began with those academic standards. After several years, however, the primary teachers requested a change in this practice. WPS found that students who did not attend preschool needed the opportunity to work on those precursor skills. This change allowed teachers to address, assess, and ensure the critical preK skills were fully covered throughout a student's kindergarten year.

Another key insight from placing new students was the timing of those initial decisions. New student schedules are initially developed based on their Renaissance Star Assessment results. However, during the first two weeks of school, additional assessments and teacher judgment play a critical role in finalizing a student's placement into a performance level. If a student is deemed too low or high during that window, performance level adjustments are made. With this said, WPS leadership advises practitioners to exercise caution when placing new students whose Renaissance Star Assessment scale scores suggest they are above grade level. Ideally, these potentially high-performing students should start at grade level to build confidence and learn to navigate the PCBS effectively.

Performance level cut scores are useful for placing students not meeting grade-level expectations. For all other content areas below the tenth-grade level, the WPS LMS automatically places students for efficiency based on the chart in figure 3.8 (page 76). The abbreviations in the chart are as follows.

- **PK:** Prekindergarten
- **PR:** Primary (kindergarten through second grade)
- **IN:** Intermediate (third through fifth grade)
- **MS:** Middle school (sixth through eighth grade)
- **Teacher placement:** Indicates that placement into these courses is determined by teacher evaluation rather than automated systems
- **Records (09):** Refers to data entries in the LMS based on transcripted scores from the receiving school
- **BOE:** Stands for "body of evidence," a collection of assessment data, student work, and teacher observations used to confirm a student's placement level

Grade	Math	Literacy	Science	Social Studies	Physical Education	Technology	Visual Arts	Performing Arts	World Language
Preschool	PK	PK	PK	PK	00	PR	00	00	*Teacher Placement*
Kinder	PK	PK	00	00	00	PR	00	00	*Teacher Placement*
1st	Level placements is completed at the building level based on Star scores and BOE	Level placements is completed at the building level based on Star scores and BOE	01	01	01	PR	01	01	*Teacher Placement*
2nd			02	02	02	PR	02	02	*Teacher Placement*
3rd			03	03	03	IN	03	03	*Teacher Placement*
4th			04	04	04	IN	04	04	*Teacher Placement*
5th			05	05	05	IN	05	05	*Teacher Placement*
6th			06	06	06	MS	06	*Teacher Placement (OS)*	*Teacher Placement*
7th			07	07	07	MS	07	*Teacher Placement (OS)*	*Teacher Placement*
8th			08	08	08	MS	08	*Teacher Placement (OS)*	*Teacher Placement*
9th			09	09	*Teacher Placement*				
10th			*Records (09)*	*Records (09)*	*Teacher Placement*				
11th			*Records (09)*	*Records (09)*	*Teacher Placement*				

Source:

FIGURE 3.8: Westminster level placement guidance.

For example, if a student transitioning into middle school scores at an intermediate level for mathematics (for example, level 05), the student would be assigned to the appropriate mathematics level in the LMS based on their performance on the district assessment. However, for noncore content areas such as performing arts or world languages, teacher judgment plays a larger role in determining placement to ensure students are in courses suited to their skill levels and interests. For high school students entering the system, credits earned at their previous school are honored based on the received records in the form of transcripts. This careful approach ensures accurate placements while allowing flexibility for adjustments as additional data become available, supporting student success and confidence as they transition into the PCBS framework.

All other placements must be manually completed at the building level, based on teacher judgment and records from the previous district. At the high school level, administrators and counselors review incoming transcripts and honor incoming credits from other schools as denoted for tenth and eleventh grade for science and social studies in figure 3.8. If learning gaps are found in a student's knowledge from previous courses completed in other districts, adjustments are made to instruction to meet the needs of the new learner.

Structuring Assessments Based on Proficiency Scale Indicators

What distinguishes assessment in a personalized competency-based classroom from a traditional one? In traditional settings, assessments often provide an overall percentage calculated from points earned compared to points possible that indicates whether a student has passed or failed, but this can obscure a student's specific knowledge and abilities. For example, consider an assessment covering the mathematics level 02 addition scale and the mathematics level 02 subtraction scale. Assume the assessment comprises ten questions, and the student scores 60 percent. Typically, this might not be deemed a passing score, but a closer examination linked to the proficiency scales might reveal a different story. If the assessment included five questions on addition and five on subtraction, and the student answered all addition questions correctly but only one subtraction question, this suggests proficiency in addition but a need for further support in subtraction. This assessment item-to-proficiency-scale mapping is a step in the right direction but not the entire solution.

The next step involves developing questions for each proficiency scale at the 2.0, 3.0, and 4.0 levels. An aha moment occurred in WPS during a training session on *The New Art and Science of Teaching* model (Marzano, 2017). The book presented a simple yet effective assessment approach. Rather than complicating assessments with randomized questions or multiple versions, which increases teacher workload, assessments can be structured sequentially: start with score 2.0 items, followed by score 3.0 items, and end with at least one opportunity for students to demonstrate score 4.0 understanding. When scoring, if a student answers all score 2.0 items correctly, the individual is at least at score 2.0 for the scale, and the teacher can proceed to the next section. If more than 50 percent of these questions are missed, the teacher can stop scoring there, assigning a score 1.5. This process continues with the score 3.0 section. But how many questions do they need to create for each score level? The district provided initial guidance to include at least four questions per score level, requiring correct answers to at least three to demonstrate understanding at the scores 2.0 and 3.0 level.

Another shift in practice was the move to include score 4.0 items. Classroom assessments and projects at that point typically only requested demonstrations of understanding at the score 2.0 and 3.0 levels. WPS identified always providing an option for students to strive for a score 4.0 as an essential practice, especially knowing students rarely aim for this level unless prompted. However, starting an assessment with a score 4.0 item could discourage students—thus the importance of the sequential structure. A simple idea is to place score 4.0 items on a separate sheet, allowing the teacher to discreetly distribute the opportunity to students ready for that stretch goal without discouraging students who are not ready yet. This reimagining of assessment design, aligned to proficiency scales, marked a significant transformation in the WPS approach.

Integrating Item Frames Within Cumulative Learning

The final shift in the WPS assessment practice was using item frames as a component of a cumulative learning process. Item frames, which Robert J. Marzano, Christopher W. Dodson, Julia A. Simms, and Jacob P. Wipf (2022) offered in *Ethical Test Preparation in the Classroom*, are structured templates that assist teachers in creating practice items for students, simulating the format and content of state and national tests and ensuring students develop schemas for and experience with the types of questions they will encounter. Item frames have become a critical tool within our learner-centered classrooms, aimed at preparing students for classroom assessments and standardized testing environments.

Integrating item frames into instructional practices supports the cumulative learning process by reinforcing key concepts throughout the year and aligning with personalized competency-based progression. Item frames enable teachers to design assessments that gauge basic understanding, application, and advanced mastery (scores 2.0, 3.0, and 4.0), while offering a detailed measure of student progress and a strategic focus on content mastery. Teachers have incorporated item frames into the teaching and learning cycle through initiatives like Throwback Thursday, where every Thursday class time is allotted toward assessment items based on an item frame that aligns with a proficiency scale from a previous unit. The outgrowth of teachers utilizing frames "to help students think the way our state assessments make them" is for students to eventually develop their own assessment items. This step is the most powerful way to support students in developing the schema to demonstrate their knowledge on high-stakes assessments.

Item frame folios are available for various item types commonly found on state assessments, such as big idea, meaning, detail, function, evidence, and purpose in English language arts, and 2-D and 3-D shapes, volume, fractions, place value, and coordinate planes in mathematics (Marzano et al., 2022). Each folio includes sample released items, guidelines for creating items, strategies to instruct students about the content, instructions to teach students about the specific type of item, and supplemental activities, as illustrated in figure 3.9 and figure 3.10 (page 80).

Third Grade | Example of Teacher-Generated Big Idea Item Frame
Part A What is a main idea of "A Howling Success"? a. Wolves have been missing from Yellowstone for over 70 years. b. Many people feared wolves and wanted them out of the park. c. Wolves helped control the number of elk living in the park. d. Scientists helped increase the number of wolves in Yellowstone. **Part B** Which detail from the article best supports the answer to Part A? a. "They worried that the predators would attack their cows, sheep, and horses . . ." (Paragraph 4) b. "Then things began to change." (Paragraph 5) c. ". . . living wolf-free in Yellowstone for many years . . . " (Paragraph 8) d. ". . . captured 17 more adult wolves in Canada and released them into the park." (Paragraph 12)
Third Grade | Directions for Creating Selected Response Items
1. Select a text with a relatively clear structure that conveys basic cause and effect, simple problems and/or chronologies, and single storylines. Formatting and linguistic clues that signal its structure should be present as well. 2. Write part A using one of the following stems: a. What is a central idea of ____________________? b. What is the main idea of ____________________? c. What is a theme of ____________________? 3. Create a correct choice. 4. Create alternative choices that are incorrect. 5. Write part B using one of the following stems: a. What evidence best supports the answer to part A? b. What information best supports the answer to part A? 6. Create a correct choice. 7. Create alternative choices that are incorrect.
Third Grade | Directions for Creating Constructed Response Items
1. Pick a passage. 2. Write an item using the stem: a. What is the author's message? 3. Add a prompt for evidence, such as: a. Support your answer with details from the text. b. Use details from the text to support your answer. c. Use two details from the source to support your explanation. d. Be sure to use details to support your answer from both texts.

Source: © 2024 by Westminster Public Schools, adapted from Marzano et al., 2022. Used with permission.

FIGURE 3.9: English language arts big idea item frame directions.

Big Idea Frame | Item Analysis **** Analyze the items students will encounter and answer the following questions of each:**
What will I directly teach students about the content?
The "big idea" of a passage is the overarching structure or frame of the passage. A passage can have a smaller structure or frames embedded in the big idea structure. The various types of structures that might be the big idea of a passage include: • Basic cause and effect (e.g., observing that in *Because of Winn-Dixie*, the entrance of a dog into a young girl's life causes many changes that help her grow) • Simple chronologies (e.g., recalling the correct order of the people Opal meets in *Because of Winn-Dixie*) • Problems with basic solutions (e.g., observing that Gloria Dump's problem of blindness is solved by seeing with her heart in *Because of Winn-Dixie*) • Plots with single storylines (e.g., observing that the storyline of *Because of Winn-Dixie* follows the adventures of a young girl and her dog and that the plot follows her growth throughout the story and her coming to peace with her mother's absence)
What will I directly teach students about this type of item?

When trying to determine the main ideas of a passage, your first job is to determine the overall structure of the information in the text.
 	
You should consider the structure of a text that presents simple sequences or chronologies:
• Texts that have a sequence-based structure contain clues as to what the big idea is. These clues include:
    + Certain words and phrases are commonly used: First, second, next, last, before, after.
    + Look for headings, subheadings, or other textual clues that indicate a sequence of events. For example, chapter titles might provide a clue about the events that happen in the chapter.
• Try to recognize the clues about this structure and mark sections of the text that have them.
• When you are finished reading, try to describe the major events or steps in a sequence or chronology in a few sentences.
 	
You should consider the structure of a text that presents basic cause/effect relationships:
• Texts that have a cause/effect structure contain clues as to what the big idea is. These clues include:
    + Certain words and phrases are commonly used: Cause, because, due to, result, sequence, consequence.
• Try to recognize the clues about this structure and mark sections of the text that have them.
• When you are finished reading, try to describe a main causal relationship in a few sentences.
 	
You should consider the structure of a text that presents a simple problem that can be solved:
• Texts that have a problem/solution structure contain clues as to what the big idea is. These clues include:
    + Certain words and phrases are commonly used: Issue, problem, cause, challenge, obstacle, strategy, solve, solution, resolution, fix.
    + Headings and subheadings often indicate the presentation of a problem followed by discussion of one or more solutions.
• Try to recognize the clues about this structure and mark sections of the text that have them.
• When you are finished reading, try to describe the problem and its solution in a few sentences.

You should consider the structure of a story with one main storyline:

- Texts that have one main storyline contain clues as to what the big idea is. These clues include:
    + A story with one narrator or one main character may also have one main storyline.
    + A story with illustrations or pictures that take up most of a page may also have only one storyline.
- Try to recognize the clues about this structure and mark sections of the text that have them.
- When you are finished reading, try to describe the storyline in a few sentences.

Source: © 2024 by Westminster Public Schools, adapted from Marzano et al., 2022. Used with permission.

FIGURE 3.10: English language arts big idea item frame instructional guides.

Cumulative learning is an adaptation of Marzano's cumulative review process (Marzano & Kosena, 2022). It emphasizes the continuous review of critical concepts throughout the academic year, ensuring students not only review material but also have opportunities to relearn and deepen their understanding of key concepts. This approach goes beyond mere practice tests, involving a structured three-phase learning process aimed at enhancing the retention of previously learned content through formal reflection on understanding. The phases include the following.

- **Recording:** Students document their learning on a topic, utilizing various methods such as informal outlines, summarizing techniques, and pictorial notes to organize and capture the main ideas and details of the content.
- **Reviewing:** Through questioning, presented problems, and sample items, students assess their understanding of the content, engaging in activities that challenge them to recall, apply, and infer based on what they have previously learned.
- **Revising:** Students refine their notes and understanding, employing strategies like sentence stems, quick writes, peer feedback, and visual symbols to correct and enhance their grasp of the content.

Key to this process is ensuring students have an accessible archive for their notes, facilitating effective review sessions. Techniques for recording include creating informal outlines, summarizing content, and using pictorial notes. The reviewing phase encourages active engagement with the material through various questioning techniques and problem-solving exercises. The revising is most important as this is where the student should engage with the previously learned content in a new and different way. This phase focuses on making corrections and refining understanding, with strategies such as quick writes and peer feedback aiding in this reflective process. This structured approach to cumulative learning fosters a deeper, more meaningful interaction with content, moving beyond traditional assessment methods to create a dynamic environment where students are continually encouraged to reflect on and improve their understanding.

Westminster Instructional Model

Believing outside perspectives can provide useful insights not readily apparent to those conducting the work, WPS has welcomed external reviewers to provide feedback on what was working and areas for improvement across all aspects of the system. A common theme identified in each review was the lack of a common instructional language. This realization led WPS to adopt a research-based instructional model. The district chose Marzano's (2007) *The Art and Science of Teaching* as the official adopted model. Later, WPS included adaptations for competency-based instruction that Marzano made in the instructional model for the Marzano Academies (Marzano & Abbott, 2022). As the district's understanding of what it meant to run a learner-centered classroom grew, the need to better understand how different instructional practices influenced this became evident. The district consulted Robert J. Marzano, who conducted interviews with WPS teachers and reviewed over ninety hours of instruction to identify the unique aspects of a learner-centered classroom. A few areas of distinction emerged from the study. One key finding was the strategic use of instructional groupings, ranging from whole groups to small groups to individuals. Such grouping is only feasible if teachers are equipped with precise data at the student level to make intentional groupings, which is achieved in WPS via the Empower LMS detailed later in this chapter. An early misunderstanding within the system was the perception that whole-group instruction was inherently bad or inappropriate in a personalized competency-based classroom. Instead, the study found that whole-group direct instruction was appropriate when all or most students were working toward proficiency on the same learning target during a given lesson segment. However, if fifteen of the twenty-six students in the class have already shown competency, time was wasted for over half of the class if whole-group instruction was provided. Eleven students may need direct instruction, but the remaining should be working on other proficiency scales or stretch goals to achieve a 3.5 or 4.0 on the targeted lesson segment.

The study also highlighted distinctions in the areas of assessment and student agency, with a key shift from the teacher being the centerpiece of the teaching and learning process to learners playing a crucial role in the classroom. The inclusion of the elements using student-centered assessments and generating summative scores from the instructional model shifted the focus away from traditional, end-of-unit assessments toward a more nuanced, learner-centered approach. The addition of generating summative scores was particularly important; unlike a traditional teacher gradebook, which typically averages scores earned over a semester, a competency-based classroom tags each piece of evidence to a specific proficiency scale. A summative score is only entered once a student demonstrates competency in multiple ways over time, as articulated in the scale for element IId, shown in figure 3.11.

Element IId: Generating Current Summative Scores in a CBE Classroom	
Design Area II. The Teacher designs and administers assessments that accurately measure students' status on proficiency scales and helps students understand the relationships between scores on assessments and overall status on a proficiency scale.	
Element IId Planning Question: How will I generate current summative scores for individual students?	
Teacher Evidence for Level 2 (Developing) The teacher is: • Systematically entering multiple (formative) scores for students on specific proficiency scales • Periodically translating the set of formative scores into current summative scores for students on specific proficiency scales When asked, the teacher can: • Explain how often they enter formative scores and the overall logic used to assign current summative scores	Student Evidence for Level 3 (Applying) or 4 (Innovating) Students are: • Using the feedback provided by current summative scores to make judgments about what they know and don't know • Talking to the teacher about the meaning of their current summative scores and how they relate to specific proficiency scales When asked, students can: • Explain what the current summative scores they received mean relative to specific proficiency scales

Source: © 2024 by Westminster Public Schools, adapted from Marzano & Abbott, 2022. Used with permission.

FIGURE 3.11: Element IId, generating current summative scores in a CBE classroom scale.

The following sections describe the WPS instructional model and its use as a teacher development tool.

Understanding the Structure of the Model

The Westminster Instructional Model is a robust, multilayered framework central to WPS's personalized competency-based instructional system. It is organized into five domains that anchor the entire model: (1) feedback, (2) content, (3) context, (4) agency, and (5) professionalism. Within these domains are twelve design areas, each addressing a key aspect of instructional practice, from proficiency scales to planning and preparing. These design areas encompass thirty-eight categories, of which thirty-one are observable, allowing for visible assessments of instructional practice, while seven focus on the underlying professional competencies. See figure 3.12 (page 84).

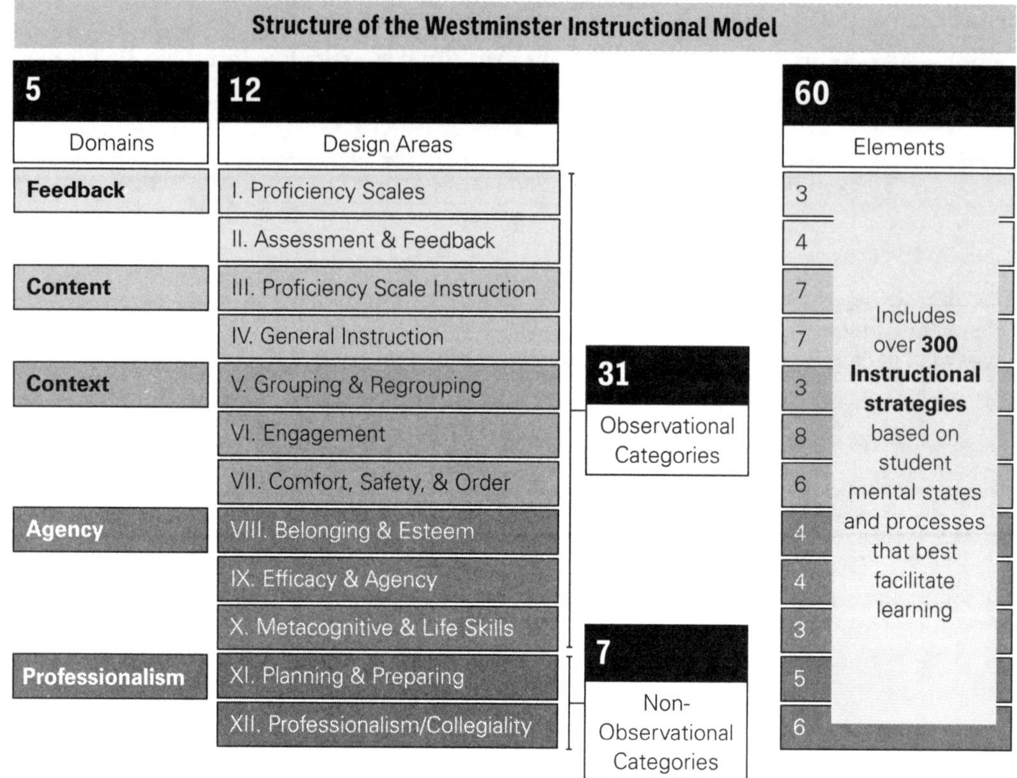

Source: © 2024 by Westminster Public Schools, adapted from Marzano & Abbott, 2022. Used with permission.

FIGURE 3.12: Structure of the Westminster Instructional Model.

The model further breaks down into sixty elements, providing a granular focus on specific instructional tactics and behaviors. See figure 3.13. Over three hundred instructional strategies are associated with these elements, offering an extensive tool kit for educators to draw on. These strategies are formulated to engage with students' mental states and processes, thereby optimizing the learning experience. This structure ensures every facet of teaching is aligned with the principles and tenets of personalized competency-based learning, providing a cohesive and comprehensive approach to education.

Each element in the model is supported by a 4.0 proficiency scale, like those used with WPS students. The scales define the behaviors teachers must demonstrate to achieve score 2.0 and, more importantly, the student behaviors required to demonstrate competency at scores 3.0 and 4.0. Also included are questions for teachers and students when practices are not immediately observable, enhancing clarity in feedback (see figure 3.14, page 87).

	Teacher Effectiveness Rating Elements: Year 1 | Year 2 | Year 3	
Feedback	**I. Proficiency Scales** *Communicating Scales | Y1* **Ia. Providing Proficiency Scales** *Tracking Progress | Y1* **Ib. Tracking Student Progress** *Celebrating Success | Y2* **Ic. Celebrating Success**	**II. Assessment & Feedback** *Obtrusive | Y2* **IIa. Using Obtrusive Assessments** *Student-Centered | Y3* **IIb. Using Student-Centered Assessments** *Unobtrusive | Y2* **IIc. Using Unobtrusive Assessments** *Summative Scores | Y1* **IId. Generating Current Summative Scores**
Content	**III. Proficiency Scale Instruction** *Direct Instruction | Y1* **IIIa. Chunking Content** **IIIb. Processing Content** **IIIc. Recording & Representing** *Structured Practice and Knowledge Deepening | Y1* **IIId. Using Structured Practice** **IIIe. Similarities & Differences** *Complex Tasks | Y3* **IIIf. Cognitively Complex Tasks** *Supporting Claims | Y3* **IIIg. Generating & Defending Claims**	**IV. General Instruction** *Reviewing and Revising | Y1* **IVa. Reviewing Content** **IVb. Revising Knowledge** **IVc. Examining & Correcting Errors** *Highlighting and Elaborating | Y1* **IVd. Highlighting Critical Info** **IVe. Previewing Content** **IVf. Elaborative Inferences** *Extending | Y3* **IVg. Extending through Homework**
Context	**V. Grouping & Regrouping** *Group Interaction | Y1* **Va. Supporting Group Interaction** *Group Transitions | Y2* **Vb. Supporting Group Transitions** *Group Support | Y2* **Vc. Providing Group Support**	**VI. Engagement** *Attention | Y1* **VIa. Noticing & Reacting** **VIb. Increasing Response Rates** *Energy | Y1* **VIc. Using Physical Movement** **VId. Maintaining Lively Pace** **VIe. Intensity & Enthusiasm** *Interest and Intrigue | Y3* **VIf. Present Unusual Information** **VIg. Using Friendly Controversy** **VIh. Using Academic Games**

FIGURE 3.13: Complete Westminster Instructional Model with notations of the year categories included in teacher effectiveness ratings.

continued ▶

<table>
<tr><th colspan="3">Teacher Effectiveness Rating Elements: Year 1 | Year 2 | Year 3</th></tr>
<tr><td>Context</td><td colspan="2">VII. Comfort, Safety, & Order
Comfort | Y2
VIIa. Organizing Physical Layout
Safety | Y1
VIIb. Demonstrating Withitness
VIIc. Adherence to Rules and Procedures
VIId. Lack of Adherence to Rules and Procedures
Order | Y1
VIIe. Establish Rules and Procedures
VIIf. Display Objectivity and Control</td></tr>
<tr><td>Agency</td><td>VIII. Belonging & Esteem
Showing Affection | Y2
VIIIa. Using Verbal and Nonverbals
VIIIb. Demonstrate Value and Respect
Understanding Students | Y1
VIIIc. Student Backgrounds
VIIId. Talking About Self

IX. Efficacy and Agency
Inspiration | Y1
IXa. Inspiring Students
Student Agency | Y1
IXb. Enhancing Student Agency
The Reluctant Learner | Y3
IXc. Asking In-Depth Questions
IXd. Probing Incorrect Answers</td><td>X. Metacognitive & Life Skills
Self-Reflection | Y2
Xa. Reflecting on Learning
Long-Term Projects | Y3
Xb. Using Long-Term Projects
Metacognitive Skills | Y3
Xc. Metacognitive and Life Skills
Professionalism</td></tr>
<tr><td>Professionalism</td><td>XI. Planning & Preparing
Progressions | Y1
XIa. Instructional Progression & Pacing
Lessons and Units | Y1
XIb. Organizing Lessons for Deeper Learning
XIc. Multidisciplinary Planning
Materials and Resources | Y1
XId. Enhancing With Traditional and Digital Materials
Special Populations | Y1
XIe. Adapting for Special Populations</td><td>XII. Professionalism and Collegiality
Parent and Community Involvement | Y1
XIIa. Interacting With Students, Parents, and Community
XIIb. Setting and Implementing Professional Goals
XIIc. Reflecting on Teaching
XIId. Seeking or Providing Mentoring
District and School Development | Y1
XIIe. Adherence to Rules, Procedures, and Policies
XIIf. Participation in District and School Initiatives</td></tr>
</table>

Source: © 2024 by Westminster Public Schools, adapted from Marzano & Abbott, 2022. Used with permission.

The Marzano Compendium of Instructional Strategies and the expansion of this compendium for the Marzano Academies model (Marzano Resources, n.d.b) serve as another crucial resource, offering a deep dive into each element, including instructional strategies, methods for determining status and growth, and student surveys for a comprehensive view of the practice. These tools are used by teachers in achieving their professional goals.

<table>
<tr><th colspan="2">Element IIIg (E14): Generating and Defending Claims in a CBE Classroom</th></tr>
<tr><td colspan="2">Design Area III: The teacher designs and executes instructional activities in real time and virtually that help students progress through the levels of specific proficiency scales.</td></tr>
<tr><td colspan="2">Element IIIg Planning Question: How will I help students generate and defend claims?</td></tr>
<tr><td>Teacher Evidence for Level 2 (Developing)

The teacher is:
• Introducing the concept of claims and support
• Presenting the formal structure of claims and support
• Providing students opportunities to generate claims, provide grounds and backing for their claims, and generating qualifiers to their claims
• Having students formally (orally or in writing) present their claims

When asked, the teacher can:
• Explain how generating and defending claims is addressed in real time and virtually
• Describe the most common strategies used for generating and defending claims</td><td>Student Evidence of Level 3 (Applying) or 4 (Innovating)

Students are:
• Generating claims
• Providing grounds for their claims
• Providing backing for the grounds
• Providing qualifiers to their claim

When asked, students can:
• Describe why generating and supporting claims helps them learn more deeply and rigorously
• Explain the claim on which they are currently working and the support they generated</td></tr>
</table>

	4 Innovating	3 Applying	2 Developing	1 Beginning	0 Not Using
Generating and Defending Claims	The teacher engages in all behaviors at the Applying level. In addition, the teacher identifies those students who are not developing logical arguments regarding their claims. The teacher designs alternate activities and strategies to meet their specific needs, leading to almost all students developing logical arguments regarding their claims.	The teacher engages students in activities that help them generate and defend claims, AND the majority of students are able to develop logical arguments regarding their claims.	The teacher engages students in activities to help them generate and defend claims and provides adequate guidance and support without significant errors or omissions. Evidence for this level of performance includes: 1. Explicitly teaching students how to make and defend claims 2. Having students formally present their claims 3. Etc. . . .	The teacher engages students in activities that help them generate and defend claims but does not provide adequate guidance and support, such as providing a clear model of the nature of an effective argument with its related parts and providing adequate practice in analyzing and constructing arguments.	The teacher does not engage students in activities that help them generate and defend claims.

Source:

FIGURE 3.14: Guide sheet for element IIIg, generating and defending claims in a CBE classroom.

Setting Teacher Goals

The folios, seen in figure 3.15, serve as a crucial tool for teachers in achieving their professional goals. In alignment with the district's competency-based approach, each teacher is required to maintain three professional goals throughout the year, rather than setting just three annual goals as in the past. This continuous goal-setting process ensures that once a goal is achieved—such as completing a goal related to element VIIa: Organizing the Physical Layout of a CBE Classroom by December 18—the teacher immediately sets a new goal. This new goal is identified through self-reflection, potentially informed by the teacher survey included in the folio, and further refined by conducting a student survey to gather baseline feedback. This approach mirrors the district's emphasis on ongoing development, where the tracking of professional progress continues beyond the traditional school year.

Generating and Defending Claims

Introducing the Concept of Claims and Support

Even though people make claims and provide support quite naturally, it is important to introduce the concept of claims and support to students so that they might engage in this actively more consciously and rigorously. At first, it is enough to introduce the idea that a claim is simply something one believes to be true. Students should be able to provide reasons for their beliefs and be able to provide evidence for those reasons. Reasons and evidence for claims are referred to as support.

Teacher Actions

- Explaining and exemplifying claims or beliefs
- Explaining the relationship between claims, reasons, and evidence
- Exemplifying reasons and evidence

Desired Student Responses

- Being able to explain and exemplify claims
- Being able to explain and exemplify reasons and evidence
- Generating claims with accompanying reasons and evidence

Extra Support

- Providing students with practice exercises in which they identify claims, reasons, and evidence

Extension

- Asking students to find examples of claims with reasons and evidence in the media

Frames for Claims and Support

One of the easiest ways to help students generate claims and support is to provide them with sentence prompts like the following.

Claim: I believe that ____________.

Reasons: I believe this because ____________.

Evidence: My evidence for this is ____________.

Students can complete these sentence stems and share them with the whole class or in small groups.

At the primary level, students might use versions of the prompts such as the following.

Claim: My new idea is ____________.

Reasons: I think this because ____________.

Evidence: What I actually saw was ____________.

These stems are designed to be used with things students can actually observe, such as what happens to a plant growing in the classroom, the behavior of ants in an ant colony, or the habits of birds nesting in a tree outside the classroom.

MARZANO COMPENDIUM OF INSTRUCTIONAL STRATEGIES
5

Source: © 2016 by Marzano Resources. Used with permission.

FIGURE 3.15: Page from the Marzano Resources Generating and Defending Claims folio.

Each school monitors teacher goals in slightly different ways, but one of the most effective practices involves using the Tracking Progress Charts found at the back of each element's folio (see figure 3.16). As teachers attempt the instructional strategies highlighted in the compendium, they track how implementation of the strategy went using the associated proficiency scale. Once they self-assess several instructional strategies from the compendium at a score 3.0, they then request their evaluator to observe one or more of those strategies during an upcoming classroom visit. Upon successful classroom observation, the teacher finalizes that professional goal element as complete and looks to the WIM to identify their next goal element. Principals often encourage teachers to publicly track their progress on these sheets, which are prominently displayed either on their classroom door or on a bulletin board at the front of their classroom. This not only allows visitors to provide targeted feedback on their goal element but also acts as a modeling technique for students who are engaged in their own goal setting and tracking of progress cycles.

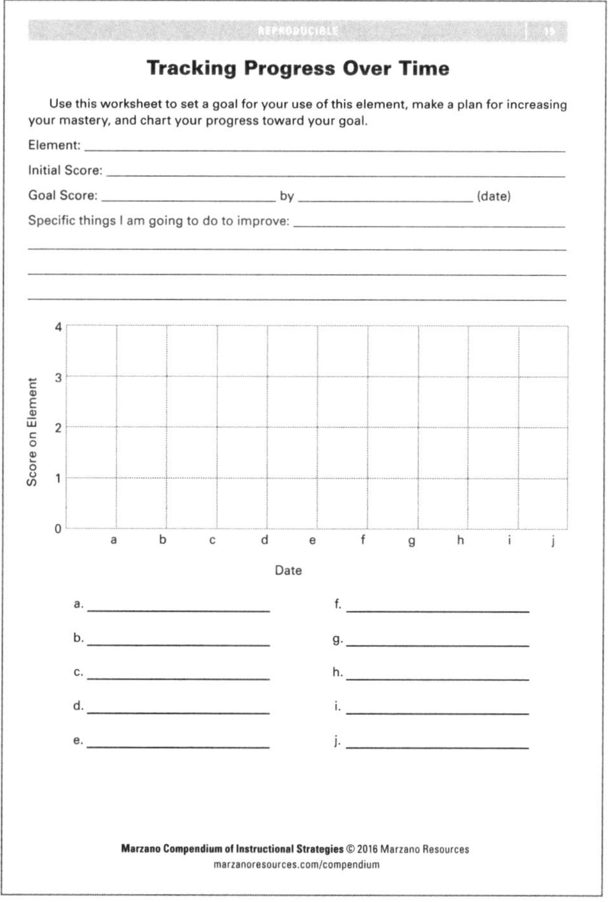
REPRODUCIBLE

Tracking Progress Over Time

Use this worksheet to set a goal for your use of this element, make a plan for increasing your mastery, and chart your progress toward your goal.

Element: ______

Initial Score: ______

Goal Score: ______ by ______ (date)

Specific things I am going to do to improve: ______

a. ______ f. ______

b. ______ g. ______

c. ______ h. ______

d. ______ i. ______

e. ______ j. ______

Source: © 2016 by Marzano Resources. Used with permission.

FIGURE 3.16: Sheets used by teachers to track progress on instructional goals.

Shifting to a Feedback and Development System

WPS believes promoting a PCBS requires the district to promote a personalized competency-based workforce. This belief led to the development of a teacher evaluation system grounded in the same tenets as a personalized competency-based education model. Wanting to highlight the ethos of continuous improvement over time, district leaders were intentional in referring to the model not as an evaluation system but rather as a feedback and development tool to shift teacher perception of what "evaluation" meant in WPS.

The district collaborated with the state department of education to gain approval for a customized evaluation system that exceeded the state's requirements. Leveraging the superintendent's teacher leadership cabinet and the district's instructional advisory committee, WPS embarked on developing a custom educator evaluation system aligned to the district's instructional model.

The first step involved aligning the instructional elements of the Westminster Instructional Model with the Colorado Model Evaluation System indicators. This process highlighted a gap in the WIM, specifically teacher expectations surrounding instructional planning and professionalism. This led to the creation of an additional WIM domain, termed the "professionalism standards." The original four domains were observable instructional elements, while the newly added professionalism domain was unobservable. Even though these elements cannot be seen directly in classroom instruction, they are critical to becoming an effective teacher. And their incorporation into the WIM allowed for the WPS Educator Feedback and Development system to meet and exceed the state's expectations, paving the way for state approval. Once the WIM domains, categories, and elements were finalized, WPS needed to determine how the teacher effectiveness rating would be calculated. During discussions among teacher leaders, school administrators, district administrators, and union members, a key realization emerged: expecting a teacher to demonstrate proficiency across an entire instructional model in their first year of teaching is unrealistic. In most evaluation systems, if a teacher does not meet every element in the adopted model, they may be labeled as "Unsatisfactory" or "Does Not Meet." WPS recognized that it should typically take three years for a teacher to demonstrate proficiency on all WIM elements, allowing supervisors ample time to document the full scope of the instructional model. As a result, WPS established a three-year ramp-up period to meet the model's expectations while respecting the professional growth process. Given that demonstrating proficiency in all sixty WIM elements can be overwhelming for both teachers and administrators, the WPS evaluation system was structured around gradual progress in specific observation categories, or instructional elements that can be grouped together.

The research of Robert J. Marzano, Cameron L. Rains, and Philip B. Warrick (2021) confirmed that a teacher does not need to demonstrate mastery of every instructional element within an instructional model. Their book *Improving Teacher Development and Evaluation* (Marzano et al., 2021) emphasized teacher flexibility and individual strengths within instructional practices. For instance, consider the WIM category of Interest and Intrigue within the Engagement design area. This category includes three elements: (1) presenting unusual information, (2) using friendly controversy, and (3) using academic games. An effective teacher does not need to employ all three elements to create interest and intrigue in the classroom effectively but can focus on just one. This approach acknowledges the uniqueness of each teacher and provides flexibility for educators to demonstrate competency in Interest and Intrigue through different WIM elements.

Observational categories also group elements that covary, where mastery of one element demonstrates mastery in others. For example, in the Comfort, Safety, and Order design area, the WIM element of Demonstrating Withitness inherently addresses the WIM element of Lack of Adherence to Rules and Procedures. This concept of covariance allows administrators and teachers to score all sixty WIM elements for evaluation through a focus on only thirty-seven observational categories. This approach made adopting the model more manageable and allowed the TER to be calculated based on observational categories, reducing the burden of recording and reporting for everyone involved.

Another key shift in the WPS Educator Feedback and Development system is the use of "evergreen" data. In this model, a teacher's previous demonstrations of competency on specific instructional elements are not erased at the start of a new school year. Instead, all data from a teacher's past evaluations remain in the system year after year. WPS believes this approach shifts administrative practice from merely checking boxes of instructional aptitude during annual formal observations to genuinely observing and supporting a teacher's practice over time. This allows evaluators to focus on instructional elements where a teacher has not yet demonstrated competency and to provide targeted support in areas where professional growth is still needed.

Keenly aware that evergreen data persist in the system, WPS has instituted safeguards to ensure educators cannot rely on historical evaluation scores indefinitely. Acknowledging research (Darling-Hammond, Wei, Andree, Richardson, & Orphanos, 2009) that shows an educator's instructional practice may regress over time, WPS created a parameter in the TER calculations to account for this reality. While evergreen data remain in the system, any element score that remains stagnant for three years is removed from the teacher's effectiveness rating.

Scoring Elements

Referring to the WIM Instructional Element proficiency scales, a score 3.0 can be achieved by a teacher only if the students in the classroom are actively demonstrating aspects of the instructional element. This requirement creates the need for a specific observation process when evaluating a teacher on the WIM. When observing, a school leader should always begin by assessing the teacher at the score 2.0 level of every element scale. If the teacher effectively demonstrates the *teacher* look-fors (score 2.0), the principal then observes the *student* look-fors (score 3.0). If the teacher is effectively instructing an element but that instruction is not translating into student action, the principal marks a score 2.0. However, if the teacher's instruction leads to students actively engaging with the instructional element, then the principal marks a score 3.0.

For instance, consider WIM element Ib, Tracking Student Progress. If the teacher effectively tracks the class's progress on a proficiency scale using a competency tracker on the wall, they would be marked with a score 2.0, since the teacher is performing the action while the students passively observe. However, if, after an assessment, the teacher asks the students to track their progress on a proficiency scale in their student data notebooks, the teacher would be marked with a score 3.0 because the students are active participants. Beginning with the score 2.0 look-fors before moving to the score 3.0 look-fors ensures accurate scoring by confirming that a teacher is not marked as fully competent until their students demonstrate the instructional element.

One notable consideration in scoring the WIM is that not all instructional elements are easily observed during formal or informal classroom observations. For example, WIM element IId, Generating Current Summative Scores, is not necessarily a daily instructional practice. Even if a principal conducts multiple observations of a teacher throughout the school year, they may not directly observe this element in action. To ensure a teacher's TER accurately reflects the entirety of their instructional practice, teachers are encouraged to upload instructional artifacts and evidence for any WIM elements that are actively being utilized but not directly observed during the year. For instance, a teacher can upload evidence of assessments and assignments used to generate summative scores, enabling the principal to provide official evaluation scores based on this evidence, even without direct observation. This practice ensures every WIM element is accurately scored each year, providing a comprehensive assessment of the teacher's effectiveness.

Monitoring Implementation of the Instructional Model

Recognizing that teaching can be a private practice and that school or districtwide instructional initiatives can sometimes be ignored without notice, WPS implemented

CBS learning walks—informal, nonevaluative classroom observations conducted by school and district administrators. These learning walks were designed to monitor classroom instructional practices aligned with the WIM, with the goal of achieving consistent application of learner-centered practices across the system. Over the years, WPS has gone through several iterations of the learning walks, continually adjusting them to meet current needs.

The initial round of learning walks included leaders from both the instructional and noninstructional sides of the district, each bringing a unique perspective to classroom observations. For example, WIM element VIIa, Organizing the Physical Layout of the Classroom, allowed the executive director of procurement to gain insights into the classroom furniture layout needed to support teachers in successfully implementing this WIM element. After participating in several learning walks, the approach to selecting classroom furniture and designing instructional settings shifted, resulting in many classrooms being furnished with flexible seating that more closely resembles a local coffee shop than traditional desks in rows. This inclusion of noninstructional administrators in the learning walks served its purpose, and after several years, WPS modified the format to include only school administrators and learning services directors from the central office.

The next iteration of learning walks was designed to collect observational data from each school several times throughout the year to pinpoint successes and areas for growth in WIM implementation. Observing strong instructional practices in one classroom provided administrators from different schools with examples of how various WIM elements could be successfully deployed. In addition to fostering a collaborative culture among principals, it also provided real-world examples for building leaders to take back to their own schools. This helped increase overall teacher effectiveness on WIM elements across the district while deepening administrators' knowledge and experience in observing the WIM. This focus on developing administrator expertise led to WPS's most recent iteration of learning walks.

Learning walks are always conducted by observation teams, where two to four administrators observe the same classroom lesson for fifteen to twenty minutes. Following the observation, debriefs are held to discuss what was observed, including the specific WIM elements seen and how they were scored. During these discussions, interrater reliability issues emerged, particularly when administrators disagreed on which WIM elements were observed or on the appropriate scores to assign. In response, the CBS learning walk design shifted its focus from observing high-quality instruction to be shared across the district to instead helping develop school and district administrators' skills in accurately observing and scoring WIM elements.

Scoring on Proficiency Scales

Scoring student work on proficiency scales is a nuanced process that involves three types of scores, all occurring throughout the school year and grounded in the clear expectations outlined in the WPS proficiency scales. As seen in figure 3.17, the three types build on each other: (1) evidence scores, (2) overall proficiency scale scores, and (3) overall performance level or course scores.

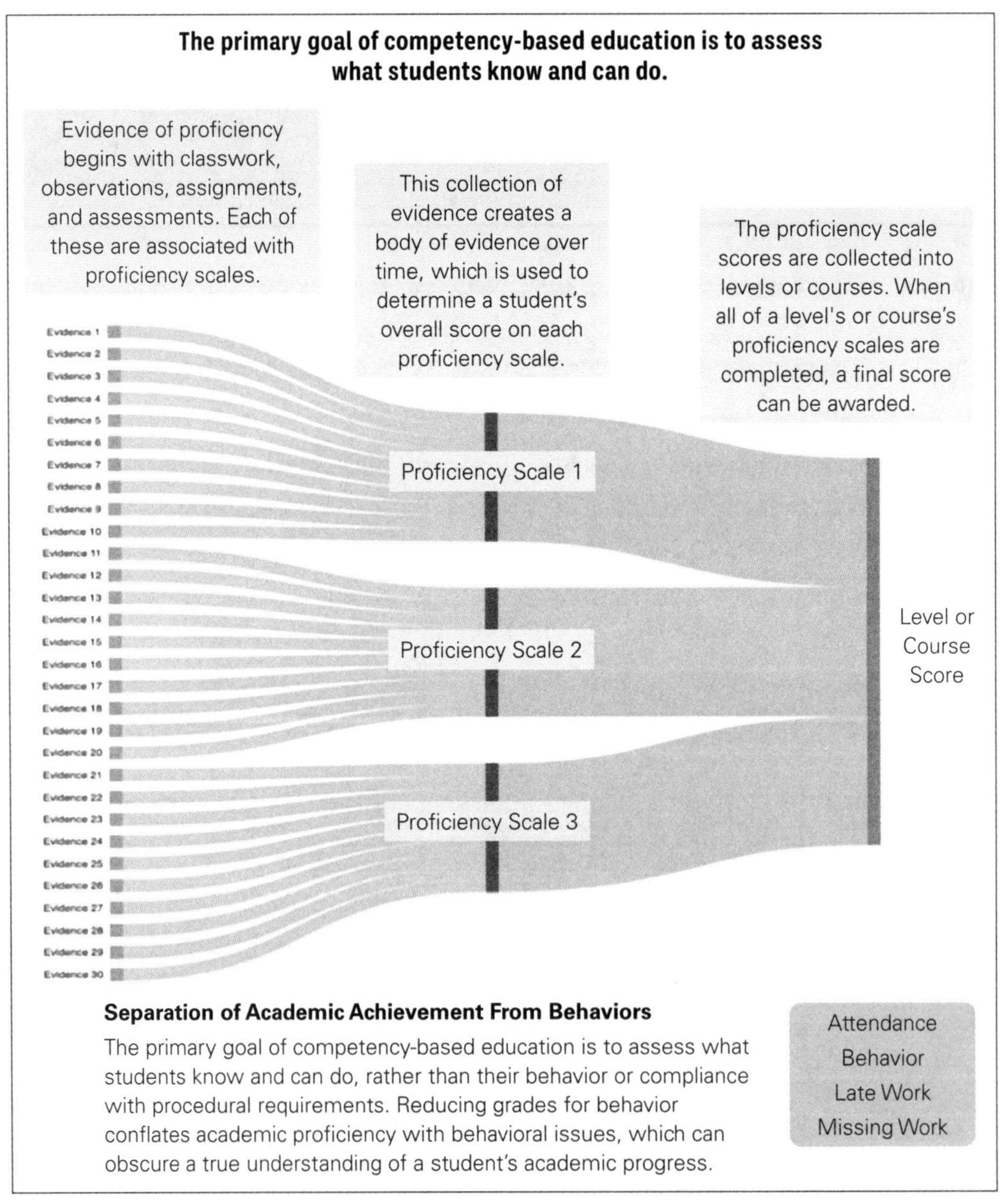

Source: © 2024 by Westminster Public Schools. Used with permission.

FIGURE 3.17: Breakdown of scores in the WPS version of PCBS.

The shift from using terms like "assignments" and "assessments" to a more inclusive term, "evidence," underscores this approach. Every score entered must be linked to at least one proficiency scale, though in practice, most pieces of evidence provide opportunities to demonstrate proficiency across multiple scales. Each proficiency scale requires a separate score, ranging from 0.0 to 4.0, including half points.

Scoring at the Bottom of a Proficiency Scale

The lower scores of the proficiency scale present challenges in shifting educational practices. Assigning a score of 0, often used as a form of punishment when a student does not turn in an assignment, is based on the misconception that it will motivate students to improve. Joe Feldman (2024), in *Grading for Equity*, highlighted how such punitive grading practices disproportionately harm struggling students and create barriers to their learning and engagement. Similarly, Douglas B. Reeves (2004) argued in "The Case Against the Zero" that these practices fail to provide meaningful feedback and often demoralize students.

Scoring evidence of student learning in relation to proficiency scales removes the ability to weaponize points. According to the language of a WPS proficiency scale, a score 0.0 is given when "even with help, no understanding or skill is demonstrated." If a student has not submitted work for review, the absence of evidence makes assigning any score, including 0.0, inappropriate. Instead, such situations require teachers to focus on encouraging submission and offering opportunities for reassessment. This approach shifts the emphasis from compliance to mastery, aligning grading practices with the principles of equity and personalized learning.

In such cases, when a student misses an assignment, a teacher can instead submit a "no evidence" score, represented by an *M* for missing. This score indicates the absence of the assignment without inaccurately reflecting the student's academic abilities on the overall proficiency scale. In other words, an *M* represents the student's work habits rather than their demonstration of competency against a particular standard.

Scoring in the Middle of a Proficiency Scale

In the middle of a proficiency scale, another common scoring challenge arises with score 2.0 standards. By design, the score 2.0 content of a proficiency scale includes the scaffolded standards that a student must first master before achieving the score 3.0 standards. These prerequisite understandings or abilities might include academic standards that require a lower DOK level, which serve as the foundation for the higher DOK levels of the score 3.0 standards. Often, these are essential skills or knowledge, such as key vocabulary terms.

For instance, when a student earns a perfect score on a vocabulary test, the teacher does not mark them with a score 3.0 on that assessment. Since vocabulary is considered a prerequisite skill, it is always awarded a score 2.0, even when the student scores perfect on the test. When a student earns an overall score of 2.0 on a proficiency scale, it indicates that they have mastered all the prerequisite skills and understandings that scaffold to the score 3.0 standards of the same scale.

Marking a score 2.0, even for a perfect test, can be confusing for students and parents, especially when a score 3.0 is typically seen as demonstrating mastery. To help clarify that, in this case, a score 2.0 is the highest score a student can achieve on a vocabulary test, it is important that the system allows for a "maximum achievable score" (MAS) to be represented in the gradebook. When a vocabulary test is marked with a MAS of score 2.0, it ensures that others viewing the grade understand that the student did exactly what was expected and that a score 2.0 is, in fact, a demonstration of their mastery of the prerequisite skills.

Scoring at the Top of a Proficiency Scale

At the top of the proficiency scale, the score 4.0 also often leads to misunderstandings. A common refrain in WPS is "A score 4.0 does not mean doing more." In other words, a score 4.0 is not earned when a student completes fifteen single-digit multiplication problems when the assignment requires ten. Simply demonstrating competency more frequently on a score 3.0 learning target is not sufficient for achieving a score 4.0. Instead, a score 4.0 reflects a student's ability to make more in-depth inferences that extend beyond classroom teachings, embodying the full spectrum of skills and knowledge outlined in the scale, often applied in real-world contexts. Early misapplications included assigning a score 4.0 for perfect test results or awarding it as extra credit for completing additional work, pitfalls of which any system transitioning to a personalized competency-based model must be aware.

Leveraging Evidence to Determine Student Competency

Determining when a student has truly demonstrated competency, as well as deciding the adequate amount of evidence required, remains a topic of ongoing discussion. Initially, WPS required students to submit three separate pieces of evidence for each learning standard before a teacher could mark proficiency. However, this approach proved problematic.

Proficiency scales vary in their depth and complexity, meaning that not all scales are equal in terms of what students must know or be able to do to demonstrate competency.

Some scales require multiple forms of evidence, while others might need only one. WPS guidance to instructional staff is to compile a body of evidence demonstrating proficiency in a variety of ways over time.

To assist teachers in determining the precise competence levels of their students across the proficiency scales, the Empower LMS employs three separate algorithms, each using a different mathematical calculation to evaluate a student's current proficiency level based on the body of evidence submitted by the teacher. These algorithms serve as reference only, with all final marks of student competency and scoring decisions made only by the teacher of record.

Updating Overall Scores on Proficiency Scales

Considering that different proficiency scales require different amounts of evidence before a student can be marked as competent, the process of updating scores on these scales throughout the academic year becomes integral. Since most proficiency scales necessitate multiple pieces of evidence, the ability to assign a current overall score to the proficiency scale is crucial. This score helps measure where a student resides in the scale's progression and identifies which standards the student still needs to master.

After thorough discussions with teachers, WPS established a protocol where a student earns an overall score of 1.5 on the first entry of student evidence toward a particular scale, regardless of the specific standard the evidence is aligned with. For example, a student might earn a score 2.0 after completing a class vocabulary assignment but still be missing evidence for the other standards embedded within the proficiency scale. In this case, the evidence score will be recorded as a score 2.0 for the vocabulary assignment, while the overall proficiency scale score will be listed as score 1.5, indicating that work on the scale has begun but is not yet complete. This automatic scoring method was designed to streamline the recording process to signify scale work has begun without requiring the teacher to mark an Update Overall Score each time.

Once a student effectively demonstrates competence on all the score 2.0 standards, the teacher can then update the overall score on the proficiency scale from score 1.5 to score 2.0. The updating of overall scores for all subsequent levels of a proficiency scale after the initial score 1.5 is no longer automatic. Only after a teacher believes a student has provided enough evidence for a particular score, and often in consultation with the Empower algorithms, does the teacher update the student's overall score to 2.0, 3.0, or 4.0.

Updating Overall Course Scores

Now that students have overall scores marked for each proficiency scale within a performance or grade level, it is possible to measure progress toward an overall course score. The individual evidence scores accumulate to form overall proficiency scale scores, and these proficiency scale scores can, in turn, be compiled to calculate an overall course score. This is the only instance within the WPS scoring methodology where an average is used.

For example, in mathematics level 04, the overall course score is calculated by averaging the overall scores for all sixteen proficiency scales that are at a 3.0 or higher. This averaged score can then be rounded to a 3.0, 3.5, or 4.0. Additionally, it is possible to convert this averaged score of proficiency scales into a grade-level equivalent (GLE) score, a topic that will be discussed in detail in an upcoming discussion regarding class roster scheduling.

Regarding overall course scores, once a student has earned a score 3.0 or higher on all proficiency scales in a particular course, an averaged score of those scales is generated and marked as the overall course score. This score then becomes the final "grade" for the class or course.

Recording and Reporting

In the early days of WPS's implementation of a PCBS, one significant barrier was the lack of a technological system capable of managing the substantial data involved, particularly in recording and reporting student scores across numerous standards and proficiency scales. This challenge was formidable and, in truth, impractical for teachers. Throughout those initial years, two essential principles emerged: (1) the necessity for a student-centric system and (2) the importance of data continuity across academic years.

First, personalized competency-based education diverges from traditional course-centric systems that confine teachers to a specific set of content standards. In a competency-based system, teachers are granted flexibility and are expected to teach and assess proficiency scales across different content areas and performance, or grade levels. This flexibility is crucial for truly personalizing learning for every student, as not all learners in a classroom are necessarily at the same point in a particular content progression. Traditional schooling only requires a teacher to instruct, assign, and assess student work from one grade level and content area, rendering most gradebook software inadequate for a PCBS.

Another critical issue with traditional grading practices is the end-dating of student work and associated academic competencies from year to year. From a teacher's standpoint, all evidence of student learning in conventional systems is permanently deleted once final grades are submitted at the end of the term. This practice erases any record of historical student performance, leaving future teachers without the valuable information of students' past performance to plan instruction effectively. Consequently, existing learning gaps may go unaddressed, or content previously mastered may be redundantly covered, either of which hinders student growth.

The need for a nontraditional gradebook that allows teachers to access and score student learning across all academic standards, while also maintaining evidence of student mastery from year to year, became pivotal to the success of WPS's PCBS. To address this need, WPS collaborated with a developer for over fifteen years to design a system that can meet these requirements, ensuring the sustainability and effectiveness of the personalized competency-based approach.

Evergreen Data Model

The Center for Competency-Based Education by Empower Learning (https://cbe.empowerlearning.net) has developed an LMS founded on the evergreen data model, enabling districts to fully embrace competency-based learning. Unlike conventional systems where student data are archived or reset after the grading term, Empower maintains evergreen data on all student performance as it relates to proficiency scales. This approach facilitates a seamless transition for students across academic periods and settings, allowing all teachers to access a comprehensive view of a student's work.

To combat the persistent issue of social promotion—where students automatically advance to the next grade level at the end of the school year—personalized competency-based schools require a flexible recording and reporting tool. Empower's system allows students to advance to the next grade level at any point during the school year while also freezing their progression at the year's end. This feature enables the next year's teacher to pick up exactly where the student left off in the spring. Maintaining a continuous, living gradebook from kindergarten through high school graduation is essential for achieving a truly personalized competency-based education.

A significant difference between traditional systems and Empower is the ability for any teacher to enter evidence of student learning toward any proficiency scale, regardless of their subject area. For instance, a student who has demonstrated competency at a score 3.0 or better on twelve of the sixteen proficiency scales for mathematics level 07, and at a score 2.0 on an additional three scales, will have their comprehensive body of evidence accessible to all educators. A science teacher, for example, might contribute to a student's mathematics level 07 proficiency based on a mathematical computation completed in a lab assignment, while other proficiency scales could be addressed by an interventionist, summer-school teacher, or the next year's mathematics teacher.

The evergreen data model not only aids teachers in tailoring instruction for individual students but also supports strategic planning for whole-group instruction. The Empower Target Browser provides teachers with quick visibility of proficiency scale completion across all grade levels for each student in their class. When planning a lesson, a teacher can see any previous student data related to that proficiency scale, as well as data from earlier grade levels that directly scaffold the learning. This allows teachers to identify the appropriate starting points for their instructional planning.

With access to detailed data from the outset, teachers can create customized Year at a Glance (YAAG) documents or course scope-and-sequences based on their incoming students' previous scores on proficiency scales. Throughout the year, teachers can make informed decisions about the appropriateness of whole-group, small-group, or individualized instruction.

Figure 3.18 displays the Empower Target Browser, where a teacher has selected all mathematics proficiency scales from grades 4 and 5 to be displayed. Each row displays tiles of the grades 4 and 5 proficiency scales for the different mathematics domains, while a tile's colored bars represent previous student scores on those scales.

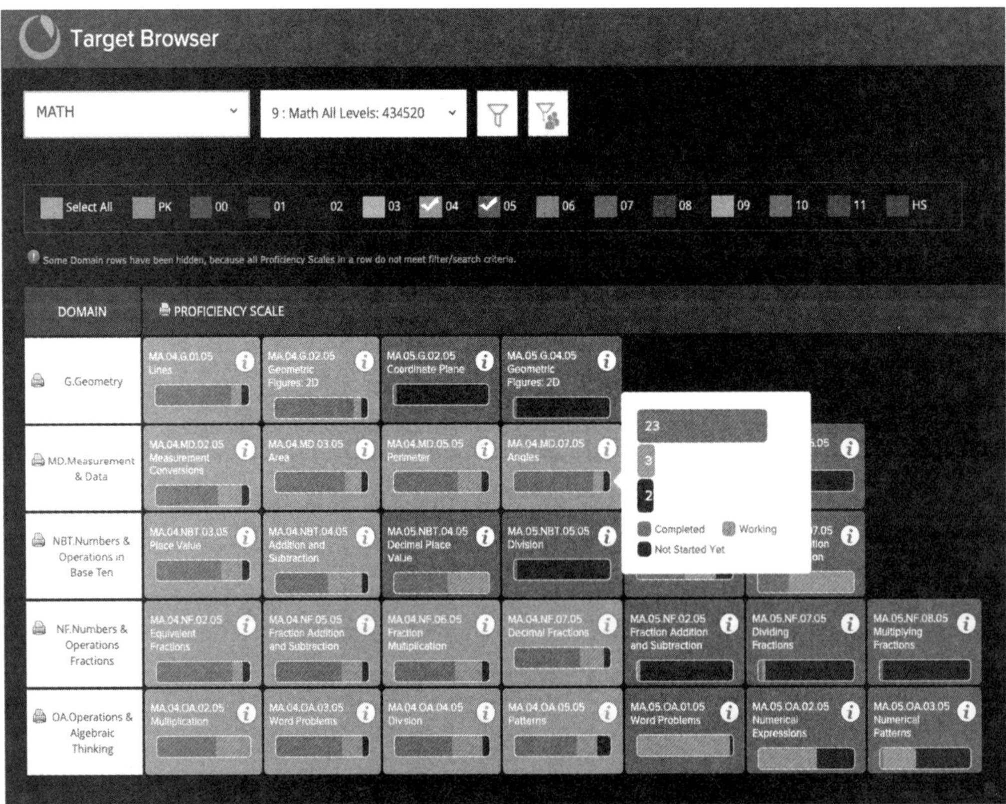

Source: © *2024 by Empower Learning, LLC. Used with permission.*

FIGURE 3.18: The Empower LMS target browser.

For instance, the target browser data reveal that most students in the class (twenty-three in the example) have already mastered or achieved a score 3.0 on a specific proficiency scale. This indicates that whole-group instruction on this scale might not be the most efficient use of time. Instead, the teacher could focus on advancing these students toward a score 4.0 or move them forward to the next aligned proficiency scale in grade 5. Meanwhile, the remaining students who have not yet demonstrated competency (three in progress and two not started) would benefit from small-group instruction, beginning with the scale's learning progression to achieve a score 3.0 proficiency.

Access to detailed evergreen data exemplifies how educators in WPS have leveraged Empower LMS to transform educational practices, providing a more personalized and effective learning experience for every student.

Access for All

Traditional gradebook software typically limits teachers to viewing only their current students, meaning they are only responsible for the academic growth of those students. However, Empower allows staff to access every student's gradebook across all content areas and performance levels, enabling the principle of collective efficacy to be realized in meaningful ways. Collective efficacy, in this context, refers to the shared belief among teachers that they can collaboratively influence student achievement and improve outcomes for all students. This capability reinforces WPS's shared commitment to the educational progress of all students, regardless of any given school year's class rosters.

For instance, a reading interventionist can enter scores on any proficiency scale for the students with whom they work. This ensures the learning achieved during small-group pullout instruction is integrated into a student's overall body of evidence toward competency. Such integration allows this vital information to be readily accessible to all stakeholders, ensuring a holistic view of each student's progress.

In a PCBS, the primary objective is for students to accumulate a comprehensive body of evidence that accurately reflects their demonstrated competency on the proficiency scales required for high school graduation. To achieve this, it is imperative that all student work, regardless of where or with which teacher it was produced, is accounted for. Finding a gradebook system like Empower is critical to meeting this goal, because it supports the continuous tracking and updating of students' progress throughout their educational journey.

This system is particularly beneficial for project-based learning, as it allows teachers to tag and score proficiency scales across various content areas and performance levels. Unlike traditional systems, where, for example, a U.S. history teacher would only have access to a specific set of content standards, the Empower LMS provides the teacher access to all content standards and performance levels. This enables the teacher to design a cross-curricular project-based learning unit, and upon completion, the ability to provide students with evidence toward competency on proficiency scales beyond the social studies content area.

Consider a scenario where a teacher is developing a unit centered on the social studies level 09 Historical Inquiry scale. In the process of identifying evidence that students could provide to demonstrate competence, it becomes apparent that they could also highlight skills relevant to the literacy level 09 Analyzing Claims, Evidence and Reasoning proficiency scale, and the personal relational competency level 09 Cultural Responsiveness scale. Utilizing the Empower system, the teacher can tag and score across all three proficiency scales as they compile evidence on their project-based assignment. Those scores will then be viewable to the student's literacy and homeroom teacher.

By providing access to all content and performance level standards, along with the mandate that every teacher is empowered and encouraged to provide instruction and assess student learning on any proficiency scale their teaching happens to address, collective efficacy is realized in dynamic ways. The outcome is that students earn credit for all their learning experiences, with every teacher actively participating in each step of a student's educational journey. While all teachers are encouraged to contribute evidence toward proficiency, the final proficiency scale score of 3.0, 3.5, or 4.0 is determined by the highly qualified teacher in the relevant content area.

Progress Reporting and Transcripts

In the WPS PCBS, developing and maintaining transcripts required careful consideration and ongoing adjustments to ensure effective communication with external stakeholders and systems. Key challenges included determining when credit is awarded, handling partial credit, managing the implications of recording zeros, and reflecting courses not completed within a traditional school year. These issues raised important questions about the role of time in assessing student progress and its impact on student motivation, particularly regarding the potential for empty transcripts due to differences in yearlong versus semester-long reporting. This consideration is especially crucial for high school students entering the system with few credits.

Initially, at the high school level, course credits were awarded upon completion of all the proficiency scales for that course, providing flexibility for both teachers and students within the teaching and learning cycle. This approach allowed students to move naturally through a course's academic progression, ensuring they advance to the next proficiency scale of instruction only after demonstrating competency on the previous one.

This mirrored the WPS belief that learning should be the constant, while time is the variable—in this case, students and teachers should not be constrained by traditional, time-based grading periods or school years. However, challenges arose when colleges and scholarship funds required a seventh-semester transcript. To address this, WPS adapted its practice by organizing proficiency scales into semesters, allowing for the awarding of 0.5 credits. While this adjustment artificially made time the constant and not the variable, it was necessary to meet the demands of external entities—a lesson that demonstrates personalized competency-based best practices are not always possible.

A key principle in the WPS transcript policy is to avoid discouraging students from early setbacks, particularly freshmen who might struggle with the transition to high school. In a traditional GPA system, poor grades earned early in a student's high school career can have a lasting negative impact on their GPA, potentially closing doors and limiting future opportunities, even if the student later excels. Through its PCBS, WPS aims to prevent this outcome, ensuring students who improve their academic habits can still achieve success without being permanently penalized by early struggles.

For example, to prevent a student who has not completed all the proficiency scales for Integrated Mathematics 1 by the end of their freshman year from receiving a score 0.0 on their transcript—which could negatively define their high school experience—WPS experimented with designations like "NG" (no grade), "IP" (in progress), or "-". Currently, WPS transcripts use a "-" to indicate that coursework is not complete. In keeping with the ethos that time should be the variable, this "-" mark has no impact on a student's GPA. Instead, a high school course score is only included in a GPA when 100 percent of the proficiency scales are attempted, with 80 percent at a 3.0 or higher. It is important to note that this flexibility, allowing a student to progress to the next level without demonstrating competency on every proficiency scale, is only available for high school–level courses. Students in K–8 levels are expected to achieve competency in 100 percent of the proficiency scales in each content level.

During one of the superintendent's student leadership cabinet meetings, concerns were raised by some high-performing students about the transcript model. Because a student's GPA was calculated only on completed courses, some students were posting on social media that they had a 4.0 GPA—while true, in some cases, this was based solely on completing one physical education course during their freshman year. This led to a discussion about the fairness of GPA calculations and a broader conversation about the purpose of GPA and the honor roll system. Rather than debating the need to rank students, the high school leadership developed a standard operating procedure for honors recognition, which was outlined in the student handbook. To be eligible for honors after freshman year, a student must have completed at least six credits, with the requirement increasing respectively to twelve, seventeen, and finally twenty-two credits by senior year. This approach allowed students to recover from a challenging year, offering a more forgiving and motivational framework compared to traditional models while still maintaining high expectations for course completion to be considered for honors recognition.

Professional Learning on Empower

As mentioned previously, WPS spent many years collaborating with the developer of the Empower LMS to help design and, in many instances, pilot new competency-based learning features embedded into the ever-evolving LMS software. Recognizing the critical role Empower played in facilitating WPS's PCBS, the need arose to provide responsive professional learning for all teachers. To address this, WPS created a training model in the form of a teacher committee named the Empower Targeted Specialists. This committee included at least one educator from each school who provided feedback to the district and Empower about the LMS's functionality and learned about new features in a train-the-trainer model.

Additionally, the committee meetings offered a platform for collaboration among the WPS Empower Targeted Specialists, allowing them to share best practices, identify specific needs, and foster a collaborative and responsive approach to the district's professional development. Often, these conversations led to feedback about the Empower LMS itself, which district officials would relay to the Empower development team for review. This collaboration between teachers and an external partner like Empower not only improved the LMS but also helped teachers across the district quickly learn how to use and appreciate the unique benefits of such a responsive system that the district relied on to provide a high-quality PCBS to each student.

LMS Onboarding for New Teachers

As mentioned in chapter 2 (page 35), WPS recognizes the unique challenge of onboarding and developing new educators to become proficient in personalized competency-based teaching. Understanding how much teachers rely on Empower to facilitate classroom learning, WPS developed a tool to support teachers' use of the LMS while being realistic about the pacing of this work. This tool, illustrated in figure 3.19, provides a comprehensive overview of the LMS's functionality, highlighting areas that new teachers should prioritize with the support of their school's Empower Targeted Specialist. Importantly, the tool covers not only recording and reporting topics but also instructional actions. It represents the intersection of every aspect of the competency-based design component of the Westminster learning model, including proficiency scales, assessments, instructional elements, recording and reporting, and scheduling. This robust tool has been a critical component in the success of our PCBS implementation.

Empower Teacher Reflection	
Pacing	☐ Pacing is set for classes or groups so that students can see their pace in all content areas. ☐ Playlists and activities are assigned to the group in which pacing is set. ☐ **Pacing is appropriate for all students in the class or group** (1 year growth for students on grade level, approx. 1.5 years growth for students below grade level). ☐ Pacing displayed matches teacher's expectations based on student work and progress.
Use of Classes and Groups	☐ Manually created groups are necessary and utilized. ☐ **Group names include level and content area.**
Playlist Organization	☐ Playlists are in order, following the progression of learning. ☐ **Activities in playlists and sub-playlists are related learning experiences (such as units), follow a progression, and build off each other.** ☐ Big Idea section of playlist is completed.
Playlist Instructional Components	☐ **Playlists are assigned to classes and groups based on the students' instructional needs.** ☐ Playlists contain a variety of activities. ☐ Playlists include activities aligned to the 4.0 descriptor on the proficiency scale in order to provide opportunities for students to score a 3.5 or 4.0.
Activity Organization	☐ **Activities are in order, following the progression of learning.** ☐ Activity is a single chunk of learning. ☐ Activities have images in icons. ☐ Activities have descriptions that provide an overview of the task. ☐ **Activities have learning targets based on the primary focus of the task** (minimum 1 LT per activity). ☐ **MAS** (Maximum Achievable Score) aligns to the proficiency scales (matches the level of rigor in the learning objective). ☐ **Action steps are clear, student-friendly, and include a call to action** (for example, submit Doc through locker). ☐ Resources are attached to provide instructional support or reinforcement of the learning target. ☐ Due dates are set (or time frame for activity is stated).
Activity Instructional Components	☐ Lessons include a combination of: + **Direct instruction** (videos, readings, and so on) + Targeted practice + Modeling + **Assessment** + Student reflection + Student choice
Naming Conventions	☐ Playlist names include content or learning goal. ☐ **Activity names include topic or skill addressed.** ☐ **Names display well on student home page.**

FIGURE 3.19: Teacher reflection guide highlighting key features to be covered in ongoing training for deep implementation of the Empower LMS.

continued ▶

Empower Teacher Reflection	
Quizzes	☐ Quiz names include topic or skill addressed. ☐ **Quiz has learning targets assigned.** ☐ Type of quiz (formative or summative) is appropriate based on the quiz content. ☐ **Each question has a learning target assigned.** ☐ **Maximum achievable score on quiz questions aligns to the proficiency scales** (matches the level of rigor of the question).
Scoring Practices	☐ **Work submitted by students is scored in a timely manner** (low number in Scoring Inbox). ☐ Activity scores are updated weekly. ☐ Activity scores are valid and varied. ☐ Activities marked Missing (M) as needed to inform parents and student of need for additional work or support. ☐ **Overall standard** (Proficiency Scale) scores are updated beyond a 1.5, as appropriate (based on student progress through the proficiency scale).
Student Home Page View	☐ **Classes and groups not in use are filtered to be hidden from student home pages.** ☐ A manageable amount of classes and groups are displayed on the home page for students and parents. ☐ **Group names are clear to students and parents.**

Source: © *2024 by Westminster Public Schools. Used with permission.*

Instructional Shifts Based on Empower

Recognizing the benefits that one-to-one technology can bring to the classroom learning environment, WPS invested in providing a Chromebook laptop for each student. This initiative allowed teachers to offer more blended learning opportunities, including greater integration with the Empower LMS. To ensure these technology tools were utilized effectively, WPS adopted the substitution, augmentation, modification, and redefinition (SAMR) model (Puentedura, 2006).

The SAMR model helps educators envision how to leverage technology to enhance student learning. At the substitution level, technology simply replaces a traditional process or learning tool without making changes to the task (for example, using a word processor instead of pen and paper to take notes in class). At the augmentation level, technology enhances the functionality of the task, such as automatic grading and feedback in an online quiz. The modification level is where existing practices begin to transform because of the technology. This level includes redesigning a task in a manner that would not be possible without technology, such as real-time collaborative editing of a document stored in the cloud. Finally, the redefinition level begins to imagine entirely new processes or tasks that were previously inconceivable without technology, such as students taking virtual field trips to faraway places or conducting simulations to understand concepts like molecular biology.

At WPS, the SAMR model provides the framework for teachers to integrate technology into their instructional practices, especially when moving beyond substitution tasks to more transformative applications. For example, teachers used online collaborative tools to facilitate peer feedback on writing assignments (modification) and integrated virtual science labs that allowed students to conduct experiments beyond the limitations of a physical classroom (redefinition). These strategies not only support the goals of personalized competency-based education but also enable students to interact with content in ways that deepen their understanding and engagement.

The SAMR model is one of many frameworks that enable teachers to focus on different ways the technology in their classrooms can enhance and ultimately redefine the learning experiences provided to their students. By using the SAMR model as a guide, educators can strategically implement technology to meet their unique instructional goals and the diverse needs of their students.

One key element of technology integration at WPS is the playlist tool within Empower's LMS, which allows teachers to personalize learning pathways for students. These playlists serve as instructional guides for teachers and enable students to self-pace through identified proficiency scales. See figure 3.20.

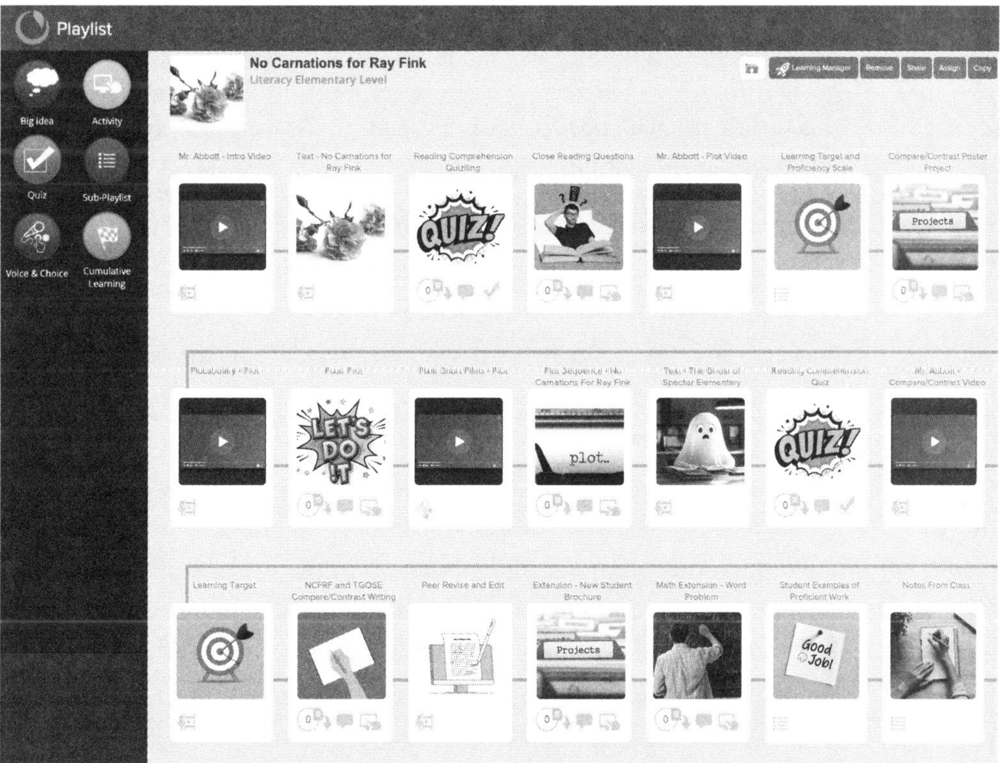

Source: © *2024 by Empower Learning, LLC. Adapted with permission.*

FIGURE 3.20: Sample Empower LMS playlist.

Teachers can design entire unit plans within playlists, incorporating unique instructional strategies, classroom activities, assessments, and access to various open educational resources. When a teacher effectively builds their coursework into a playlist, students who successfully complete it can demonstrate proficiency in all required competencies within a performance level.

Recognizing the potential of playlists and acknowledging that some teachers were more naturally suited to designing effective ones, the district provided financial incentives for teachers willing to develop playlists for both individual units and complete performance levels. These high-quality playlists were then made available across WPS, ensuring every teacher, regardless of technological aptitude, could leverage the power of the Empower LMS. This professional sharing not only reduced the workload for teachers by eliminating the need for each educator to design their own playlists but also fostered a collaborative and cooperative teaching community within WPS.

Scheduling for Performance-Based Groups

A critical step toward achieving a personalized competency-based education model is redefining how students are grouped into learning environments. Traditional systems typically group students by their chronological age into grade levels, as if all eight-year-old students perform at the same academic level and therefore require the same instruction. However, this age-based grouping can be limiting—it often results in advanced students feeling unchallenged and disengaged, while students who need more support may feel overwhelmed and fall behind.

Personalized competency-based education challenges this assumption, recognizing that each student is unique, and that academic ability often does not align with age. To better address these individual differences, schools must adopt alternative grouping methods, such as organizing students by skill level, mastery of specific competencies, or learning styles. Research supports these approaches. A meta-analysis by Yiping Lou and colleagues (1996) showed how using student ability within subjects as the grouping mechanism improved academic performance and increased motivation when combined with differentiated instruction. Similarly, Carol Ann Tomlinson and Tonya R. Moon (2013) highlighted that grouping students based on their readiness and interests enhanced student engagement and promoted successful learning outcomes by appropriately challenging each learner. By grouping students based on their individual needs rather than their age, schools can create more cohesive and effective learning environments that truly support each student's growth and success.

Elementary and K–8 Master Schedule Design

Each school within WPS is tasked with the critical responsibility of creating a master schedule that allows students to smoothly transition between teachers and subjects at various levels. In a traditional school setting, particularly in elementary and K–8 schools, students typically spend most of their day with the same teacher, surrounded by age-similar peers. However, in schools that employ an academic grouping model, even elementary students must be regrouped at least once during the day. For example, a second-grade student might attend mathematics at level 03 with one teacher, move to literacy level 01 with another, and then proceed to science level 02 and social studies level 02 with different instructors.

Some WPS elementary and K–8 schools are departmentalized, allowing for these types of transitions throughout the day, while others remain more traditional, with each teacher responsible for instructing all four core content areas. Most elementary and K–8 schools in WPS follow the latter model, typically grouping students by literacy levels in the mornings—where social studies is also taught—and then regrouping them into mathematics levels in the afternoon. This model minimizes transitions for younger students while still maintaining a commitment to performance-based, rather than age-based, groupings.

The introduction of midday transitions adds a layer of complexity to master schedule design that is not typically encountered in traditional elementary schools. Specifically, the placement of the specials block—physical education, music, art, and the like—for different groups of teachers (primary versus intermediate) can limit which students are available for those classes during certain times. For example, if a student is grouped into a classroom for literacy in the morning and then attends specials before lunch, that student cannot be placed in a mathematics classroom in the afternoon that also attends specials during that time. This scheduling constraint arises because each student must receive specials instruction only once per day.

This requirement creates an artificial "firewall," or a scheduling boundary, that restricts the classrooms into which a student can be regrouped. The need to navigate these constraints made scheduling much more complex. Initially managed on paper, this process posed significant logistic challenges, such as ensuring all students were correctly grouped and that instructional time was optimized. These challenges prompted our elementary principals to develop advanced scheduling skills, evolving into master schedulers like secondary school leaders.

Looking at figure 3.21, firewalls are denoted by the gray bars between teachers 6 and 7 and teachers 10 and 11. Symbols representing a primary student and middle school student (MS Student) illustrate how students might be scheduled throughout the day.

Breakfast | Homeroom | Dismissal

Staff	(P1) 7:50-8:45	(P2) 8:45-9:30	(P3) 9:30-10:15	(P4) 10:15-11:00	(P5) 11:00-11:45	(P6) 11:45-12:30	(P7)12:30-1:15	(P8) 1:15-2:00	(P9) 2:00-2:50
Teacher 1	ELA & Writing (0)		WIN	S.S./Science (0)	Lunch	Math (0)		Elective/Plan	Cumulative Review
Teacher 2	ELA & Writing (0)		WIN	S.S./Science (0)	Lunch	Math (0)		Elective/Plan	Cumulative Review
Teacher 3	ELA & Writing (1)		WIN	S.S./Science (1)	Lunch	Math (1)		Elective/Plan	Cumulative Review
Teacher 4	ELA & Writing (1)		WIN	Elective/Plan	Lunch	S.S./Science (1)	Math (1)		Cumulative Review
Teacher 5	ELA & Writing (2)		WIN	Elective/Plan	Lunch	S.S./Science (2)	Math (2)		Cumulative Review
Teacher 6	ELA & Writing (2)		WIN	Elective/Plan	Lunch	S.S./Science (2)	Math (2)		Cumulative Review
	Lower level	Higher level	Porous Firewall Between Lower and Upper Elementary				Lower level	Higher level	
Teacher 7	ELA/S.S. (3)		WIN	Science (3)	Elective/Plan	Lunch	Math (3)		Cumulative Review
Teacher 8	ELA/S.S (4)		WIN	Science (4)	Elective/Plan	Lunch	Math (4)		Cumulative Review
Teacher 9	ELA/S.S (4)		WIN	Science (4)	Elective/Plan	Lunch	Math (4)		Cumulative Review
Teacher 10	ELA/S.S (5)		WIN	Science (5)	Elective/Plan	Lunch	Math (5)		Cumulative Review
	Lower level	Higher level	Porous Firewall Between Upper Elementary and Middle School Ages				Lower level	Higher level	
Teacher 11	ELA/S.S (6)		Elective/Plan	ELA/S.S (7)		Lunch	ELA/S.S (8)		WIN
Teacher 12	Science (7)		Elective/Plan	Science (8)		Lunch	Science (6)		WIN
Teacher 13	Math (8)		Elective/Plan	Math (7)		Lunch	Math (6)		WIN

Primary Student | MS Student

Source: © 2024 by Westminster Public Schools. Used with permission.

FIGURE 3.21: Fairview PK–8 master schedule (360 students).

The primary student spends most of the day at learning level 02, which corresponds to second-grade content. However, for mathematics, this student is at performance level 03 and transitions to teacher 7's classroom for that subject before returning to teacher 5 for a cumulative review at the end of the day.

Now consider the middle school student (MS Student). They begin their day at performance level 05 for ELA and social studies and then transition to level 08 or 06 content for the rest of the day. The gray bars, labeled "Porous Firewalls," are critical to the schedule's flexibility. These firewalls are permeable, allowing students to move up or down in performance levels because the ELA, social studies, and mathematics blocks are vertically aligned, enabling smooth transitions through the schedule.

Just-in-Time Teaching Model

In the initial stages of WPS's personalized competency-based education implementation, the focus was on ensuring students mastered one performance level before progressing to the next. For instance, a student would advance from mathematics level 03 to mathematics level 04 only after achieving a score of 3.0 or higher on all sixteen proficiency scales in that level. This approach had several advantages, the most important being that it allowed teachers to focus on a single performance level.

To motivate students, schools organized monthly celebrations to acknowledge the completion of a performance level, with varying intervals and unique forms of recognition, such as level-up assemblies, certificates, bracelets, and dog tags. While this method provided a solid foundation for moving away from traditional, age-based groupings, it soon became clear that it had limitations. A significant challenge was overcoming the entrenched belief that a performance level, similar to a grade level, should be completed within a year—a mindset deeply rooted in traditional educational practices. Shifting away from this assumption proved daunting for staff, students, and parents alike.

As student needs became more diverse and evolved, particularly in the aftermath of the COVID-19 pandemic, it became evident that a more adaptive approach was necessary. The pandemic brought unique challenges such as gaps in learning and varying levels of student readiness. Finding inspiration from strategies highlighted in The New Teacher Project (TNTP, 2021) report *Accelerate, Don't Remediate*, WPS began providing rigorous grade-level content while simultaneously addressing essential skill gaps only when they directly scaffold to the current learning. The strategy reflects lessons learned from post–Hurricane Katrina education reforms in New Orleans, which demonstrated the importance of balancing grade-level rigor with targeted supports to ensure student progress in disrupted educational environments (Harris & Larsen, 2018).

The just-in-time teaching model is a strategic approach that addresses learning gaps by scaffolding current grade-level content with aligned standards from previous grades. This method allows students to receive the foundational knowledge they need when they need it, ensuring they can fully engage with new learning targets. Using the Common Core State Standards (National Governors Association Center for Best Practices & Council of Chief State School Officers, 2010a, 2010b), educators can create a coherence map, which tracks the progression of each standard through grade levels. This mapping provides a vertically aligned thread of standards, making it possible to see how concepts build on one another over time. For example, a level 04 mathematics teacher can use coherence mapping to identify that the fourth-grade standard 4.NBT.A (Place Value) is directly supported by the third-grade standard 3.NBT.A (Estimation) and the second-grade standard 2.NBT.A (Place Value).

With this mapping in hand, teachers can design lessons that incorporate scaffolded instruction from second- and third-grade standards alongside the fourth-grade standard. For instance, in a lesson on fourth-grade place value, a teacher might begin with a quick review or targeted instruction on the second- and third-grade place value concepts, ensuring students have the necessary foundation to grasp the more advanced fourth-grade material. This just-in-time delivery of earlier content fills any learning gaps, providing students with the background knowledge they need to succeed with the current grade-level standards.

The shift to just-in-time teaching led to a significant transformation in the performance-based grouping model that WPS was employing. Originally, students were organized into performance levels based on their beginning-of-year (BOY) ability level. Student ability can be measured in many ways, so an early decision for any school or system implementing performance-based groupings is to determine which metric will be used for grouping. Before the shift to just-in-time learning, WPS used the EOY (end-of-year) Empower level data and state and district assessment data as the mechanism for creating class rosters. This approach ensured all students began the school year grouped with others who were at or around the same place in a particular learning progression.

However, to fully realize the benefits of just-in-time instruction, WPS implemented a new student grouping method that focused on where it wanted a student to finish the year, rather than the starting point. Instead of grouping students based on their BOY academic ability, WPS began grouping them according to where they aimed to be by the end of the year. This new method, which WPS termed the "EOY Goal GLE" (grade-level equivalent), represented the point of academic progression within a specific content area that a student should achieve by year end with successful instruction.

Competency-Based Grade-Level Equivalent

In the WPS system, each student is assigned a grade-level equivalent score for every content area, indicating their position on the learning continuum from prekindergarten (PK) to level 12. This GLE score helps track a student's progress over time in comparison to state standards. As students improve their scores on proficiency scales, their GLE increases, with points being added each time they earn a score of 1.5, 2.0, 2.5, or 3.0 on a proficiency scale.

WPS uses a mathematical algorithm to track a student's progression across every proficiency scale within a particular content area. Each proficiency scale contributes 3 points toward the GLE. When a student demonstrates full competency on a proficiency scale (a score of 3.0), they earn all 3 points. Recognizing that proficiency scales represent a progression of learning, WPS also awards partial points for intermediate scores: a score of 1.5 is valued at 0.75 points, and a score of 2.0 is valued at 1.5 points.

This system allows for a more nuanced understanding of student progress. To convert these proficiency scale points into an actual GLE score, the total points a student has earned are divided by the total points needed to complete a particular level. Figure 3.22 provides further details on this process.

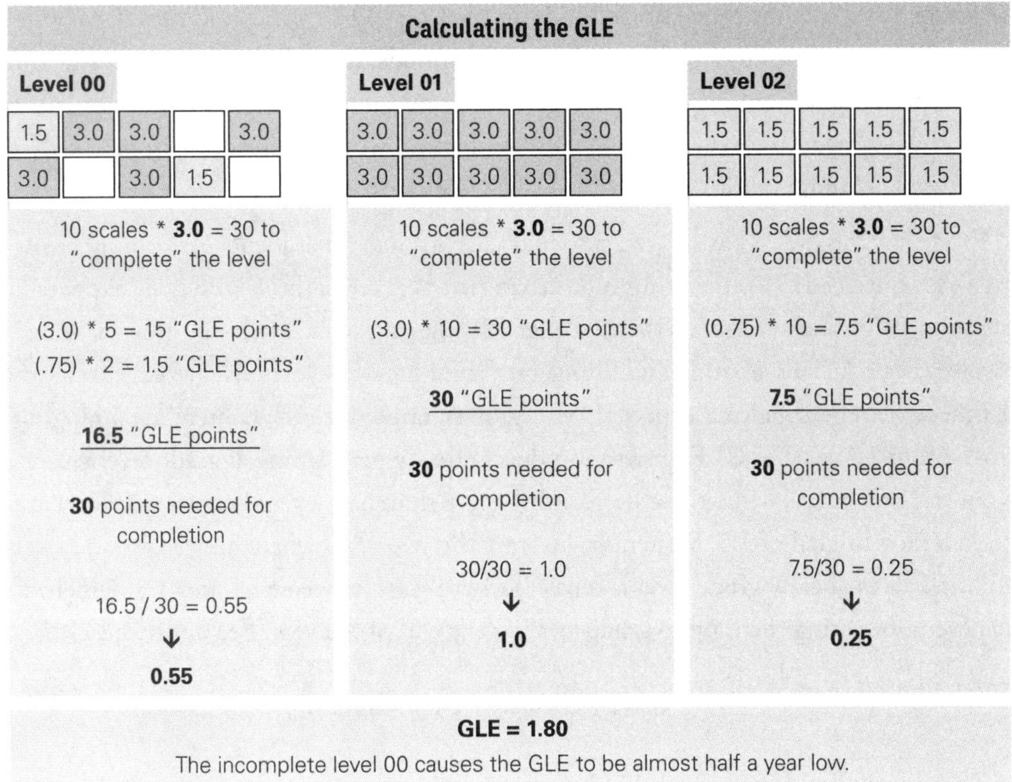

Source: © 2024 by Westminster Public Schools. Used with permission.

FIGURE 3.22: Explanation of GLE calculation.

It is important to note that while WPS proficiency scales include scores of 0.0–1.0 and 3.5–4.0, these scores do not impact a student's overall GLE. These scores are crucial for understanding a student's mastery of specific content, but they are excluded from the GLE calculation to maintain consistency in tracking overall progress.

Creation of Expected or Goal GLEs for Students

Now that a student's grade-level equivalent can be calculated for all content areas, this metric can be used to create performance-based class rosters. As mentioned previously, WPS's just-in-time model requires starting with the end goal in mind, specifically by setting an expected, or goal, GLE. Simply put, this is the GLE a student is expected to reach by the end of the school year. To calculate a student's goal GLE, you add their beginning-of-year GLE to the expected GLE growth for the year. The sum of these two numbers becomes the student's goal GLE for the school year.

It is important to note that WPS does not automatically set a student's expected GLE growth at 1.0, which represents one grade level's worth of progress. Because of the lingering impacts of disrupted schooling from the COVID-19 pandemic, as well as other external factors related to students' diverse backgrounds, many WPS students are below their expected grade level. If WPS were to set the expected GLE growth at only 1.0, a student who began the year half a grade level behind would still finish the year half a grade level behind, even if they met the expected growth.

To address this, WPS ensures the expected GLE growth for students performing below grade level exceeds 1.0, meaning more than one year's worth of growth is expected. However, WPS also recognizes the challenge of achieving such "catch-up" growth, which involves both current learning and filling gaps from previous years. Therefore, every student receives a personalized expected GLE growth target for each content area, ranging from 1.0 to 1.5 years of GLE growth. Students already performing at grade level receive a growth goal of 1.0, while those performing more than half a year below grade level are given a growth goal of 1.5. Students who start the year somewhere between grade level and half a year below grade level receive a growth goal between 1.1 and 1.4, which, if achieved, will bring them up to grade level by the end of the year. See figure 3.23.

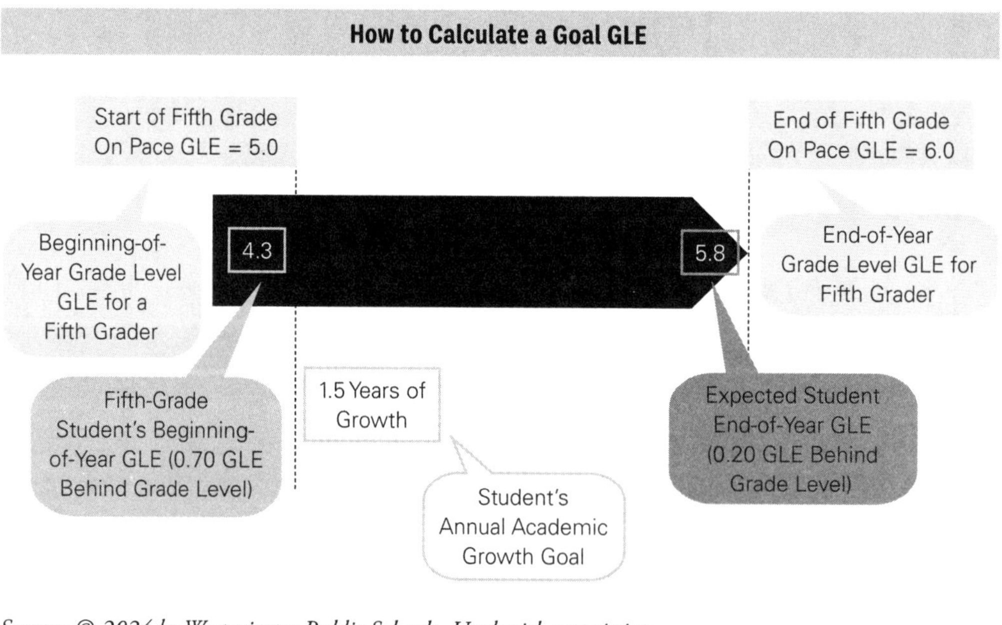

Source: © 2024 by Westminster Public Schools. Used with permission.

FIGURE 3.23: How to calculate expected GLE growth.

Armed with a student's current or beginning-of-year GLE and their expected GLE growth for the year, WPS can calculate a predicted or goal GLE representing the target learning level a student is expected to reach by the end of the school year. This calculation is done through simple addition of the current GLE and the expected GLE growth.

To effectively support the just-in-time teaching model—which focuses on delivering prerequisite content just when it is needed to support current grade-level learning—WPS now uses student goal GLEs as the primary mechanism for grouping students into performance-based classroom rosters. See figure 3.24.

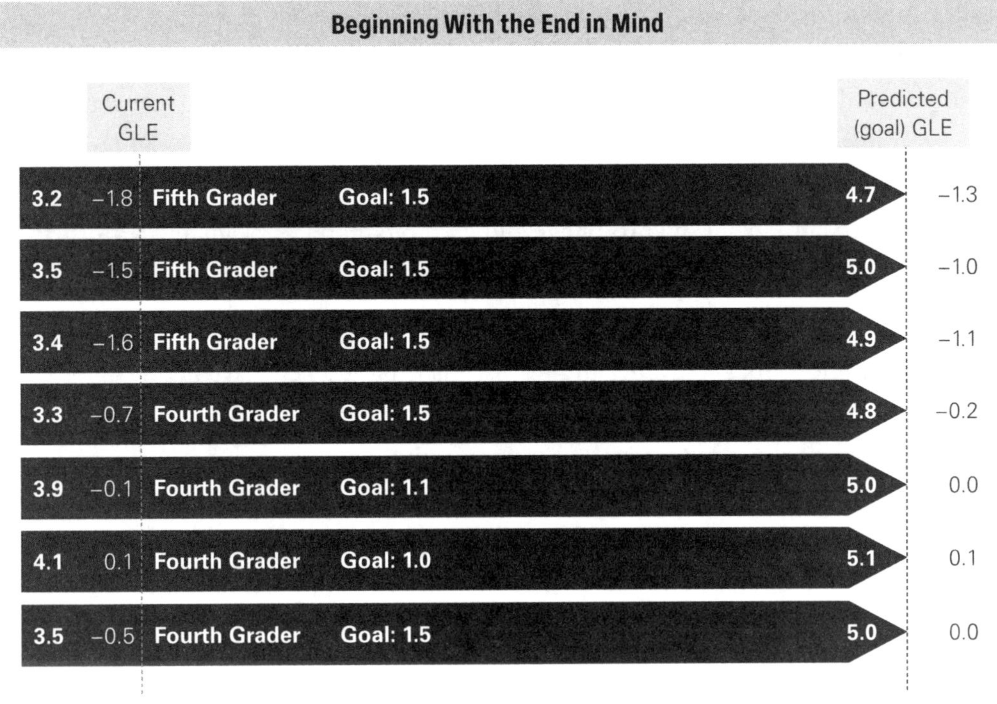

Source: © 2024 by Westminster Public Schools. Used with permission.

FIGURE 3.24: Smart Scheduling grouping concept.

Starting with the end in mind allows for the creation of class rosters where students are generally at the same point in a content area's preK–12 learning progression. Importantly, for the just-in-time model, these students also share similar learning gaps, which reduces the need for extensive differentiation. This enables the classroom teacher to concentrate on shared instructional needs while strategically providing multilevel scaffolded instruction.

This intentional backfilling of missing proficiency scale competencies only when that content directly supports current grade-level instruction is how a student who is behind grade level can realistically achieve a year and a half's worth of growth. The adage "work smarter, not harder" certainly comes to mind.

Scheduling Considerations

In addition to the factors already discussed, several other key considerations underpin the scheduling strategy in WPS's competency-based model. Central to this approach is optimizing educational outcomes by carefully balancing teacher workload, addressing student needs, fostering student agency, and ensuring thorough planning. WPS makes significant efforts to reduce the number of performance levels that teachers are expected to instruct and to eliminate the artificial divides between grade levels that can complicate class groupings, especially in smaller schools. The goal is to create balanced class compositions that consider both age and academic needs, ideally limiting classrooms to no more than two chronological years of age and no more than two academic performance levels per classroom.

Furthermore, the scheduling process emphasizes the importance of strategic planning time for both individual educators and teams, ensuring teachers have many opportunities to prepare and collaborate. This approach necessitates a departure from traditional scheduling practices, which typically begin in early spring. Instead, the competency-based model requires waiting until the close of the academic year to make more informed decisions about student placement. As a result, the scheduling methodologies differ between high school and elementary levels, reflecting the tailored flexibility needed to meet the unique demands of each educational stage.

Final Thoughts

As highlighted throughout this chapter, WPS's journey toward implementing a personalized competency-based education model has evolved over time, constantly being reiterated to adjust to lessons learned and to meet ever-changing needs. By moving away from traditional notions of grade levels and into performance-based class groupings, redefining curriculum into proficiency scales, aligning assessments to standards, implementing a dynamic personalized competency-based LMS and gradebook, and adopting just-in-time instructional practices, WPS has created a school environment that honors the individuality of students and ensures all learners have the opportunity to reach their full potential.

The success of WPS's PCBS model is not in its innovative design but instead in the district's commitment to continuous improvement. From the iterative development of proficiency scales to the strategic use of tools like the Empower LMS and the introduction of the just-in-time teaching model, WPS has shown that adaptability and responsiveness are essential in meeting the evolving needs of students.

WPS knows the shift to a PCBS presents many challenges, but it believes the benefits gained through increased student engagement and improved academic outcomes are well worth the struggle that second-order change brings.

CHAPTER 4

Learner-Centered Classroom

The world that students will graduate into is ever changing, including the knowledge and skills that the workforce will require. This reality makes WPS's motto of "Preparing students for the day after graduation" a complex challenge. However, the district believes empowering students with agency and instilling a desire for lifelong learning will equip them to become active participants in a global society. The WPS personalized competency-based model is designed with this goal in mind, placing student agency at the core of the classroom experience. Central to this approach is the WPS learner-centered classroom—an interactive and cooperative learning environment where students are active participants in their educational journey. This chapter explores the principles and practices that define the WPS learner-centered classroom and how schools can structure their classrooms to ensure each student becomes a self-actualized learner.

Above all else, the goal of the WPS personalized competency-based model is to generate student agency in meaningful ways. When the learning environment is designed with this goal in mind, a student-centered classroom becomes inevitable. In WPS, this is called the *learner-centered classroom*, wherein:

> Learners and teachers respond to and reflect on progress in order to build ownership and independence by involving teachers and other learners to become problem solvers, move through performance levels, meet their goals, and figure out their own path to success; learners have the opportunity to make choices and demonstrate proficiency throughout the learner-centered classroom. Teachers instruct and guide individual learners, small groups, as well as the whole class to set high expectations for all learners and determine the most effective instructional strategies for each learner in the classroom. (Westminster Public Schools, n.d.)

The learner-centered classroom is a model that every teacher in WPS is expected to implement, regardless of their role or the student level they teach. Although top-down directives can be challenging, WPS believes this approach is crucial to ensuring every student becomes a self-actualized learner. To achieve this goal, the district is deliberate in its expectations, ensuring such a critical initiative is not left to chance.

Introducing New Teachers to the Learner-Centered Classroom

WPS's commitment to the learner-centered classroom model begins with New Teacher Orientation and Training week. As noted in chapter 2 (page 35), WPS introduces new staff to the district through a tailored orientation that includes an introduction to its PCBS with a specific focus on the fundamentals of the learner-centered classroom and strategies for implementation. Each principal is also asked to identify a returning teacher to set up a "CBS Model Classroom" before the school year begins (secondary schools may choose several across different departments). On the first day of NTOT, new teachers visit this model classroom, where learner-centered classroom principles are highlighted, giving them the opportunity to envision how they might implement these ideas in their own classrooms.

CBS Model Classroom teachers not only prepare their classrooms before NTOT week but also provide guidance and mentoring to new teachers on learner-centered classroom practices throughout the year. On day 1 of NTOT, teachers first receive formal learner-centered classroom training at a districtwide location and then visit their schools for a lunch-and-learn session with their principals and the CBS Model Classroom teacher in their model classroom. This session offers a practical view of learner-centered classroom implementation, allowing for the exchange of questions, tips, and ideas. The remainder of the afternoon is dedicated to new teachers setting up their own learner-centered classrooms with support from school administrators and the model classroom teacher.

A defining feature of the WPS learner-centered classroom is its focus on individual mastery and student agency. During NTOT, teachers receive detailed explanations of the key characteristics of a learner-centered classroom, along with practical steps for implementation, while also being encouraged to collaborate with colleagues to develop their own interpretations.

However, achieving a learner-centered classroom is far more challenging than merely describing it. Ensuring all students develop into self-actualized learners who demonstrate strong self-agency is a significant undertaking for any school district. Recognizing that the expectations for a learner-centered classroom apply to all schools and teachers, WPS has established several non-negotiables within its PCBS to cultivate student agency and create learner-centered environments. The following sections outline these non-negotiables and their importance.

Developing a Classroom Shared Vision

Each classroom within a school functions as its own community, much like each school forms a unique community within the larger school district. Within the classroom, teachers and students, as members of this community, establish the customs, norms, and expectations that shape the character of their learning environment. Classrooms with strong, healthy communities are well positioned to promote academic growth, fostering trust, acceptance, and a safe space for risk taking without fear of failure. These traits are also key objectives of the WPS PCBS. When successfully cultivated, they lead to confident learners who exercise agency both within the classroom and in their broader communities. To support this, WPS places a strong emphasis on creating shared visions within the classroom.

A classroom shared vision is more than just an extension of a school's mission and vision; it is a powerful tool for cultivating a healthy learning environment. It clarifies the roles of students and teachers by explicitly outlining the responsibilities each member holds in creating and maintaining that environment. To ensure this practice is consistently applied across all classrooms, the district must emphasize its importance and support the uniform implementation of shared visions in every school.

In WPS, the district's shared vision is to prepare future leaders, learners, and thinkers for a global community, with the belief that the most important day in a student's life is the day after graduation. While classrooms are not expected to directly replicate this districtwide vision, the aim is for the essence of WPS's vison to be reflected and integrated into each classroom's unique shared vision. More broadly, the district expects every classroom's shared vision to include central tenets such as a culture of collaboration and inclusivity. It is paramount that students see themselves as valuable contributors to their classroom community.

WPS requires teachers to start the school year by collaboratively developing a shared vision with their students. The district encourages teachers to begin this process with a brainstorming session focused on identifying the components of a healthy community. This allows for a larger conversation that embraces the diverse backgrounds and perspectives within each classroom. By encouraging students to share who they are and what strengths they bring, a sense of belonging and mutual respect is fostered.

One particularly popular approach to creating a shared vision begins with storytelling or reading a book that emphasizes community values. This method helps students visualize their classroom as a community. When the chosen story highlights collective achievement and the importance of individual contributions, it creates rich dialogue about the creation of a shared vision.

In addition to collaboration and inclusivity, WPS believes a classroom's shared vision must include core values and principles that serve as guideposts for behavior and decision making. To this end, many schools implement classroom codes of conduct. While WPS recognizes the importance of these codes, in a PCBS, the emphasis on collective responsibility might lead to renaming the *code of conduct* to the *code of collaboration*. This deliberate choice highlights the importance of teamwork and community, fostering a culture of collective efficacy and clarifying each student's role in the learning process.

In the spirit of collective responsibility and efficacy, WPS believes that classroom shared visions must incorporate specific and relevant goals for the entire group. These goals can include academic targets, such as increasing reading fluency, mastering a set of mathematical concepts, and achieving a particular level of proficiency in a content area. Additionally, classwide goals may focus on developing critical thinking and problem-solving skills or nonacademic objectives, such as creating a supportive and inclusive environment where all students feel valued. Regardless of the goals chosen, it is crucial that all students contribute to setting these goals and understand their role in achieving them.

Finally, to ensure every teacher has a clear road map for creating strong shared visions, the district developed a comprehensive how-to guide that teachers are encouraged to follow. See figure 4.1.

Westminster Public Schools

Where Education Is Personal

SHARED VISION

What is it?

The shared vision establishes the collective purpose of an organization. It is derived from the commonly held beliefs and values of all the stakeholders involved with the organization and drives the daily work toward continued improvement. Westminster Public Schools has developed a rubric to help schools identify areas of improvement along their journey of implementing a Competency-Based System.

When is it used?

Beginning of Year:

- Develop a shared vision in class based on the school and district vision.
- Include "We Agree" statements, when applicable.
- Develop a plan for parent involvement and communication throughout year.
- Communicate vision with families, gather feedback, and adjust as needed.

Monthly:

- Survey students and parents on positives and changes they'd like to see in your classroom (use Plus/Delta or circle map for reflection). This can also be done each time a new student enters the classroom as a way to keep the vision alive throughout the year.

January:

- Reinvigorate shared vision and code of conduct after break to refresh memories.

End of Year:

- Begin planning for end-of-year reflections and start of new year.
- Evaluate methods; gather feedback.

Why is it used?

Shared Vision:

- Used to build community, get to know students and teacher
- Establish a healthy classroom environment.

Sample uses:

Use Shared Vision to:

- Get to know each other and what an ideal classroom looks like
- Primary—beginning to draw pictures about what school should look like
- Intermediate—more individualized, good pre-writing activity for year
- Secondary—good way to get students involved in your classroom
- Beginning of year to establish a common vision
- Adjust and review when class requires reminder
- Review at the start of second semester
- Return as needed to strengthen classroom purpose
- Tool can be used as a guide for how school can establish vision

Additional Supports (optional):

- Thinking Maps: Circle Map

FIGURE 4.1: Westminster Public Schools shared vision standard operating procedure.

continued ▶

Process

1. Teacher chooses a question for students to answer on the circle map or uses an affinity diagram. One idea per sticky note or jotted on the circle map.
2. Students can turn and talk to a neighbor (each neighbor gets a thirty-second turn to answer the question):
    a. Possible questions to guide discussion:
        i. What does a perfect student look like?
        ii. What does a perfect teacher look like?
        iii. What does a perfect school look like?
        iv. What would a perfect school be?
        v. What would make this the best class in the universe?
3. Possible strategies to develop a shared vision:
    a. Use mix around room to get students brainstorming together. Students stand up, students pair with first person by them and give high five, students without partner raise hand, and rest of class must help those who do not have a partner. Teacher asks question and gives think time. Each student has 30 seconds to give answer to open ended question. (Eliminates "Me, too.")
    b. Use a circle map to get students describing the answer to your question.
    c. Use an Affinity Diagram to brainstorm and sort ideas (see Affinity Diagram page for more information).
4. Synthesize:
    a. After all ideas are gathered, develop a statement that represents trend ideas.
    b. Post in classroom.
5. Continuously improve by "checking and adjusting" progress toward your vision:
    a. Include parent feedback as necessary.
    b. A shared vision is only as strong as the environment the students are in. Get students talking to each other in class to learn more about each other.

Group size: Up to 50

Duration: Up to 30 minutes

Shared Vision

In our class, everyone:

- Is a leader
- Takes care of each other
- Helps each other
- Learns everything
- Does awesome work
- Is kind, quiet, and safe

Because we are leaders!

Considerations:

- Your classroom vision is only as real as you make it; reflect with students when things go wrong, and adjust as needed.
- The start of second semester is a great time to start over with a new shared vision or adjusting the shared vision as needed.

Source: © 2024 by Westminster Public Schools. Used with permission.

This standard operating procedure outlines key steps, including optimal times during the year to create or modify the classroom shared vision, suggestions for visual thinking tools (such as a circle map) to help classes organize their ideas, and strategies for regularly "checking and adjusting" the shared vision's implementation throughout the year. This guide is provided to all educators and is an integral part of the district's NTOT week.

Drawing From the WPS PCBS Tool Kit

In addition to developing a classroom shared vision and a code of collaboration, WPS encourages teachers to be intentional about how they cultivate student agency in their classrooms. Recognizing that classroom wall space is limited and valuable, it is important to ensure every item displayed serves a meaningful purpose. To this end, the district provides specific instructional tools designed to foster student agency within a learner-centered classroom. Central to this effort is the WPS "PCBS tool kit," an assortment of competency-based tools that, when utilized effectively, help create a successful learner-centered classroom.

Included in this tool kit are focus boards, which feature learning targets and success criteria; class competency trackers; anchor charts; choice boards; exemplars of student learning; consensograms; and parking lots, to name a few. Some tools, like competency trackers, are unique to CBE, while others, such as anchor charts, are common in both traditional and competency-based classrooms. Each tool plays a specific role in fostering the principles of a learner-centered classroom. Let us examine each one more closely.

Focus Boards

In the WPS PCBS framework, the classroom focus board is a crucial instructional tool. While teachers have the autonomy to design their focus boards in numerous ways, they must adhere to certain core principles. Primarily, focus boards should clearly convey essential daily learning information, highlighting key concepts, goals, and associated success criteria. WPS encourages teachers to include the relevant proficiency scales the class is working toward, either on or near the board itself. Since academic progression in the WPS system is measured solely by student competency on these scales, clear and effective communication of them is vital. This topic is explored in more detail later when discussing student-friendly proficiency scales, but it is important to note that learner-centered classroom tools often intersect and support one another.

One vital component of the focus board is defining the daily lesson's success criteria. While these criteria are often aligned with a proficiency scale, there are instances when they may not be. The primary goal of success criteria is to communicate learning objectives and expectations to students. This typically begins with a class discussion about the daily learning objective and what constitutes student success. When success criteria are associated with a proficiency scale, they help students understand the progression of learning, particularly how to demonstrate competency from a score 2.0 to a score 3.0 and potentially up to a score 4.0. Although achieving a score 4.0 is not required, all students are encouraged to strive for this level on each proficiency scale. Providing students with a clear distinction between a score 3.0 and score 4.0 is the first step in ensuring every student can aim for a score 4.0. Offering concrete examples and illustrations of what success looks like is critical. This clarification of learning expectations fosters student agency by giving students specific targets and benchmarks to work toward.

Finally, WPS advises teachers to start each lesson at the focus board. This practice highlights the day's learning objectives and reinforces the focus board as a continuously accessible resource for students to reference throughout the day. While not mandatory, many teachers find success in having a student explain the contents of the focus board to their classmates. This simple yet effective approach further promotes student agency in a learner-centered classroom. Figure 4.2 shows a sample focus board in a primary classroom.

Focus Board

Objectives	Vocabulary	Focus Question
Literacy Identify letters and sounds	Letters P—Pumpkin T—Turtle I—Iguana	Can you match the letter with the picture?
Math Count patterns Sequence by size	Count Patterns Small Medium Large	Can you count pumpkins and turkeys? Can you sort small, medium, and large?
Social and Emotional Making friends Being thankful	Friend Share Happy Teamwork Thankful	Can you identify how someone feels by their face?
Social Studies and Science Life cycle of a pumpkin Night and day on a globe	Life cycle Pumpkin Night Day	How does a pumpkin grow? Why does Earth have night and day?

Source: © 2024 by Westminster Public Schools. Adapted with permission.

FIGURE 4.2: Sample focus board, primary.

Choice Boards

Often positioned alongside the focus board is an associated choice board. Choice boards include a range of learning activities students can choose from. These activities are intentional and provide differentiated options for students to determine how they prefer to demonstrate their learning. Giving students a choice to select an activity best suited to highlight their strengths or preferences helps promote student ownership in the task at hand. Choice boards are not specific to a personalized competency-based classroom;

however, they can be easily modified to serve a personalized competency-based design. Let us explore these adaptations more.

To begin, all choice board activities must be aligned with specific competencies or learning targets embedded within the proficiency scales. Given that personalized competency-based learning is often self-paced, it is essential for the choice board to clearly indicate which activities correspond to score 2.0, score 3.0, and score 4.0 targets. This alignment provides students with clear criteria for mastery and offers a visual representation of the learning progression within the proficiency scale. By clearly defining the criteria and learning options for each score level, students can select activities that meet their current needs and help them progress successfully. When thoughtfully designed, personalized competency-based choice board activities also allow students opportunities to revise or improve their understanding without penalty.

PCBSs recognize that learning is a process that often requires multiple attempts before competency is fully realized. To support this, teachers should ensure every activity on the choice board allows students to submit multiple versions or drafts, especially after receiving feedback. While teacher review is always preferred, fostering a collaborative culture where students can receive peer feedback both during and after the completion of an activity is highly recommended. Ultimately, providing students with multiple opportunities to refine their work and demonstrate competency enhances their ownership of the learning process. Figure 4.3 shows a sample choice board for literacy activities in a primary classroom.

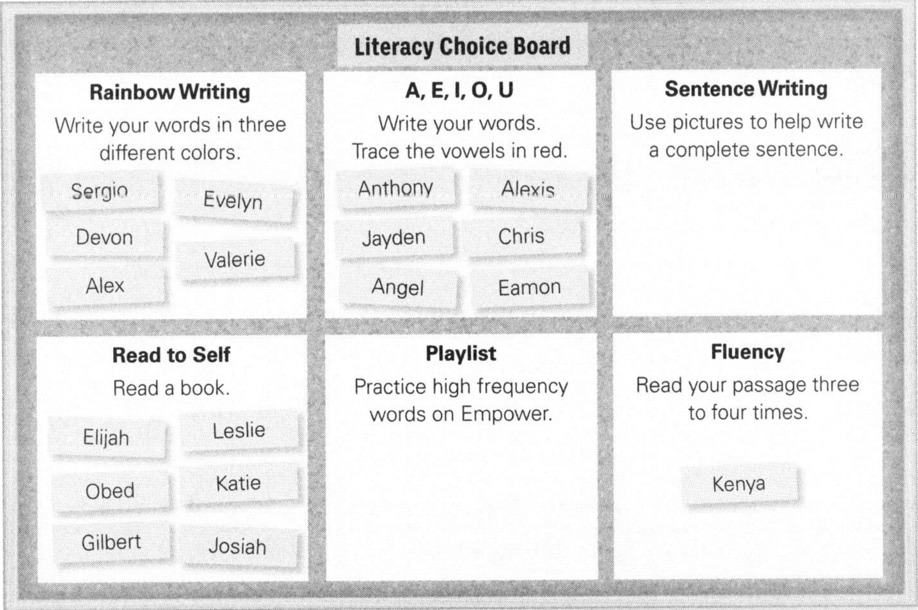

Source: © 2024 by Westminster Public Schools. Adapted with permission.

FIGURE 4.3: Literacy choice board, primary.

Competency Trackers

Another essential component of the WPS learner-centered classroom is the use of class competency trackers. These tools visually display the learning progressions on specific proficiency scales, offering a clear representation of the journey students will take toward mastery. Competency trackers may include charts or graphs that outline the expected learning targets or skills, along with the subsequent steps in the learning process.

The effectiveness of competency trackers lies in their interactivity. They should allow students to physically mark their individual progress, which fosters engagement and ownership of their learning journey. Teachers can further enhance this tool by including mechanisms that track the class's collective progress, adding a collaborative element to the learning process.

Competency trackers play a pivotal role in motivating students by making learning targets relevant and understandable while also highlighting their connection to larger learning goals. WPS encourages teachers to incorporate celebrations or student recognition into the competency tracker process. This can be as simple as the class collectively offering a "Good job!" to a student who moves up on the tracker or as engaging as allowing students to ring a bell after completing a learning target.

Regardless of the specific method used, competency trackers are a critical component of a learner-centered classroom. They help build student agency by providing a visual representation of the learning progression and fostering an awareness of competency, which in turn nurtures ownership of learning.

Anchor Charts

Next in the WPS PCBS tool kit is the use of anchor charts. These charts offer visual representations of important ideas and key learning points and are commonly used in both traditional and competency-based classrooms. When displayed strategically, they serve as easily accessible reference points for students throughout the day.

Generic anchor charts can be purchased by the school or district, particularly when uniformity is desired—examples include double-bubble maps and Venn diagrams. These professionally produced charts are visually appealing and made with high-quality materials, factors worth considering when selecting classroom tools.

However, WPS strongly recommends that teachers, when possible, collaboratively create anchor charts with students during a lesson. This collaborative effort invites students into the creation process, fostering a sense of ownership that is often lacking with premade materials. Designing an anchor chart together helps students draw connections and emphasizes preferred ways to visually represent their thinking. Co-created anchor charts are an effective way to build student ownership in both academic and nonacademic endeavors. For example, class-created anchor charts are particularly useful for drafting, communicating, and displaying classroom routines and procedures. Figure 4.4 displays a sample anchor chart for the topic of measurement at the primary level.

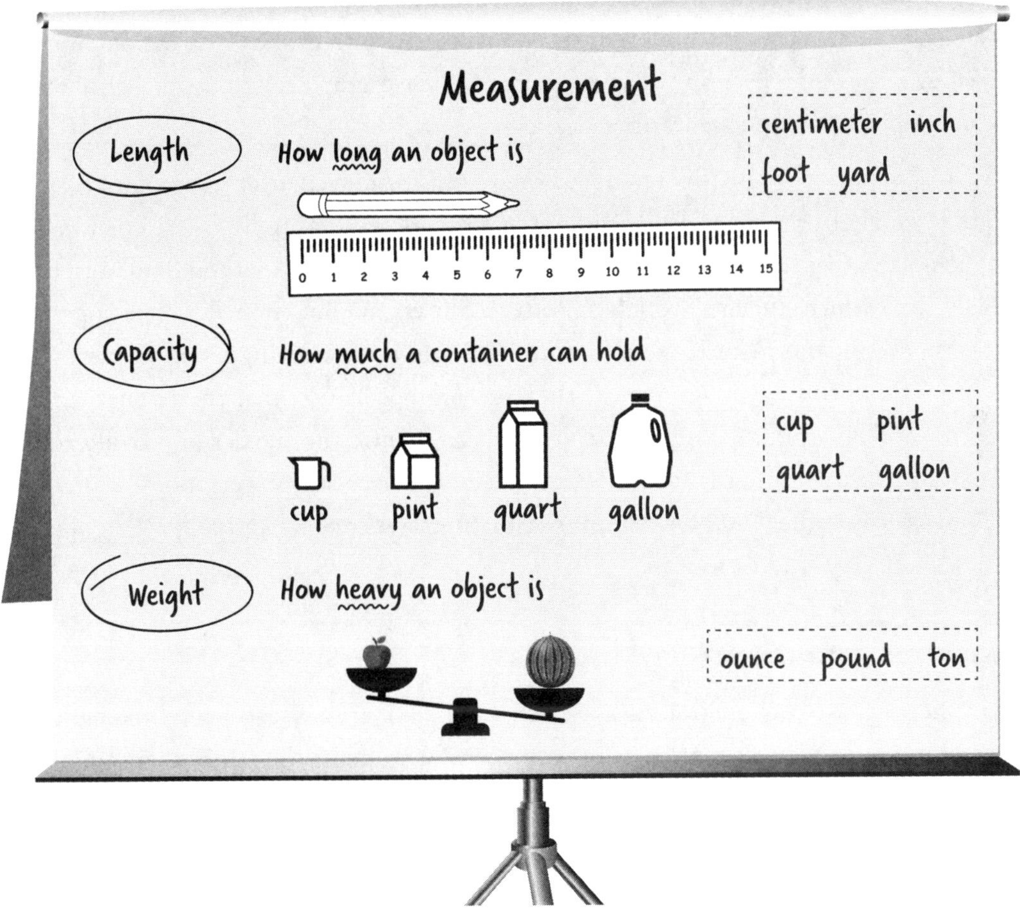

Source: © 2024 by Westminster Public Schools. Adapted with permission.

FIGURE 4.4: Measurement anchor chart, primary.

Exemplars of Student Work

In addition to providing success criteria on focus boards, WPS emphasizes the importance of including examples of student work in a learner-centered classroom. These exemplars serve several critical functions in fostering student agency within a personalized competency-based classroom.

First, student exemplars set clear expectations for high-quality work. This is particularly beneficial for learning targets that require higher-order thinking or involve complex tasks. By displaying what a score 3.0 on a proficiency scale looks like, students have a concrete example of what they should be striving to achieve. This is especially valuable when defining score 4.0 work, as this level of proficiency often extends beyond what is explicitly defined by the learning target itself.

Teachers are encouraged to use exemplars for student self-assessment purposes. Beyond simply measuring proficiency on a learning target, exemplars can guide students in identifying additional areas for improvement. When paired with explicit instruction on how to self-evaluate and reflect on their performance, these exemplars become powerful tools for developing introspective learners.

It is important for all students to see their work displayed as an exemplar at some point throughout the year. While some student work will naturally rise to the level of an exemplar, other students might need teacher support to reach that standard. Teachers should track which students' work has been recognized and intentionally create opportunities for all students to be acknowledged. This might involve giving a student advanced notice of an upcoming assignment with clear communication that the teacher would like to use their work as an exemplar. It may also require the teacher to provide additional support to ensure the student's work meets the necessary expectations. Fostering inclusivity within the classroom community often means creating and supporting opportunities for every student to shine.

Consensograms and Parking Lots

The next items to explore from the WPS PCBS tool kit are consensograms and parking lots. These classroom tools offer structured ways for students to express their opinions and feelings, making them effective methods for teachers to gather feedback on how the class is progressing. While many versions of these tools exist, and WPS does not mandate a specific design, there are benefits to a school adopting a uniform consensogram or parking lot format across all classrooms. This consistency provides students with continuity from one period to the next and from year to year. Regardless of the version chosen, certain key principles must be incorporated to ensure these tools effectively contribute to creating a learner-centered classroom.

A *consensogram* is a visual tool that allows students to record their opinions, feelings, or knowledge about a specific topic, while also enabling teachers to collect and assess this information. Consensograms are excellent for fostering a sense of community and gauging collective understanding. For example, a consensogram can be used for class voting by having students place a sticky dot next to their choice from a menu of voting options displayed on chart paper or a scale. This approach quickly generates a visual representation of the class's collective thinking while also highlighting individual perspectives. Such visuals can lead to rich discussions about student opinions and the numerous factors that influence individual choices.

Another effective use of a consensogram is to check for understanding. By asking students to mark where they believe they are on a learning chart, the tool encourages self-assessment and reflection on learning. Also, it provides teachers with valuable insights into the class's overall progress and the development of individual students.

Another essential tool from the WPS PCBS tool kit is the *parking lot*. This tool typically takes the form of a dedicated section on a door, the whiteboard, or a poster-sized sheet of paper where students can "park" questions, ideas, or opinions about the day's learning that do not require immediate attention. When integrated into the daily classroom routine, the parking lot ensures that important thoughts and questions are not forgotten. It provides teachers with a convenient way to collect reminders about specific items or student feedback, allowing them to address these topics at a more appropriate time.

By offering a formalized method for students to ask questions and express their opinions, the parking lot helps foster curiosity and promotes a sense of belonging—both critical components of creating a learner-centered classroom. This tool also ensures off-topic questions or ideas can still be included in the classroom discussion, even if they are addressed at a different time or on a different day.

Cooperative Learning

Over time, research has consistently demonstrated the benefits of active versus passive learning (Freeman et al., 2014; Kagan, 1994). Despite this, typical classroom instruction still tends to minimize student involvement in the learning process. While teacher-centered instruction has its place, students too often find themselves passively listening to teacher-delivered lectures. This is problematic as passive learning leads to significantly lower retention rates compared to active learning. Louis Deslauriers, Ellen Schelew, and Carl Weiman (2011) found that students who participated in active learning environments performed almost twice as well as those in lecture-based settings. One effective way to make learning more active is by implementing formalized cooperative learning strategies that encourage student engagement and interaction, leading to better understanding and long-term retention of material (Johnson, Johnson, & Smith, 2014).

Cooperative learning is defined as an instructional approach where classrooms are organized into small groups that work together to achieve shared learning goals, typically through structured activities or guided frameworks (Davidson, 2021; Slavin, 2010). These strategies promote social interaction among students, leading to deeper understanding and diverse engagement with content. Although some teachers naturally incorporate cooperative learning into their lesson design, many do not. To ensure every student has opportunities to become an active learner, districts must identify and implement specific cooperative learning frameworks. While districts or schools can purchase cooperative learning resources, any classroom can achieve its goals by adhering to key principles, such as positive interdependence, individual accountability, and group processing (Johnson et al., 2014).

First, the composition of each small group must be intentional. One common strategy is to mix students of varying abilities, pairing "high" and "low" achievers to foster mutual growth. The "low" students benefit from the support of their "high" achieving peers, while teaching the content enhances the learning of the "high" achievers. However, ability is not the only criterion for grouping. Other strategies include student choice, random assignment, or a strengths-based approach that considers each student's natural tendencies and places them with peers who complement their strengths. For example, some students may excel as leaders, others may be highly organized, and others may be effective communicators. Grouping these students together creates a strong team dynamic that is well suited to tackling challenging learning objectives. Regardless of the grouping strategy used, it is essential to ensure the group activity aligns with and supports the intended learning goals.

Once the learning target is established, teachers should set clear objectives and roles for each group. Assigning specific roles—such as group leader, recorder, and communicator—is essential for ensuring active participation from all students, as the group's success depends on each member's contribution. Skipping this step can undermine the effectiveness of the activity. Additionally, having groups self-assess at the end of the activity reinforces the expectation of collaborative work and equal contribution. This process allows students to reflect on the effectiveness of their group dynamics and understand how strong relationships enhance cooperation.

It is recommended for districts to develop or select a set of cooperative learning frameworks for teachers. When a uniform framework is selected, district-level support can be tailored to ensure these instructional practices are consistently implemented across all schools and classrooms. Specific to cooperative learning, providing teachers with various effective student grouping strategies and step-by-step protocols for different learning goals (for example, engaging with new content versus reviewing existing knowledge) can significantly increase student engagement, bolstering the learner-centered classroom approach.

Student Data Notebooks

Moving beyond the physical classroom walls and into the student workspace, a critical component of the learner-centered classroom is student data notebooks. These notebooks serve as a personal record of each student's learning journey, documenting academic progress over time. Although digital LMS platforms provide a centralized location for students to house their academic data, WPS believes physical notebooks are also crucial due to the tactile nature of engaging directly with the content of a data notebook. The process of writing, organizing, and reflecting in a physical format promotes ownership and metacognitive skills that can be less intuitive in a purely digital environment. While teachers provide initial guidance on how to use these notebooks, the responsibility for maintaining and updating them lies with the students.

Key elements of data notebooks include references to classroom content, such as proficiency scales, along with records of classroom activities and assessment results. WPS emphasizes the importance of incorporating goal-setting and self-reflection practices within these notebooks. Here, students set their learning objectives, devise action plans to achieve them, track their progress, and reflect on their performance. Additionally, data notebooks can serve as structured agendas for student-led parent-teacher conferences, allowing students to take ownership of their learning and communicate their progress effectively. Let us explore the multifaceted role that student data notebooks play in a learner-centered classroom in greater detail.

To begin, it is important to customize data notebooks according to different age groups. For younger students (four to eight years old), incorporating visual elements such as bar charts or line graphs can help them connect more easily with the data, while older students (fourteen to eighteen years old) may prefer more complex methods of data analysis. Regardless of the instructional level, in WPS, student data notebooks typically take the form of one-inch three-ring binders. This format allows for easy insertion of loose-leaf sheets and the use of prepurchased section dividers for organization.

One ongoing challenge observed is maintaining an orderly notebook. While some students are naturally tidy, many require direct instruction on notebook upkeep. Teachers should be encouraged to establish clear routines for maintaining data notebooks and conduct regular spot checks. An effective method for ensuring organized notebooks is through regular student-teacher miniconferences—a strategy that will be discussed in more detail shortly. To ensure timely maintenance, consider designating the first Monday of each month for students to update their progress toward long-term goals.

To maximize the potential of student data notebooks, it is essential that they are integrated with classroom content. Specifically, the notebooks should align directly with class learning objectives, or in a competency-based system, the proficiency scales. A highly effective practice is for students to include a copy of the relevant proficiency scales in their data notebooks at the start of each new instructional unit. This provides an ideal opportunity to discuss the learning objectives as a class and for students to visualize what success will look like. While using a copy of the proficiency scale is a good start, the use of student-friendly proficiency scales as the central feature of a student data notebook is strongly advised.

Student-Friendly Proficiency Scales

In the WPS PCBS, students demonstrate competency as outlined in the WPS proficiency scales. These scales are based on the Colorado Academic Standards (Colorado Department of Education, 2025a), which are often written in complex language not easily understood by young learners. WPS commonly refers to this as "eduspeak," meaning language typically understood by adult educators but not by students. Simply providing students with a proficiency scale filled with eduspeak is unlikely to achieve the intended goal of effectively communicating the learning target. Therefore, it is essential to create alternative versions of these proficiency scales that are student friendly.

Student-friendly proficiency scales begin with translating academic standards into language that is age appropriate, often referred to as "kidspeak." The translation process varies depending on the age of the students. For example, kindergarten-friendly standards might simplify or omit complex vocabulary and technical terms, or even replace all text with images. In contrast, high school–friendly standards may require little to no modification.

When writing in student-friendly language, it is important to retain essential vocabulary and preserve the core meaning of the standards. Simplifying the language should not result in lowering the expectations of the standard. Even unintentional omissions or excessive alterations can confuse students, making it harder for them to understand the content and visualize their learning path.

WPS encourages its teachers to rewrite proficiency scales themselves. This task compels educators to engage deeply with academic standards, leading to a thorough understanding of what is expected of students—a process that naturally enhances instructional planning. However, requiring every teacher to rewrite each proficiency scale they teach is a time-consuming endeavor. Recognizing this, a district might choose to centrally create student-friendly proficiency scales to be distributed to schools. If this option is preferred, the recommendation is that the creation of these scales should be integrated into the scale development process described in chapter 3 (page 53). This integration ensures a consistent approach to developing student-friendly scales, with alignment across grade levels and subject areas. Figure 4.5 and figure 4.6 (page 136) display sample student-friendly scales for primary and intermediate students, respectively.

My Learning: **Level 01:** Counting and Writing Numbers			
Score	**My Learning Goals**	**My Rating Before**	**My Rating After**
4.0	I can use numbers up to 120 to solve problems, like finding patterns or counting by 10s or 5s starting from any number.		
	I can also show numbers in different ways and explain my answers to others.		
3.0	I can count forward from any number, up to 120, without having to start at 1.		
	I can read and write my numbers from 1–120 and can show those numbers using objects.		
2.0	I can count by 10s up to 120.		
	When given a number between 1–120, I can say the number that comes before or after.		
	I can write all my numbers from 1 to 120.		

Vocabulary	
	I can describe using my own words.
Number	
Before	
After	
Count	

How will I remember this target?

Source: © 2024 by Westminster Public Schools. Adapted with permission.

FIGURE 4.5: Student-friendly scale, level 01.

Science Level 06: Water Cycle					
Self-Rating		**1**	**2**	**3**	**4**
Score 4.0	I can analyze and evaluate the impact of human activities (such as urban development, deforestation, and climate change) on the water cycle, including changes to specific pathways, stores, and the balance of freshwater and saltwater, and propose solutions to mitigate these impacts while maintaining the sustainability of Earth's water system.				
Score 3.0	I can develop a model to explain the water cycle and the sources of energy that power it.				
Score 2.0	I can explain how Earth's closed system relates to the cycling of water on Earth and the various paths water can take once it is on the surface of the Earth (for example, snowmelt, runoff, streamflow, interception, percolation) and explain how water on the surface of the Earth enters the atmosphere (evaporation and transpiration).				
	I can describe the different states of water (ice, liquid, vapor) and how water moves from the atmosphere to the surface of the Earth (condensation and precipitation).				
	I can compare the relative sizes of stores of water on Earth (for example, clouds, oceans, glaciers, snowpack, lakes, rivers, streams, watersheds, soil, water tables, aquifers) and explain the ratios of fresh and saltwater on Earth by comparing the size of their stores (for example, compare the amount of saltwater in the ocean to freshwater in glaciers and streams).				
	I can explain the role of the sun, gravity, and organisms (plants and animals) in the water cycle.				
	I can explain how life on Earth relies on water provided by the water cycle.				

Vocabulary		
Word	**Meaning**	**Rating**
atmosphere		1 2 3 4
cloud		1 2 3 4
condensation		1 2 3 4
evaporation		1 2 3 4
precipitation		1 2 3 4
glacier		1 2 3 4
groundwater		1 2 3 4
water cycle		1 2 3 4
water vapor		1 2 3 4
snowmelt		1 2 3 4

Evidence	Possible Score	Score

Why is this important?

Goal: I will be a score ____________ on weather and climate by ______________________.	
One thing I don't understand (or am not good at) yet:	Key Concepts (Most Important Parts):

Revision: How has your thinking changed? What did you learn?

Source: © 2024 by Westminster Public Schools. Adapted with permission.

FIGURE 4.6: Student-friendly scale, level 06.

As evidenced in these examples, beyond simply translating academic standards into kidspeak, WPS advocates that student-friendly proficiency scales serve multiple functions, including student self-assessment, goal setting, progress tracking, and self-reflection on learning. Let us explore each of these functions in more detail.

Student Self-Assessment and Goal Setting

In addition to communicating learning objectives, student-friendly proficiency scales provide students with an opportunity to self-assess their understanding along the learning continuum. To support this, these scales should include a dedicated section specifically for self-assessment, designed to be age appropriate. For example, younger students (four to eight years old) might circle different face emoji to represent their current level of understanding, with a smiley face indicating "I got this" and a frowny face signaling "I don't have this yet." As students mature, they can transition to self-assessing on a 1–4 scale, which helps them internalize the meanings of proficiency scale scores. Regardless of the method used, it is essential that each student actively assesses their knowledge before beginning their competency journey on those standards.

Once a student has self-assessed their initial status on a proficiency scale, the next step is to set goals related to the learning targets or standards embedded within that scale. This helps the student understand the learning progression and identify tangible ways to track their progress throughout the lesson or unit. It is recommended that students set both macro and micro goals within the scale. For example, they might establish a weekly goal to learn the critical vocabulary terms required at the score 2.0 level, which are foundational for achieving the ultimate score 3.0 targets later in the unit. Additionally, students can review the academic standards and set incremental goals that, when accomplished, will lead to score 3.0 competencies. This process of student action planning is an effective way for students to visualize their learning path as they progress toward competency. Once goals are established, the next step is for students to track their progress toward achieving them.

Given the importance of progress monitoring, it is essential for student-friendly scales to include a section where students can track their progress in relation to the academic standards. Teachers should provide tools that let students visually track their performance across the annual scope and sequence of proficiency scales and within the more detailed scoring of individual targets. Offering both broad and detailed views helps students monitor their short- and long-term progress.

There are various methods to achieve this, with age appropriate tracking being a key consideration. For younger learners (four to eight years old), coloring bar charts that indicate the completion of academic standards can be particularly effective. Older students (nine to eighteen years old) might use classroom assessments or self-assessments to track their progress toward meeting the score 2.0, score 3.0, and, where applicable, score 4.0 targets. It is recommended that after each informal and formal assessment, students record their scores and engage in thoughtful reflection on their performance. This leads to the next crucial component of the student data notebook: reflection and self-assessment.

Student Journaling

In a learner-centered classroom, student reflection serves as a powerful tool for fostering student agency. Every student data notebook should include a journaling section where students can reflect on their learning, effective strategies, areas for continued growth, and potential improvement plans. Encouraging students to think critically about their learning and consider how they can apply these insights to future assignments or units cultivates genuine student ownership of their educational journey.

WPS advocates for students to extend their journal reflections beyond academic performance to include considerations of classroom decision making, particularly those decisions that either supported or hindered their learning. Reflecting on classroom behavior, personal dispositions toward learning, or attitudes toward specific subject contents helps students gain a deeper understanding of how their beliefs and mindsets influence their learning outcomes. Developing these metacognitive skills benefits students beyond the immediate classroom and school year. Also, in alignment with the collective nature of the class shared vision, self-reflection fosters awareness of how individual behavior impacts the classroom environment.

It is recommended that student journaling occurs daily, or at least weekly, as part of the classroom routine. This simple practice leads to more self-aware and empowered learners, contributing to the overall success of the learner-centered classroom.

Student-Led Parent-Teacher Conferences

Student data notebooks, as their name suggests, serve as the centralized repository for student data. However, WPS advocates for a broader definition of what constitutes "data." Beyond assessment results, students are encouraged to include various academic artifacts that document their performance over time. These can include class assignments, projects, or any work products they are particularly proud of. Ultimately, data notebooks become a curated collection of student work that showcases each student's learning journey.

When utilized as described, data notebooks transcend their role as a mere learning tool; they also become the centerpiece of student-led parent-teacher conferences, a key element of the learner-centered classroom. In a PCBS, these conferences focus on student progression within specific competencies as measured by the proficiency scales. Since competency-based systems are inherently personalized, each student has a unique story to share about their individual learning journey through the content standards.

During student-led conferences, the student is the facilitator, with parents and the teacher participating as listeners. The student discusses their academic progress, future learning goals, and any personal insights they wish to share. While the format of these conferences may vary, they should include a collection of student work that highlights competencies and academic exploration. Student data notebooks should be used as the central organizing tool for these conferences. When notebooks include sections for self-assessment, goal setting, academic tracking, and self-reflection, students can effectively use them to narrate their school experience, presenting their data and work samples as evidence. This approach enhances student agency in parent-teacher conferences and throughout the school day.

Student-Generated Assessments

The goal of a learner-centered classroom is to foster student agency, and perhaps the best way to exemplify this is through student-generated assessments. When students engage with learning objectives by actively participating in designing the means to showcase their knowledge and skills, they exercise student agency. For example, in a unit focused on persuasive writing, a student might decide to demonstrate their ability by creating a multimedia presentation or writing an op-ed about a topic of interest. Given the characteristics of a learner-centered classroom, the essential ingredients are in place for students to design high-quality, personalized demonstrations of competency. Student-friendly proficiency scales communicate learning targets in accessible language, encouraging students to self-assess and set personal learning goals for each proficiency scale. Through action planning, students establish tangible steps to follow, while reflective journaling offers opportunities to evaluate their real-time performance toward these goals. With this foundation, the transition to student-designed assessments becomes highly feasible. These scaffolds—self-assessment tools, action plans, and reflective practices—prepare students to confidently transition into designing their own assessments.

The primary aim of student-generated assessments is to deepen students' understanding and mastery of content. When students are empowered to determine how they will demonstrate competency, it requires a level of critical thinking that goes beyond traditional teacher-provided assessments. For instance, to demonstrate an understanding of interdependent relationships in a science unit on ecosystems, a student might design a hands-on experiment, while another might choose to create a visual infographic explaining the flow of energy. Creating their own assessments challenges students to analyze and evaluate content critically and, more importantly, to consider how to best leverage their personal strengths during the evaluation process. This process encourages students not only to recall basic information but also to analyze key components and make judgments about what they deem most important.

While there is no strict rule for implementing student-generated assessments, some important considerations should guide the process. First, the co-creation of student-friendly proficiency scales between teachers and students enhances understanding of learning goals and success criteria. For example, students might collaborate with their teacher to define what "competency" or "mastery" of particular topics might look like—such as explaining important concepts, applying them to new or different scenarios, and being able to justify their reasoning. A natural extension of this process is for students to consider how they might demonstrate competency on the identified success criteria. Another strategy is to integrate student-generated assessments into the self-assessment process. While it can be challenging to design an assessment before learning occurs, asking students to envision the result of their learning during self-assessment can lay the groundwork for effective personalized assessments later in the unit. For instance, when studying government systems in social studies, groups of students can choose how they demonstrate their understandings—such as writing and acting out a role-play scenario, drafting a policy brief to solve a community problem, or designing a graphic organizer. Additionally, co-creating rubrics for learning targets with students can serve as a first step toward encouraging them to think critically about how they will demonstrate competency.

Student-generated assessments can also be incorporated into the learning journals discussed earlier. Alongside reflecting on their learning, students can be prompted to consider how they might best demonstrate their newfound understanding or skills as the instructional unit progresses. For example, weekly journal prompts might ask, "How could you show your understanding of this concept to someone else?" or "What format would best suit your learning style to present your work?" Regular reflection, whether daily or weekly, encourages students to continually think about how to best showcase their learning.

Student-generated assessments may best exemplify the goals of a learner-centered classroom. Allowing students to critically engage with learning standards to the extent that they determine how to demonstrate competency epitomizes student agency. Through self-assessment, students gain awareness of their starting point on a particular learning target. By setting personalized goals, devising action plans to achieve them, and monitoring their progress, students develop tangible ownership of their learning process. This type of agency not only encourages academic growth but also builds metacognitive skills such as self-regulation, critical thinking, and creativity, ultimately preparing students for success on the day after graduation.

Final Thoughts

Reflecting on WPS's commitment to preparing future leaders, learners, and thinkers for a global community, it became essential to ensure a learner-centered classroom was established across all schools. This involved the integration of key components such as the classroom shared vision and code of collaboration, the PCBS tool kit, student data notebooks, student-friendly proficiency scales, student-led self-assessment and goal setting, journaling, student-led parent-teacher conferences, student-generated assessments, and cooperative learning strategies.

When these elements are effectively implemented, they create an environment that genuinely fosters student agency. The goal extends beyond mastering the content of any single unit or class. It is about developing the skills that enable students to become self-aware, confident, and empowered individuals. More important than any test score or isolated demonstration of competency is the creation of self-actualized individuals who are prepared to positively impact their communities. This is the result of a learner-centered classroom.

CHAPTER 5

Continuous Improvement

To realize their potential, even the best-designed systems inevitably require iteration. This is especially true when implementing transformative changes, such as PCBE, in organizations as complex as school districts. WPS's own PCBE journey required constant monitoring and adjustment, as demonstrated by examples provided throughout this book. Systematic continuous improvement forms the foundation for the sustained success of any PCBE effort. By creating a culture that embraces iterative growth and data-driven decision making, continuous improvement enables organizations to respond and adapt effectively to the complexities that inevitably accompany second-order change. For schools and districts beginning the work of becoming a PCBE system—or those who have already started—continuous improvement provides a framework to ensure systems are aligned with the innovative practices of PCBE while maintaining accountability to drive systemic growth.

This chapter chronicles the evolution of continuous improvement within WPS as it embarked on its personalized competency-based journey. Initially, the district relied on a traditional and often fragmented approach to systematic improvement in district operations. However, by looking beyond public education to successful practices in other industries, WPS adopted a continuous improvement process that allowed the district to remain agile as it navigated the profound changes required by a transition to a PCBS. This chapter delves into the implementation of continuous improvement across the district, the challenges encountered along the way, and the strategies that led to sustained improvement. Readers will gain insights into how WPS managed significant systemic changes, balanced innovation with accountability, and responded to unprecedented challenges such as the COVID-19 pandemic.

The concept and application of continuous improvement originated from the factory model of production, aiming to enhance efficiency and reduce costs. In the 1980s, Toyota introduced the Toyota Production System (TPS), which became a pioneer in successfully leveraging continuous improvement strategies, setting a benchmark for global competitiveness in the automobile industry (Liker, 2004; Shingo, 1989). Since then, continuous improvement practices have been adopted by companies across a wide range of industries, all seeking operational excellence through data-driven decision making. As these concepts transcended industries, they eventually found their way into the realm of education, transforming traditional practices. However, the transition into school districts faced challenges due to the fragmented nature of traditional schooling models, the inherent complexity of educational institutions, and the difficulty of defining the factors that genuinely determine the quality of an outstanding educational institution.

Since 2009, WPS has undergone a significant shift in its approach to continuous improvement. What began as a series of isolated events and reactive measures has evolved into a deeply embedded and integral component of the district's daily operations and long-term strategy. This chapter addresses the evolution of continuous improvement within WPS, detailing the applied practices, strategic alignments, and systemic changes that have driven this transformation. Through this exploration, readers will understand how continuous improvement has moved from a peripheral concept to a core principle that underpins the district's commitment to excellence.

Shifting Toward Continuous Improvement

Before the introduction of the PCBS in the 2009–2010 school year, WPS operated with a conventional mindset regarding achievement data and improvement cycles. This prevailing practice treated these processes as a yearly routine tied to the school calendar, often overlooking the importance of continuous assessment and multiyear strategic planning. Class schedules were traditionally established during the spring semester, primarily based on factors such as gender (ensuring an equal number of boys and girls) and teacher recommendations regarding student interpersonal relationships. High school schedules were heavily influenced by course selections rather than by past student performance data. Achievement data were used primarily to describe and justify the existing situation, which was seen as fixed rather than a tool for driving sustainable improvement. Systematic monitoring of perceptual or operational data was notably absent. However, despite this fragmented approach, WPS did develop two innovative K–8 internal grade-level assessments in reading and writing, which later catalyzed a shift toward a more systematic approach to performance data over the long term.

In the early 2000s, the district acquired the Northwest Evaluation Association assessments and integrated them alongside the homegrown district reading assessment and district writing assessment. Schools began to see the value in tracking a student's score trajectory throughout the school year, using both status and growth results to highlight academic and program improvements. This marked a pivotal moment in the district's evolution, as thinking evolved further with the implementation of practices developed through the Colorado Consortium for Data-Driven Decisions initiative. Leaders and staff became familiar with Victoria Bernhardt's (1998) "Multiple Measures of Data" framework, which emphasized the importance of ongoing data collection related to student and staff demographics, perception data, school processes, and student learning. Additionally, the work of Bruce Wellman and Laura Lipton (2004) on data-driven dialogue provided a collaborative method for staff to analyze multiple measures of data, fostering a culture of continuous improvement through a four-step cyclical process. See figure 5.1.

Source: Wellman & Lipton, 2004. Adapted with permission.

FIGURE 5.1: Data-driven dialogue process.

Continued use of the district's reading and writing assessments, the Northwest Evaluation Association assessments, and corresponding training programs propelled a positive shift in attitudes toward more frequent and effective data usage. Over time, these data-driven practices became integral to the data cycles adopted by schools and laid the foundation for implementing meaningful districtwide collaborative practices, such as professional learning communities (PLCs), which further elevated the importance of data analysis for instructional planning.

However, WPS had not yet fully moved away from the traditional school calendar improvement cycle mindset. The shift to authentic, continuous improvement thinking was only fully realized during the planning and early implementation phases of the district's PCBS. This transformative period demanded a new perspective on effective data utilization over time.

Navigating Initial Implementation and Learning Opportunities

The planning and early implementation phase of WPS's PCBS was marked by collaboration with the Re-Inventing Schools Coalition; visits to the Chugach School District (as described in chapter 1, page 11); and a focused effort on understanding system structures, identifying professional learning needs, and effectively communicating the transition to a districtwide PCBS. As schools gained a deeper understanding of the model's components, they began the important work of creating classroom shared visions and codes of cooperation. These foundational tools helped establish clarity and alignment among students, teachers, and school leaders, setting the stage for consistent application of PCBS principles in daily practice. These elements became focal points during district walkthroughs, where district personnel observed current practices and provided feedback to teachers and school leaders, suggesting actionable next steps.

An observation tool was employed to assess the implementation of PCBS elements and traits along a continuum—ranging from awareness, understanding, first implementation, routine use, and refinement, to replication. This approach allowed teachers and school leaders to identify their current stage of implementation and set clear goals for advancement. This tool evolved over time, becoming a comprehensive self-assessment rubric (as described in chapter 1, page 11). The rubric was designed not only to monitor progress but also to serve as a guide for schools and districts aiming to build a robust PCBS. It ensured consistent implementation of all five components of the PCBS: (1) shared vision, (2) leadership, (3) competency-based design, (4) learner-centered classrooms, and (5) continuous improvement.

As expected, numerous initiatives, projects, and activities were unfolding concurrently within WPS during the two-year planning, communication, and initial implementation phase. It quickly became clear that a flexible and reliable decision making and communication process was crucial to prevent confusion and conflicts. This underscores the importance of clear structures for managing large-scale change. Without an adaptable system for communication and issue resolution, the complexity of simultaneous initiatives can overwhelm stakeholders and derail progress. The implementation of any new process, practice, or strategy inevitably had a cascading impact across various areas, necessitating a responsive approach to issue resolution as system improvements progressed. To address this need, WPS adopted the PDCA cycle, a methodology rooted in W. Edwards Deming's (1986) principles of *total quality management*. This cycle was rapidly integrated into all aspects of school and district operations, ensuring a consistent approach to managing and resolving issues. The PDCA cycle provides a replicable framework for addressing the inevitable challenges that arise during systemwide change. By embedding continuous improvement into decision-making processes, schools and districts can remain agile and responsive while maintaining focus on their long-term goals. The PDCA cycle follows four iterative steps.

1. **Plan:** Identify a goal or improvement area, analyze the current situation, and develop a detailed action plan to address the issue or implement a new process.
2. **Do:** Implement the plan on a small scale to test its effectiveness and gather data on its impact.
3. **Check:** Review and analyze the results to determine whether the plan achieved the desired outcomes and identify any gaps or challenges.
4. **Adjust:** Based on the analysis, refine the plan, scale it up if successful, or revisit earlier steps to make necessary adjustments.

By embedding this cycle into district operations, WPS established a consistent, repeatable framework for addressing challenges and ensuring progress. The PDCA methodology allowed the district to remain agile and responsive, aligning new initiatives with long-term goals while fostering a culture of continuous improvement.

The PDCA cycle was seamlessly woven into the district's decision-making model, providing a practical framework for addressing and resolving challenges. Strategies, outcomes, and procedures that emerged from using the PDCA cycle to tackle systemic challenges were meticulously documented in standard operating procedures. These SOPs were made digitally accessible to all internal stakeholders, serving as a valuable reference for leaders. To maintain relevance and effectiveness, the SOPs underwent annual reviews, incorporating new insights and adapting to evolving circumstances. Additionally, school leaders and classroom teachers developed their own SOPs, refining and enhancing their processes in alignment with district goals. The district-level protocol outlined in figure 5.2 illustrates this procedural approach.

	Westminster Public Schools Where Education Is Personal
	STANDARD OPERATING PROCEDURES
	What is it?
	A graphic organizer or list to help learners move through procedural steps or follow expectations to accomplish a specific goal.
	When is it used?
	Standard operating procedures are used any time learners have to follow specific steps to complete a task or follow specific expectations for classroom activities that recur frequently.
	Why is it used?
	It is used to make all required procedures and expectations transparent to the learner. **Sample uses:** Use an SOP to: • Provide clear expectations for behavior during whole-group and small-group work time • Provide instruction to differentiated groups while the teacher is occupied • Provide directions to students during centers while the teacher is occupied • Provide visual directions for any procedural task • Use SOPs any time you want students to be self-directed learners • Document a process for students to go to specials • Provide steps to solve a mathematics problem
	Additional Supports (Optional):
	You may also consider using student data to decide which SOPs need to be created. For example, if a student survey reveals that learners are not focused during small-group time, you can communicate that data to students and then create a SOP to support better engagement during small groups. 1. Name the procedural process or concept being outlined at the top of the flowchart/list. 2. Develop an intent or purpose statement for the process and write it under the title. 3. Have the students either observe the process and write the steps on sticky notes or brainstorm the steps and expectations, and the teacher can facilitate visualizing of the process. 4. Use simple symbols or a list to construct the flow of the process or relationship. 5. Have a learner explain and model the SOP with the class. 6. Ask learners if they have any questions about the SOP or the necessary resources to complete the task. 7. Post the SOP in a student-friendly place. 8. Reuse SOPs that are part of the class routines. 9. Study the SOP and determine how and where it can be improved after the initial use.

<table>
<tr><td rowspan="4">Process

Group size: Varies

Duration: 15 minutes</td><td colspan="2">STANDARD OPERATING PROCEDURES</td></tr>
<tr><td>Instruction SOP
• Computer closed
• Essential supplies only
• Limit distractions
+ Put away toys
+ No side conversations
• Active listening
+ Eye contact with the speaker
+ No interjections
+ Think about what is being said
+ Ask questions by raising your hand
+ Nod your head to show you're listening</td><td>Work SOP
• Stay in your work space
+ No wandering
• Focus on the subject
+ Collaborate with others
+ Talk about the topic
+ Limit side conversations
• Appropriate classroom behavior
+ Hands to yourself
+ Appropriate voice level</td></tr>
<tr><td>Rewards and Consequences
If you make choices that distract other learners:
• First time—Warning (Make a change)
• Second time—Move seats
• Third time—Remove from class (100GP fine)

If you make choices that support other learners:
☑ GP reward
☑ Pass
☑ Monthly celebration</td><td>Rewards and Consequences
If you make choices that distract other learners:
• First time—Warning (Make a change)
• Second time—Move seats
• Third time—Remove from class (100GP fine)

If you make choices that support other learners:
☑ GP reward
☑ Pass
☑ Monthly celebration</td></tr>
<tr><td colspan="2">Considerations:
• It is helpful to develop the procedural flowchart and collect necessary resources prior to introducing to the class.
• It is helpful to practice using a flowchart with a simple procedure first (process to go to lunch) so students understand its use prior to utilizing with a more complex task (how to write an essay).
• SOPs are more effective when they are routinely used by students.
• SOPs can be written on a board, on poster paper, or printed for student use.</td></tr>
</table>

Source: © 2024 by Westminster Public Schools. Used with permission.

FIGURE 5.2: Westminster Public Schools guidance document for developing standard operating procedures.

District-level SOPs are typically more intricate and detailed, serving as operational extensions of board of education policies. The examples in figure 5.3 (page 150) and figure 5.4 (page 151) illustrate this complexity.

INDIVIDUALIZED GOALS: STANDARD OPERATING PROCEDURE

AUTOMATICALLY SET GOALS SOPs

Goals will be automatically set for all current preK–8 students in the district at the beginning of the school year.

- These goals will be set for Mathematics, Literacy, Science, and Social Studies.
- Goals will range from 1.0 to 1.5 years growth, based on their current GLE and their traditional grade level.
- These set goals will be visible on the Teacher and School Dashboards in Empower.

Setting Individual Growth Goals

All preK–8 students will have an Individualized Growth Goal automatically set in Empower for their four core content areas.

The image below illustrates Growth Goals for six different students who are traditional third graders.

- The student who is on grade level and the two above grade level have a goal of at least one year of growth, in one year's time.
- The student that is less than half a year behind will have a goal set to bring them back on track (1.1 to 1.4 years growth).
- The two students that are more than a half a level behind will be expected to gain at least a year and a half of growth to help close their academic gaps.

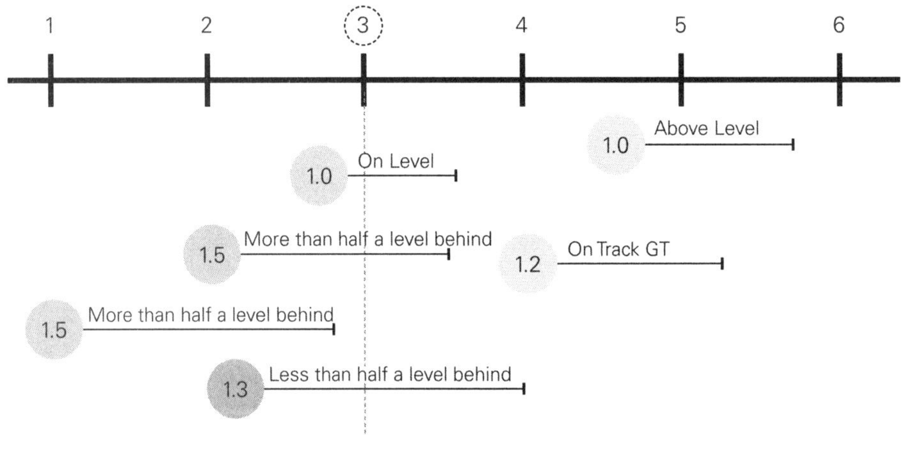

On or above expected grade level = 1.0 years of growth
Half a level or less behind = Enough growth to get on track
More than half a level behind = 1.5 year of growth
IEP students qualified for DLM = 0.5 years growth
On level Gifted and Talented students = 1.2 years growth

Once goals are set, schools do have the ability to modify goals if required.

- An ILP or other supporting evidence may be used to determine the need for a different goal.
- Student data that has been corrected may require a goal to be changed.
- All goal changes will be made in the Set Goal tool in Empower.

Set Goals Tool

Source: © 2024 by Westminster Public Schools. Used with permission.

FIGURE 5.3: Sample Westminster Public Schools standard operating procedure for individualized goals.

Westminster Public Schools Where Education Is Personal
Nonsequential Grade-Level Progression Standard Operating Procedure
By **December 1** of each school year, students and families must signal an intent for a grade-level reassignment to the school administration. After families signal the intent for a grade-level reassignment, the school principal will notify the Learning Services designee to complete an eligibility determination in **February and March**. The Learning Services designee will share the determination results with all relevant stakeholders (i.e., family, students, teachers, etc.) by **April 1**. If eligible for grade-level reassignment, during **April and May**, the student and the family will meet with the Westminster High School Leadership and their assigned counselor to develop an individualized transition plan for the student. The plan will include: 1. Performance expectations. 2. Social and emotional expectations. 3. Schools will offer and share opportunities with the student for interest-based and academic programming, sports, and extracurricular groups to help the student determine the next steps for participation (for example, recommendations for student organizations, activities, athletic participation, and check-ins with counselors). 4. The family will share ways to support their child during the transition and high school years. 5. The student will share the support needed to determine the next steps. 6. School tours are available on request. After **May 1**, schools may alter the assigned grade level in Infinite Campus for the current year.

Source: © 2024 by Westminster Public Schools. Used with permission.

FIGURE 5.4: Westminster Public Schools SOP for nonsequential grade-level progression.

In addition to monitoring through the self-assessment rubric and school walkthroughs, district leadership held regular meetings with various stakeholders, including teacher leaders, instructional coaches, data facilitators, beacon teachers, and principals. These sessions focused on discussing the implementation of the system and identifying ways to improve it. Since the teachers and staff voted in the spring of 2008 to proceed with implementing a PCBS (detailed in chapter 1, page 11), there had been a concerted effort to encourage teachers and staff to share their ideas, thoughts, and concerns to enhance the overall system. Staff were incredibly open and transparent in sharing "the good, the bad, and the ugly" about the new system from its inception. However, the spring of 2012 marked a pivotal moment for WPS as fourteen significant systemic issues emerged simultaneously. Figure 5.5 (page 152) outlines these issues and the recommendations to address them. It is important to note that while most were approved by the board of education, some were modified, and the viability of others was determined over time.

ADJUSTMENT 1: The current name of our educational system is difficult to explain to stakeholders and has several negative connotations.

RECOMMENDATION: Rename our educational model to a "Competency-Based System."

ADJUSTMENT 2: Address the amount of Recording and Reporting required due to the shift to the new Colorado Academic Standards (CAS).

RECOMMENDATION: Teachers should record student progress at the Measurement Topic level rather than the Learning Target level.

ADJUSTMENT 3: Streamline Recording and Reporting to make it more manageable for staff and user friendly for parents and students.

RECOMMENDATION: Move to a single electronic Recording and Reporting system that captures a "body of evidence" or "inventory of learning."

ADJUSTMENT 4: Address the logistic problems (time, frequency, location, etc.) of administering real-time Measurement Topic Assessments (MTAs) in Scantron.

RECOMMENDATION: Move from a real-time testing model to a benchmark model that occurs at designated intervals throughout the school year.

ADJUSTMENT 5: Parents and external stakeholders have difficulty understanding how Performance Levels correspond with grade levels.

RECOMMENDATION: Investigate how to transition toward aligning our performance levels with the Colorado Academic Standards (CAS) grade levels over the course of the 2012–2013 school year.

ADJUSTMENT 6: A large number of students are behind at the high school level and need to "catch up" by using proven strategies.

RECOMMENDATION: Reinstitute the AVID (Advancement Via Individual Determination) program at the high school level and implement it as intended.

ADJUSTMENT 7: The International Baccalaureate Programme (IB) has not yielded the results or success as intended.

RECOMMENDATION: Eliminate the Middle Years Programme (MYP) at Ranum Middle School and evaluate progress at Westminster High School during the next two years.

ADJUSTMENT 8: Review the Academy concept and develop a thorough plan to increase effectiveness and coherence.

RECOMMENDATION: Postpone the implementation of Academies until the 2013–2014 school year.

ADJUSTMENT 9: The majority of students are underperforming as evidenced by the number of students in each performance level.

RECOMMENDATION: Summer school should be mandatory for secondary students performing three or more levels below the expected level.

ADJUSTMENT 10: Alternative structures are needed to accommodate learners at both ends of the Learning Continuum in the absence of (or in combination with) a matriculation process.

RECOMMENDATION: Develop a plan for exploring the development of a preparatory level academy for each school level.

ADJUSTMENT 11: Considerable counselor time at the high school level is used to manage "student crises" and other administrivia.

RECOMMENDATION: Develop a plan to repurpose the work of counselors so that it is focused primarily on the academic achievement and success for all students for postsecondary and workforce readiness.

ADJUSTMENT 12: Graduate more students with science, technology, engineering and mathematics (STEM) skills.

RECOMMENDATION: Explore the possibilities of implementing a STEM school.

ADJUSTMENT 13: Increase postsecondary opportunities.

RECOMMENDATION: Explore the possibilities and develop a plan for increasing the number of students participating in Advanced Placement courses and concurrent enrollment opportunities.

ADJUSTMENT 14: Accommodate the unique needs of the high school.

RECOMMENDATION: Implement a competency-based system at Westminster High School that looks different from the current SBS implementation.

Source: © 2024 by Westminster Public Schools. Used with permission.

FIGURE 5.5: List of systemic adjustments made to the Westminster Public Schools competency-based system in 2012.

The process of addressing these issues and implementing adjustments culminated in the development and approval of the initial CBS Board of Education Resolution on April 10, 2012 (see chapter 2, page 35). Additionally, to proactively handle and monitor solutions to internal systemic issues—particularly during the early years of implementation—an instructional advisory committee was established in collaboration with the district's union, the Westminster Education Association. The committee's purpose was to provide recommendations to the superintendent, suggesting solutions for issues experienced across multiple schools. This committee proved to be both effective and creative in advancing the shared vision, and their responsibilities were formalized in the licensed negotiated agreement, as outlined in figure 5.6.

ARTICLE L36 - Instructional Advisory Committee

L36-1 The instructional advisory committee shall make recommendations to the Superintendent concerning systemic issues that are instructional in nature and impact the student achievement subsequent to actively engaging in a solution-focused collaborative process.

L36-2 The function of the committee is advisory. As a result of agenda items discussed, the committee shall make recommendations to the Superintendent of Schools, a Deputy Superintendent, or appropriate Executive Director for their consideration.

L36-3 The committee shall be composed of sixteen (16) members, consisting of eight (8) teachers and eight (8) administrators. The Deputy Superintendent of Schools and the President of the Association shall serve as ex officio facilitators. Such members shall be effective September 1.

L36-4 Teacher members of the committee shall be selected by the Association. The term of teacher members shall be staggered so that approximately fifty percent (50%) of the numbers carry over from one year to the next.

L36-5 The administrator members of the committee shall be appointed by the Superintendent.

FIGURE 5.6: Westminster Public Schools negotiated agreement article defining responsibilities for the instructional advisory committee.

continued ▶

L36-6	The committee shall use a collaborative approach to solve issues and reach a consensus on recommendations. Any operating rules shall be established by the committee.
L36-7	Meetings shall be held once monthly September through May on a schedule set by the members of the committee and the Superintendent. Meeting dates may be changed or additional meetings scheduled when necessary, by mutual agreement.
L36-8	Items for the agenda are to be written and mailed to the committee facilitators and the Superintendent for inclusion on the agenda. Minutes will be kept and distributed appropriately. The committee shall consider only those items that have not been or cannot be resolved through proper administrative channels. Items shall not be included on the agenda if they are in the process of negotiations or in any step on the grievance procedure. The fact that any item is on the agenda or has been considered by the committee does not mean that it cannot also be proposed for the negotiations package by either the district or the Association. Items may be added to the agenda at any meeting by majority vote of the committee.
L36-9	The administration shall respond to the committee on the status of any recommendation made by the committee within twenty (20) days or at the next regular scheduled committee meeting, whichever occurs first.
L36-10	Agenda items may be submitted by an employee or group of employees provided the item or items meet the qualifications for the agenda as established above.
L36-11	Inquiries concerning duplication of record lists or the gathering of data where administrative guidance might be needed should be submitted to the appropriate department head in writing, with a copy to the Superintendent. The department head shall within five (5) days respond to the inquiry in writing, either supplying the information or indicating what would be involved in obtaining the information and suggesting a time and procedure.
L36-12	The committee may appoint temporary subcommittees for study or other purposes as it deems appropriate.

Source: © 2024 by Westminster Public Schools. Used with permission.

Navigating Innovation, Accountability, and Accreditation

District and school leadership faced the complex task of driving transformative innovation within a state accountability and accreditation model that did not align with the principles of a PCBS. From WPS's perspective, accountability and accreditation are distinct yet interconnected concepts. Accountability involves aligning proactive measures and anticipating future performance, while accreditation represents retrospective evaluations of past performance. WPS defines these concepts as follows.

- *Accountability* is an ongoing continuous improvement process wherein quality is assessed, reinforced, and certified over time. It relies on clearly defined, research-based indicators for both schools and districts and is typically an *internal process.*

- *Accreditation* is the recognition that a school district meets established quality standards, enabling its graduates to qualify for admission to higher or more specialized educational institutions or professional practice fields. It is typically an *external process.*

The inaugural 2010 state assessment results for WPS were less than encouraging, serving as a sobering reality check that diverged from initial expectations. Thirteen of the district's eighteen schools were designated as "Turnaround" or "Priority Improvement," placing significant pressure on the district to address these challenges head-on. These unfavorable designations sparked resistance from parents and community members, who expressed dissatisfaction, particularly because of the number of schools falling into the two lowest categories.

Despite continuous communication about ongoing improvement efforts and forewarning about the more stringent nature of the new accountability model, the community's expectations were not met. The district had anticipated a potential implementation dip in state assessment scores due to the substantial second-order changes underway. However, despite efforts to manage expectations, the community demonstrated intolerance and impatience for this expected dip, expressing their concerns both verbally and in writing. While these results fell short of anticipated outcomes, they established a foundational benchmark against which the progress of the WPS PCBS could be measured over time. This benchmark is shown in figure 5.7 (page 156).

Despite the initial pushback, WPS persisted in leading and refining its PCBS. As illustrated in the chart (figure 5.7, page 156), significant achievement strides were made over the subsequent four years, with only two schools remaining in the "Priority Improvement" status by 2014. Simultaneously, and despite annual changes to the state's accountability methodology, WPS experienced a commendable overall accreditation score increase of sixteen points, successfully transitioning from "Turnaround" to the upper tier of "Priority Improvement." This upward trajectory reflected the district's commitment to continuous improvement and the effectiveness of its PCBS.

The following sections—Refining the Path Forward for State Accreditation and Charting the Course for District Improvement—provide context into the critical actions WPS undertook to persevere through initial setbacks, align district practices with accountability requirements, and develop the instructional capacity needed to sustain PCBS implementation. Together, they provide actionable insights for districts navigating similar challenges.

Accreditation Designations from 2010 through 2014

2010		2011		2012		2013		2014	
Schools	**Points**	**Schools**	**Points**	**Schools**	**Points**	**Schools**	**Points**	**Schools**	**Points**
Crown Pointe	82.0	Crown Pointe	80.0	Sunset Ridge ES	87.3	Mesa ES	74.7	Fairview ES	85.7
Sunset Ridge ES	66.7	Mesa ES	71.8	Mesa ES	79.2	Crown Pointe	69.4	Sunset Ridge ES	81.9
Flynn ES	53.4	Harris Park ES	59.4	Flynn ES	74.0	Tennyson Knolls ES	68.2	Mesa ES	67.0
Tennyson Knolls ES	51.6	Sunset Ridge ES	58.2	Crown Pointe	72.8	Sunset Ridge ES	65.8	Crown Pointe	65.7
Metz ES	50.6	Metz ES	51.1	Skyline Vista ES	71.6	FM Day ES	62.0	Tennyson Knolls ES	63.1
Shaw Heights MS	46.0	Skyline Vista ES	51.1	Fairview ES	64.4	Flynn ES	61.8	Flynn ES	61.9
Harris Park ES	44.5	Hodgkins ES	50.1	FM Day ES	63.5	Skyline Vista ES	61.2	Harris Park ES	56.7
Skyline Vista ES	43.8	Hidden Lake HS	54.1*	Sherrelwood ES	54.1	Sherrelwood ES	58.5	FM Day ES	54.8
Westminster ES	43.8	Tennyson Knolls ES	46.9	Harris Park ES	49.2	Metz ES	54.2	Sherrelwood ES	52.9
Westminster HS	39.5	Shaw Heights MS	45.3	Westminster ES	48.9	Harris Park ES	53.1	Skyline Vista ES	52.3
Ranum MS	39.1	Fairview ES	43.8	Tennyson Knolls ES	48.2	Shaw Heights MS	51.1	Ranum MS	51.7
Scott Carpenter MS	36.8	FM Day ES	43.3	Hidden Lake HS	57.0*	Hodgkins ES	49.6	Col. STEM Academy	51.3
Hidden Lake HS	29.6*	Flynn ES	40.3	Hodgkins ES	44.4	Westminster HS	47.4	Hodgkins ES	50.0
Mesa ES	27.1	Scott Carpenter MS	37.6	Shaw Heights MS	43.6	Hidden Lake HS	53.2*	Westminster HS	49.3
Sherrelwood ES	26.7	Westminster ES	37.6	Westminster HS	43.2	Ranum MS	46.7	Metz ES	48.7
Fairview ES	26.6	Westminster HS	36.1	Metz ES	39.7	Fairview ES	46.4	Shaw Heights MS	48.4
FM Day ES	26.3	Sherrelwood ES	28.2	Scott Carpenter MS	38.6	Westminster ES	43.8	Hidden Lake HS	48.0*
Hodgkins ES	26.3	Ranum MS	26.3	Ranum MS	38.2	Scott Carpenter MS	41.6	Westminster ES	44.3
								Scott Carpenter MS	39.5

District	30.9
Academic Achievement	25.0
Academic Growth	30.6
Academic Growth Gaps	31.1
Postsecondary Readiness	33.3

District	40.2
Academic Achievement	25.0
Academic Growth	44.4
Academic Growth Gaps	41.7
Postsecondary Readiness	41.7

District	46.4
Academic Achievement	25.0
Academic Growth	52.4
Academic Growth Gaps	49.4
Postsecondary Readiness	48.4

District	46.4
Academic Achievement	25.0
Academic Growth	52.4
Academic Growth Gaps	49.4
Postsecondary Readiness	48.4

District	46.8
Academic Achievement	25.0
Academic Growth	52.4
Academic Growth Gaps	52.2
Postsecondary Readiness	48.4

K-8 Plan Assignment	Points
Performance	>59
Improvement	47–59
Priority Improvement	37–47
Turnaround	<37

High School Plan	Points
Performance	>60
Improvement	47–60
Priority Improvement	33–47
Turnaround	<33

District Plan	Points
Performance	>64
Improvement	52–64
Priority Improvement	42–52
Turnaround	<42

**Hidden Lake High School is designated an Alternative Education Campus and lives under a separate accreditation.*

Source: © *2024 by Westminster Public Schools. Used with permission.*

FIGURE 5.7: Westminster Public Schools charts reflect the Colorado Department of Education accountability designations.

Refining the Path Forward for State Accreditation

Before the official release of the 2010 state accreditation designations, the WPS leadership team took a proactive approach by inviting personnel from the Colorado Department of Education to conduct a four-day Comprehensive Appraisal for District Improvement Revisit Audit. The main objective was to evaluate the processes and practices of the evolving PCBS implemented districtwide during its first year and to gather actionable recommendations for enhancing student achievement. The Revisit, led by the same team leader and including several original team members from the previous audit, focused on seven key areas: (1) instruction, (2) professional development, (3) curriculum, (4) assessment, (5) district culture, (6) family and community, and (7) comprehensive and effective planning.

While the team acknowledged the positive strides made since the initial CADI visit in December 2006, they identified two overarching focus areas to guide the district's improvement efforts over the next three years or more.

- Shift teachers' focus beyond mastering the structure of the PCBS to delivering highly effective, research-based instruction within a learner-centered system.
- Implement intensive, differentiated, ongoing, and job-embedded professional development for all teachers, enabling them to deliver effective instruction within the PCBS.

Charting the Course for District Improvement

Following the Revisit, WPS actively engaged in the Targeted District Improvement Partnership (TDIP) with the Colorado Department of Education. This partnership made the district eligible for federal funding through the American Recovery and Reinvestment Act, which facilitated the development of a three-year comprehensive district improvement plan. A representative team conducted a root cause analysis of the CADI Revisit findings and the latest student achievement data. As a result, the team identified the following four priority needs.

1. **Monitor and, if necessary, develop instructional models based on research:** This includes providing clearly defined expectations, focused coaching, and systematic progress monitoring to ensure effective instruction for every learner.
2. **Provide ongoing professional development:** Empower teachers to move beyond classroom management by utilizing student data to guide direct instruction and differentiated small-group work.

3. **Develop a comprehensive, ongoing professional development plan:** Focus on effective instructional strategies in mathematics and literacy content for both building administrators and teachers. Also, build leadership capacity to effectively monitor and guide improvement of instructional expertise within the schools.
4. **Provide leadership training:** Enhance capacity for facilitating collaborative groups, fostering dialogue, and evaluating effective instructional strategies within a purposeful learning community.

Participating stakeholders agreed that the continuous implementation of an authentic PCBS, along with addressing these prioritized needs, would systematically elevate student achievement to significantly higher levels in the coming years. Throughout this process, district leadership engaged in extensive conversations and negotiations with state department personnel to ensure that the TDIP fully supported the future direction and goals of WPS while meeting legislative requirements.

Embracing a Comprehensive and Evolving Strategic Plan

The board of education reengaged in a new strategic planning process with stakeholders, and by fall of 2015, WPS enthusiastically adopted a five-year strategic plan titled "Vision 2020." This strategic initiative not only prioritized academic advancements, postsecondary readiness, and staff retention but also underscored the commitment to continue modernizing and upgrading all facilities. The plan, comprehensive in nature, delineated five key areas of focus. These areas collectively embodied the shared vision of all stakeholders and permeated every facet of the district's activities. The essence of this strategic endeavor was encapsulated by the following five statements:

1. Westminster Public Schools' identity articulates the Mission, Values, and Vision that are shared by the District and community, enabling it to demonstrate outstanding quality that transcends the boundaries of the classroom walls and is personified in our staff and students.
2. Westminster Public Schools is an educational leader whose priority is to seek high academic standards, support innovative instructional programs and practices, increase academic achievement, and develop our students' learning skills.
3. Westminster Public Schools supports the personal, social, financial literacy, career exploration and development of our students in order to ensure each is professionally prepared.

4. Westminster Public Schools provides functional and safe infrastructure and facilities, which make a significant contribution to a positive student and workplace experience.
5. Westminster Public Schools is an employer of choice committed to fostering an environment of education innovation through a workplace that attracts, sustains, and inspires great people, working for a great purpose, while promoting diversity, equity, civility, and respect. (Westminster Public Schools, 2017, p. 9)

The five focus areas of this strategic plan provided a road map for the district's future while balancing innovation, operational needs, and the well-being of stakeholders. Each statement served as a guiding principle for district initiatives, ensuring alignment with WPS's commitment to continuous improvement and PCBS. In the sections that follow, key challenges and actions taken to achieve these goals are discussed, demonstrating how continuous improvement shaped decisions regarding accreditation, accountability, and instruction.

Navigating Accreditation and Commitment Challenges

As the fall of 2015 progressed, the political climate in Colorado became increasingly challenging, disproportionately affecting school districts serving large populations of students impacted by poverty. In response, WPS leadership sought alternative accreditation options. After careful consideration, WPS chose to partner with Cognia, an international accreditation agency. This decision was driven by two primary objectives: (1) securing independent accreditation and (2) validating the PCBS.

During the spring of 2016, coinciding with a pause in the state's Accountability Clock due to Colorado's transition to the Common Core State Standards, Cognia conducted an extensive review and evaluation of the district and its individual schools, resulting in a six-year accreditation. This achievement distinguished WPS as the first school district in Colorado to attain dual accreditation, renewing hope and revitalizing energy for the ongoing educational transformation.

The Cognia team was impressed by the elevated level of dedication and commitment demonstrated by all stakeholders. They recognized the clarity of the system's shared vision, which was well documented and embraced by the community. The strong culture, shaped by WPS's history in a larger urban environment, the loyalty of its alumni, and the collective determination to succeed, left an impression.

While Cognia acknowledged the considerable progress WPS had made toward fully adopting a PCBS, they provided critical feedback for further improvement. In their final report, they likened the system to a Lamborghini—well designed and high performing—but noted that most people within the system did not yet know how to "drive" it. Based on this critical feedback, WPS recognized the need to refine and deepen its approach to implementing the PCBS. The district focused on three key areas to ensure the system's success.

- **Broaden and deepen stakeholder engagement:** WPS committed to ensuring all stakeholders, including students, parents, teachers, and community members, had an equitable voice in the ongoing implementation of the system's purpose and direction. This approach aimed to create a more inclusive and representative decision-making process.
- **Ensure fidelity in implementation:** Recognizing the importance of consistent application, WPS designed and implemented a process to continually verify all instructional staff and leaders were implementing the PCBS with fidelity. This process ensured the system's principles were applied uniformly across the district.
- **Professional learning and evaluation:** To support the effective implementation of the PCBS, WPS prioritized the development and execution of professional learning and evaluation programs (highlighted previously in this book). These programs were designed to ensure all instructional staff and leaders possessed the deep knowledge and skills necessary to implement the personalized competency-based model effectively, leading to improved outcomes for all students.

The recommendations provided by Cognia were thoughtfully integrated into an updated version of the district's strategic plan and the unified improvement plans for the district and individual schools. One significant outcome from this integration was the introduction of monthly learning walks (discussed in chapter 3, page 53) at all schools by representative teams. Initially, these learning walks employed Cognia's Effective Learning Environments Observation Tool (eleot) to gather systems-level data (see Ways to Sustain the Shared Vision, page 28 in chapter 1). The use of the eleot marked a pivotal shift in focus from observing the teacher to concentrating on the students, evaluating the degree to which learners experienced an environment that was equitable, supportive, and well managed, with high expectations and active learning. This tool also assessed whether learner progress was effectively monitored, whether feedback was provided, and the extent to which technology was used to enhance learning. As WPS developed subsequent observation protocols, the district placed heightened emphasis on both student and teacher behaviors, ensuring a comprehensive approach to fostering an effective learning environment.

By responding to Cognia's recommendations, WPS strengthened its shared vision, ensured alignment with districtwide goals, and carved a new path for achieving long-term success. Implementing new systems for monitoring fidelity ensured consistent application of PCBS principles across schools, allowing the district to identify areas for support and make timely adjustments. Additionally, the focus on student actions inside the classroom shifted the instructional conversation toward establishing better skills and confidence needed to implement student-centric innovative practices effectively. Despite already being six years into the PCBE journey, these initiatives advanced WPS's PCBE transformation even further.

Navigating the Accountability Clock

In the fall of 2016, the introduction of the more rigorous Colorado Measures of Academic Success and revisions to the state's accountability system marked a significant downward shift in school performance across the state. The new methodology for determining ratings, coupled with different weightings for achievement, growth, and postsecondary workforce readiness (PWR) categories, resulted in decreased performance ratings for some WPS schools. Consequently, eight schools regressed to year 1 on the Accountability Clock, with seven being designated as "Priority Improvement" and one as "Turnaround." The district's Accountability Clock was not reset but continued its progression, leading WPS to enter its sixth year as accredited with a "Priority Improvement Plan" on July 1, 2017. This status triggered a State Review Panel (SRP) of the district.

In accordance with the Education Accountability Act of 2009, the State Board of Education was required to issue directives to the district's local school board. In April 2017, WPS leadership received written notification from the commissioner of education that a formal recommendation had been submitted by the Colorado Department of Education to the state board. The proposed "corrective actions" for WPS included the following.

- Closure of the district
- Conversion to charter schools
- District reorganization
- External management partner
- Innovation status

The commissioner recommended that WPS adopt the external management option after a thorough evaluation of the district's data, leadership, culture, academic systems, and unified improvement plan. This recommendation also considered discussions with district leadership, site visits by Colorado Department of Education staff to WPS schools, the final recommendation from the State Review Panel, and the district's own proposal for a management pathway. As part of this new "corrective action," WPS was required to develop a management pathway plan in addition to the annual district improvement plan. Despite the challenges of creating and implementing two concurrent plans, WPS leadership crafted a comprehensive management pathway plan, integrating insights from the State Review Panel, Cognia, and the district's internal evaluations. This plan outlined four overarching goals and several key supporting actions (see figure 5.8).

- **Goal 1:** Ensure consistent and deeper implementation of the PCBS in all instructional aspects.
- **Goal 2:** Attract, retain, and develop effective personalized competency-based educators and leaders.
- **Goal 3:** Foster a strong culture of academic success, including postsecondary workforce readiness for students and parents.
- **Goal 4:** Strengthen and expand early childhood education.

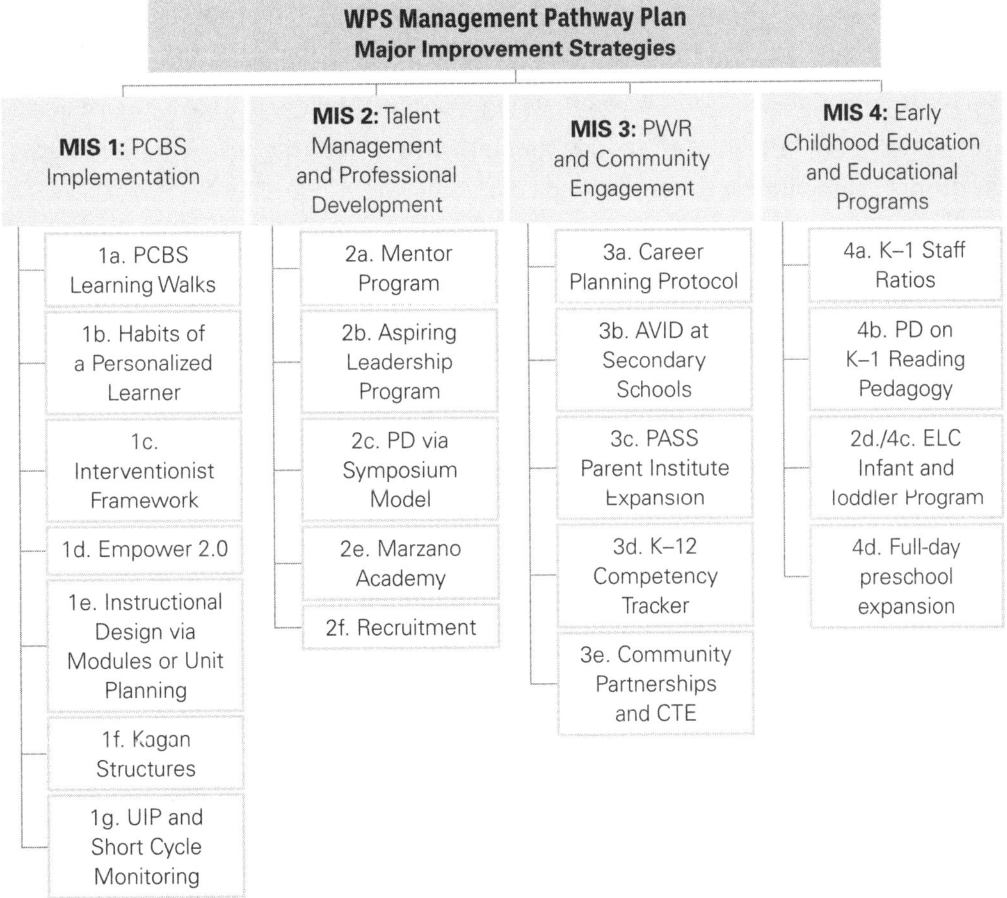

Source: © 2024 by Westminster Public Schools. Used with permission.

FIGURE 5.8: Overarching goals and significant supporting actions.

The WPS leadership presented the management pathway plan to the State Board of Education in the spring of 2017. During the hearing, the district outlined the four primary goals, detailed the aligned major improvement strategies, and emphasized its ongoing collaboration with two key partners: (1) Cognia, serving as the WPS accountability partner, and (2) Marzano Academies, acting as the WPS instructional partner. Despite facing initial confusion and resistance from the state board—including objections from two members who advocated for removing the district's accreditation—the management pathway plan was approved in a narrow four-to-three vote along political lines. This decision followed extensive discussions and the submission of written clarifications by WPS leadership.

This experience highlights the importance of perseverance and strategic collaboration while navigating high-stakes accountability systems. In spite of the contentious and politically charged process, WPS maintained focus on its shared vision and strategic plan, leveraging partnerships with Cognia and Marzano Academies to ensure the continued implementation of its goals. The approval of the management pathway plan allowed the district to integrate its continuous improvement strategies into actionable reforms, leading to significant progress. In 2018, WPS successfully moved off the state's Accountability Clock after earning an "Improvement" rating—a status the district has retained since. This achievement boosted staff morale, strengthened community trust, and reinforced the district's commitment to personalized competency-based learning. For districts facing similar challenges, WPS's story demonstrates the value of adaptability, collaboration, and a steadfast commitment to improvement, even in the face of adversity.

Navigating Pandemic Challenges

Having triumphed over the challenges posed by the state's Accountability Clock, WPS faced another major hurdle in spring 2020—the onset of the COVID-19 pandemic. This coincided with the planned release of the next generation of the WPS strategic plan, now named Destination 2030. However, due to the global disruptions caused by the pandemic, the development of Destination 2030 was paused. In response, WPS leadership shifted their focus to developing a bridge plan aimed at mitigating the immediate impacts of the COVID-19 pandemic and allowing time to fully understand the potential implications that would need to be addressed once the crisis subsided. The bridge plan was structured around the three phases of the WPS reset model.

- **Respond:** Reacting to disruptive change
- **Recovery:** Overcoming challenges, experimenting with innovative approaches, and regaining productivity
- **Renewal:** Applying learnings, innovating, and emerging stronger

The pandemic unquestionably exacerbated existing educational disparities worldwide—between rural and urban school districts, affluent and underprivileged communities, and across various gender and ethnic groups. These learning losses not only threatened the current generation but also jeopardized years of consistent academic progress. Beyond education, economic, social, and mental health challenges also emerged, with long-lasting effects on students.

Like all school districts, WPS confronted these challenges; however, the WPS's PCBS became increasingly important in minimizing the negative impacts. The greatest advantage offered by the WPS PCBS during the early days of the pandemic was its approach to student grading. As schools across the U.S. closed their doors in the spring of 2020 and many systems struggled to provide remote learning overnight, numerous districts were forced to hold student grades harmless for the remainder of the school year. This often meant that grades were frozen or students were given pass/fail marks. Additionally, as the 2020–2021 school year began, many traditional systems had no choice but to socially promote students to the next grade or course level, even though they had missed several months of instruction from the previous year. This premature advancement placed students in classrooms for which they may not have been academically prepared.

In contrast, WPS's PCBS provided a markedly unique experience for its students. As discussed in chapter 3 (page 53), the Empower LMS employs an evergreen data model, where student evidence of learning and associated scores on proficiency scales are never reset. Because academic progression in WPS is solely based on students demonstrating mastery of proficiency scales, the district was able to seamlessly continue where students and teachers had left off on returning from at-home pandemic learning. This ensured no WPS student skipped any content because of the disruptions brought on by the pandemic, maintaining the integrity of their academic progression.

This is not to suggest that WPS did not have to dramatically alter its approach to education during this time. While maintaining student outcomes remained a top priority, the primary "pivot" involved transitioning classroom learning to remote online instruction through the Empower LMS. As a one-to-one technology district, WPS was well prepared for this shift. However, new challenges inevitably arose, such as connectivity issues for some families, the need to create non-screen-intensive daily schedules, and the unique difficulties faced by students across different age groups.

Despite these challenges, WPS effectively utilized the same continuous improvement strategies that had proven successful in overcoming the state's Accountability Clock to mitigate the effects of the pandemic. The success of these efforts was evident when state accountability resumed in spring 2022. WPS remained off the Accountability Clock and experienced less regression in student performance compared to neighboring metro school districts.

Elevating Educational Excellence

In the fall of 2022, WPS reengaged with Cognia to renew its six-year accreditation contract, which included all schools and early learning centers. In addition to this renewal, WPS pursued STEM Certification and the newly introduced "Competency-Based Education Certification." Cognia conducted an in-person comprehensive review, employing the same methods used six years prior. However, this time, the review used updated quality performance standards resulting from Cognia's continuous improvement cycle. These revisions introduced three broad new concepts—learner centered, demonstration of equity, and learner well-being—which were embedded into four key quality characteristics.

1. **Healthy culture for learning:** Focused on the challenges, joys, and opportunities for learning, in coherence with the institution's mission and vision
2. **Leadership for learning:** Emphasizing the responsibility of institution leaders to positively influence and impact all aspects of the institution
3. **Engagement for learning:** Inclusive learning processes involving all learners, fostering confidence and a love for learning
4. **Growth in learning:** Measuring learners' growth in programs and curricula, ensuring readiness for successful transitions to the next levels of learning

Following a rigorous review, Cognia recommended the following.

- Reaccreditation for the district and all its schools for another six-year term
- Reaccreditation for three early learning centers and thirteen individual preschool programs for a six-year term
- Issuance of STEM Certification for Colorado STEM Academy for a six-year term
- Issuance of Competency-Based Education Certification for the district and all its schools for a six-year term

However, Cognia also identified three key areas for improvement.

1. Develop, implement, and evaluate the teacher feedback and mentoring process to increase overall quality and consistency across the system.
2. Expand opportunities for teacher leadership beyond an administrative track to include professional development and communities of practice.

3. Develop, expand, and deepen the competency-based instructional model for high-quality consistency and alignment in the system.

These findings were incorporated into the district's strategic plan and the annual district and school-improvement plans with corresponding actions taken as part of the established practice.

Navigating the Future

After a pause in development due to the pandemic, WPS transitioned from immediate crisis management to long-term planning, culminating in the completion of the Destination 2030 strategic plan. Approved by the board of education in January 2023, this seven-year plan reflects a thoughtful and robust continuous improvement process. It outlines three broad goals supported by short-, mid-, and long-term outcomes, encompassing all strategic priorities essential to leading a successful and innovative school district. The various strategic priorities and goals are as follows.

1. By 2030, WPS will provide, through innovative educational and extracurricular programs, the best student experience in the region as measured by academic achievement; postsecondary and workforce readiness; and student engagement, well-being, and satisfaction.
   + Ensure a Solid Academic Foundation
   + A Quality Teacher in Every Room/Leader in Every Building
   + A Thriving Wage the Day After Graduation
   + A Healthy Mind, Body, and Safe Environment
2. By 2030, WPS will be a public school sector leader in addressing Colorado's most pressing environmental challenges as the state moves toward a non-carbon energy future.
   + Energy Resources
3. WPS will play an active and substantial role in leading a culture of civic engagement that enhances trust in our democracy, in one another, and one that promotes social inclusion by educating a new generation of knowledgeable, inspired, and engaged citizens.
   + Develop and Sustain an Effective Internal Infrastructure to Support and Coordinate Community Engagement
   + Harness the District's Resources to Improve Economic Development in Our Local Community

These ambitious goals demonstrate WPS's continued focus on innovation, equity, and community engagement. Destination 2030 emphasized the importance of approaching education holistically—ensuring academic excellence, environmental responsibility, and civic engagement—all while preparing students for that first day after graduation. WPS's desire to maintain a forward-looking mindset, even when presented with significant challenges, hopefully offers other districts embarking down similar paths the inspiration and actionable insights leaders need to build resilient and future-ready school systems.

Final Thoughts

For WPS, the journey toward continuous improvement has been a transformative experience, marked by significant shifts in mindset and practice. Initially rooted in traditional, fragmented approaches, WPS evolved by adopting innovative practices from various industries, allowing the district to remain agile and responsive during its transition to a PCBS. This chapter highlighted the challenges WPS faced, from balancing innovation with accountability to navigating unprecedented disruptions like the COVID-19 pandemic.

The district's commitment to continuous improvement has moved from being a peripheral concept to a core principle driving its success. By embracing strategies like the PDCA cycle and the HRS framework, WPS has ensured that continuous improvement is embedded in every aspect of its operations. This dedication has allowed the district not only to overcome obstacles but also to sustain and elevate educational excellence for all students. As WPS continues to refine its practices, its journey offers valuable insights into the power of continuous improvement in driving meaningful and lasting change in education. The next chapter will delve into the details of how WPS enhanced its continuous improvement model by implementing high reliability frameworks to further strengthen its commitment to ongoing improvement and educational excellence.

CHAPTER 6

Bridging Continuous Improvement to High Reliability

In its journey toward implementing a PCBS, continuous improvement has served as the backbone for managing second-order change within WPS. The previous chapter detailed how the district evolved from a series of fragmented initiatives into a unified, data-driven approach toward system iteration. Since engaging with Cognia in 2015, WPS has demonstrated a commitment to continuous improvement, leveraging the principles and external partners to navigate the challenges of adopting a PCBS. However, as WPS advanced with its innovative system design, it became increasingly apparent that navigating multiple accountability frameworks and evaluation models was complex and challenging. While continuous improvement provided the necessary structure for measuring progress, the district recognized the need for a more robust framework to unify the various standards and practices across the system.

This realization led WPS to adopt the High Reliability Schools framework (Marzano et al., 2014), an extension of its continuous improvement efforts. HRS is derived from the principles of high reliability organizations, which are entities that excel in high-stakes environments where failure is not an option. Fields like aviation, healthcare, and nuclear energy rely on high reliability principles to achieve near-zero error rates by adhering to rigorous protocols and fostering a culture of safety and precision (Weick & Sutcliffe, 2007). Since 2019, the district has utilized the principles of HRS—through its five levels, which provide schools with a framework to align systems to goals and collect evidence to measure the efficacy of those systems—as the foundation of its continuous improvement processes.

For WPS, HRS was an opportunity to enhance its continuous improvement initiatives by consolidating various accountability and accreditation measures into a cohesive system. The framework allowed the district to meet all state and external standards while also enhancing its capacity to achieve strategic goals. Importantly, HRS provided a pathway to create consistent, scalable systems of improvement that supported excellence across all schools and departments. In the WPS learning model, HRS is not a separate initiative but a natural extension of its continuous improvement philosophy. Rather than positioning continuous improvement and HRS as distinct topics, WPS has integrated the principles of high reliability into every aspect of its continuous improvement practices. This alignment ensures schools operate cohesively, with HRS levels serving as benchmarks for achieving excellence in specific areas.

This chapter explores how WPS adopted the HRS framework and integrated it seamlessly into its continuous improvement model, making it a cornerstone of the district's transformation. It also details the creation of "The Playbook"—a comprehensive tool designed to operationalize the HRS framework in daily school practices. Through this approach, WPS streamlined processes, enhanced accountability, and fostered a culture of excellence and continuous growth districtwide.

Outlining the High Reliability Schools Framework

To provide a clear understanding of the HRS framework and its role in WPS's transformation, it is essential to establish a baseline of key concepts. Developed by Marzano and colleagues (2014), the HRS framework consists of five levels, each representing a critical area of focus to ensure schools operate as high-performing organizations.

- **Level 1: Safe, supportive, and collaborative culture**—Establishing and maintaining a safe, supportive, and collaborative school environment where students and staff can thrive

- **Level 2: Effective teaching in every classroom**—Ensuring high-quality, research-based instructional practices are consistently implemented across all classrooms
- **Level 3: Guaranteed and viable curriculum**—Developing and aligning curriculum to ensure all students have equitable access to essential content and learning opportunities
- **Level 4: Standards-referenced reporting**—Implementing reporting systems that provide clear, actionable data on student progress toward proficiency
- **Level 5: Competency-based education**—Creating systems that allow students to progress based on mastery rather than time-based grade levels

Each level builds on the previous one, creating a layered approach to systemic improvement. The framework relies on *leading indicators* to identify key processes and systems that must be in place and *lagging indicators* to measure the efficacy of these processes over time. Using leading and lagging indicators allows schools to monitor progress in real time while also evaluating long-term outcomes.

Developing a Comprehensive Set of Leading Indicators

As WPS began the initial adoption of the HRS framework, it became clear that while the district's previous continuous improvement efforts had been successful, there was still a need for a more unified and cohesive system. The HRS framework, with its structured approach to aligning systems with stated goals (leading indicators) and providing evidence of efficacy (lagging indicators), emerged as the ideal tool for this unification. However, the challenge lies in operationalizing this framework across all the district's unique schools and departments.

This recognition led to the development of the WPS HRS leading indicators into the daily operations of schools and departments across the district. This process consolidated various accountability measures, evaluation models, and continuous improvement strategies into a single, cohesive document. By unifying these elements, WPS provided clarity and focus for school and district leaders, ensuring all schools and departments were working toward the same high standards.

Historically, success in schools and districts has been narrowly defined by their ability to enhance achievement outcomes. However, common sense and experience show that much more contributes to the success of schools and districts—elements that are often the result of intentional design rather than mere chance, as evidenced by the Destination

2030 WPS Strategic Plan described in chapter 5 (page 143). Existing accountability and teacher and principal evaluation models, which focus on state test results and compliance, frequently overlook these broader designs, thereby impeding systemic innovation.

While WPS pressed ahead with its PCBS innovation, the school district and its schools were still accountable to the state's traditional accountability frameworks, as well as required to use the state's teacher and principal evaluation tools. At the same time, highlighted in chapter 5 (page 143), WPS sought dual accreditation through Cognia and partnered with Marzano Academies, both of which provided their own distinct standards. The complexity of navigating these similar but different systems became untenable for school and district leaders.

In response, WPS leadership took decisive steps to devise, develop, and implement a single master continuous improvement model that strategically leveraged the expertise and best practices from Cognia, Marzano Academies, Marzano Resources, and the Colorado Department of Education. After evaluating all guiding documents, the HRS framework emerged as the optimal method for seamlessly integrating the varying standards. Moreover, the five HRS levels effectively aligned and connected the core components and tenets of the WPS PCBS. Building on the HRS indicators as a foundation, a singular overarching framework was developed.

Aligning Varied Expectations Into a Single Set of Unified Leading Indicators

The first step in unifying the continuous improvement model was to establish a single set of leading indicators all WPS schools would be held accountable for. This process began with analyzing the existing HRS leading indicators (Marzano et al., 2014) to identify which needed modification to better align with WPS's unique goals. The hierarchical HRS framework provided a solid foundation for aligning the numerous standard operating procedures and guidance documents within the district. The initial twenty-five HRS indicators and their various sub-indicators were cross-referenced with all existing SOPs, guidance documents, and tools, allowing the district to identify significant alignments and overlaps.

Next, the district conducted a crosswalk between the Cognia and Marzano Academy standards and the evolving WPS HRS leading indicators. During this process, some standards from both models did not directly align with the HRS framework, prompting the creation of additional leading indicators to incorporate these missing elements. This thorough cross-referencing process resulted in the addition of four new WPS-specific leading indicators and several adjustments to existing indicators and sub-indicators, leading to the WPS-adapted version of HRS. By consolidating these separate models into one cohesive framework within the five levels of HRS, WPS achieved greater clarity and a unified focus for school and district leaders. This refined set of high-quality leading indicators, as shown in figure 6.1 and figure 6.2 (page 176), also included a unique set of district leading indicators for each department, which will be discussed in more detail later in this chapter.

Framework or Guiding Document	Indicator or Standard
High Reliability Schools	**HRS Indicator 2.1:** The school leader communicates a clear vision of how instruction should be addressed in the school.
Marzano School Level Indicators	**School Level Indicator 5:** Instruction and Teacher Development. The school has a Marzano Academies Inc. (MAI) approved instructional model used to provide feedback to teachers about their status and growth on specific pedagogical skills.
Cognia Performance Standard	**Leadership for Learning Standard 12:** Professional staff implement curriculum and instruction aligned for relevancy, inclusion, and effectiveness.
Cognia Competency-Based Education Certification	**Standard 3:** Learners pursue rigorous, common expectations for learning (knowledge, skills, and dispositions) that are explicit, transparent, measurable, and transferable.
Colorado Department of Education Principal Standard	**Standard III.A:** Principals establish, align, and ensure implementation of a district plan of instruction, instructional practice, assessments, and use of student data that result in academic growth and achievement for all students. **Standard IV.B:** Principals link professional growth to their professional goals.
Westminster Version – High Reliability School Indicators and Sub-indicators	**HRS Indicator 2.1:** The school has adopted the Westminster Instructional Model, which provides feedback to teachers about their status and growth on specific pedagogical skills. 2.1.1 The Westminster Instructional Model articulates the schoolwide model of instruction, which is developed and refreshed through observation and input by the users. 2.1.2 Professional development opportunities are provided for new and experienced teachers regarding the schoolwide model of instruction (Westminster Instructional Model). 2.1.3 When asked, teachers can describe the major Domains (i.e., Feedback, Content, Context, Agency, and Professionalism) and Design Questions of the schoolwide model of instruction. 2.1.4 The schoolwide language of instruction is used regularly by faculty in their informal conversations and professional learning communities. 2.1.5 New initiatives are prioritized and limited in number to support the instructional model.

Source: © 2024 by Westminster Public Schools. Used with permission.

FIGURE 6.1: Alignment of HRS indicator 2.1 to standards and indicators across the various Westminster guiding documents.

HRS Levels	Westminster Public Schools' Indicators
HRS Level 1. Safe, Supportive, and Collaborative Culture (Safety Plan, PLCs, Student Agency)	1.1 The faculty and staff perceive the school environment as safe and orderly. 1.2 Students, parents, and the community perceive the school environment as safe and orderly. 1.3 Teachers have formal roles in the decision-making process regarding school initiatives. 1.4 Teacher teams and collaborative groups regularly interact to address common issues regarding curriculum, assessment, instruction, and the achievement of all students. 1.5 Teachers and staff have formal ways to provide input regarding the optimal functioning of the school. 1.6 Students, parents, and the community have formal ways to provide input regarding the optimal functioning of the school. 1.7 The success of the whole school, as well as individuals within the school, is appropriately acknowledged. 1.8 The school allocates human, material, technological and fiscal resources in alignment with the school's identified needs and priorities to improve student performance and organizational effectiveness (time is a resource). *1.9 The school has programs and practices in place that help develop student efficacy and agency.*
HRS Level 2. Effective Teaching in Every Classroom (Westminster Instructional Model)	2.1 The school has adopted the Westminster Instructional Model, which is used to provide feedback to teachers regarding their status and growth on specific pedagogical skills. 2.2 Support is provided to teachers to continually enhance their pedagogical skills through reflection and professional growth plans. 2.3 Predominant instructional practices throughout the school are known and monitored. 2.4 Teachers are provided with clear, ongoing evaluations of their pedagogical strengths and weaknesses that are based on multiple sources of data and are consistent with student achievement data. 2.5 Teachers are provided with job-embedded professional development that is directly related to their instructional growth goals. 2.6 Teachers have the opportunities to observe and discuss effective teaching. *2.7 The school procures online resources and engages teachers in activities that help them develop and integrate online resources for score 2.0, 3.0, and 4.0 on proficiency scales.*
HRS Level 3. Guaranteed and Viable Curriculum (Proficiency Scales and Data)	3.1 The school has adopted the WPS Proficiency Scales for all levels and courses taught which adhere to national, state, and district standards. 3.2 The school curriculum is focused enough that it can be adequately addressed in the time available to teachers and flexible in time available to meet student needs. 3.3 All students have the opportunity to learn the critical content of the curriculum.

HRS Level 3. Guaranteed and Viable Curriculum (Proficiency Scales and Data)	3.4 Clear and measurable goals are established and focused on critical needs regarding improving overall student achievement and growth at the student, class, and school level. 3.5 The school engages in a continuous improvement process that produces evidence, including measurable results of improving student learning and professional practice. 3.6 Appropriate school- and classroom-level programs and practices are in place to help students meet individual achievement goals when data indicate interventions are needed. *3.7 The school has well-articulated domains and accompanying proficiency scales for cognitive and metacognitive skills that are systematically taught and assessed throughout the curriculum.*
HRS Level 4. Standards-Referenced Reporting (Empower LMS)	4.1 Clear and measurable goals are established and focused on critical needs regarding improving achievement of individual students within the school. 4.2 Data are analyzed, interpreted, and used to regularly monitor progress toward achievement goals for individual students.
HRS Level 5. Competency-Based Education (Schedules, Pacing, Anytime/Anywhere Learning)	5.1 Students move on to the next level of the curriculum for any subject area only after they have demonstrated competence at the previous level. 5.2 The school schedule is designed to accommodate students moving at a pace appropriate to their background and needs. 5.3 Students who have demonstrated competence levels greater than those articulated in the system are afforded immediate opportunities to begin work on advanced content and/or career paths of interest.
High Reliability District Level 6. District Level Systems of Support	*Board of Education, Superintendent, Learning Services, Human Resources, Finance, Communications, Student Services, Maintenance and Operations, Custodial, Transportation, Logistics, Technology, Principal Professionalism, Athletics and Activities, Education Foundation*

Source: © 2024 by Westminster Public Schools, adapted from Marzano et al., 2014. Used with permission.

FIGURE 6.2: Westminster version of the High Reliability Schools framework.

Ensuring HRS Speaks Your Language

Moreover, modifications were made to the HRS terminology to ensure stakeholders at all levels within WPS recognized the same language and saw direct connections to their work. For instance, the original HRS term "measurement topic" used in level 3 was replaced with "domain" to better suit WPS's context. Similarly, the language of HRS indicator 2.1 was updated from requiring the establishment of a schoolwide instructional model to specifying the adoption of the Westminster Instructional Model. In figure 6.3 (page 178), indicators 1.1 and 1.2 retain their original HRS wording, while 1.8 was modified to better reflect WPS expectations. Additionally, indicator 1.9 was newly introduced to incorporate WPS personalized competency-based learning into

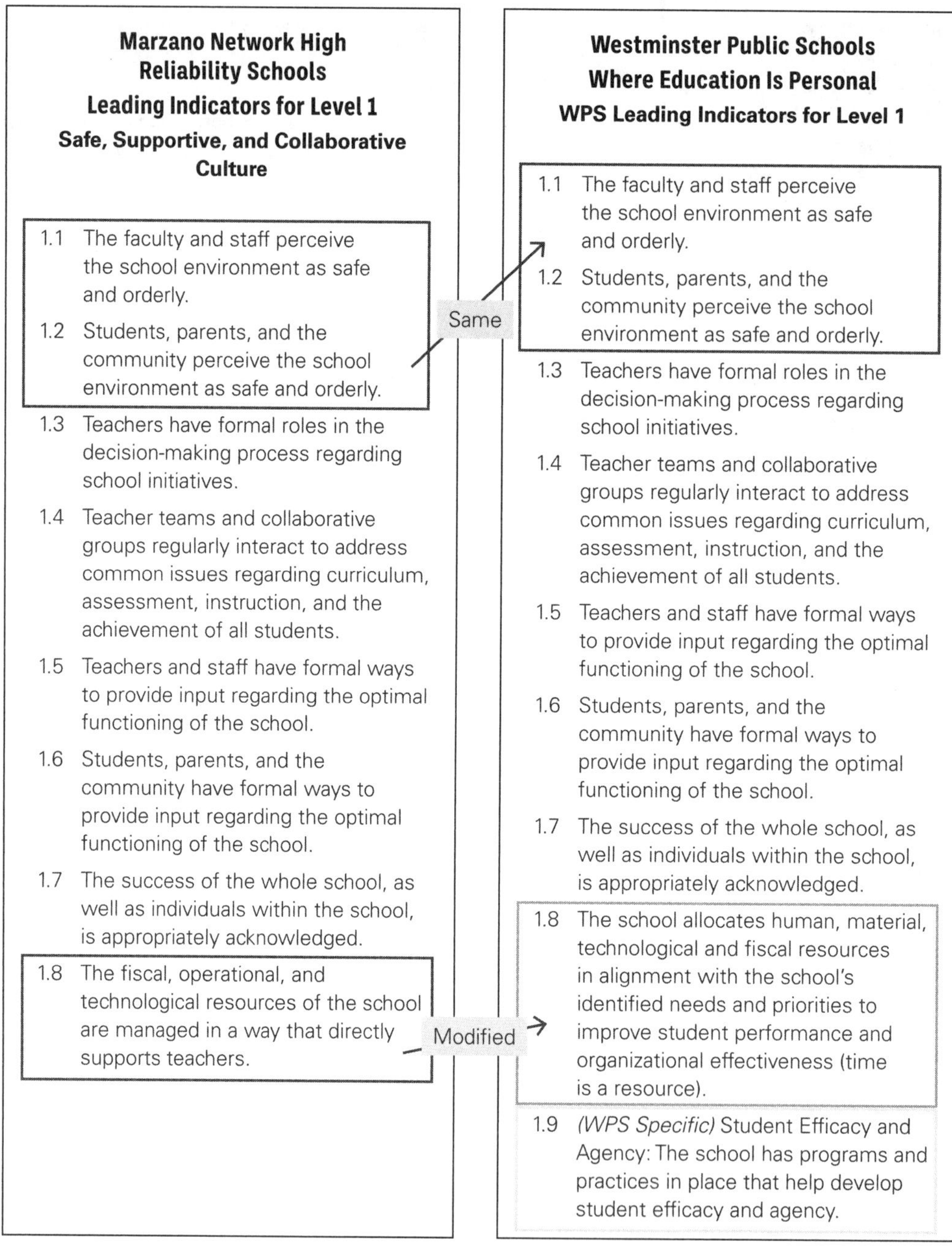

Source: © 2024 by Westminster Public Schools, adapted from Marzano et al., 2014. Used with permission.

FIGURE 6.3: Example shifts from Marzano, Warrick, and Simms (2014) to the Westminster Public Schools language.

HRS level 1. While these language modifications were minor, they significantly enhanced clarity and facilitated a deeper, systemwide implementation with intentional checks.

Integrating a PCBS Throughout the HRS Framework

The deliberate use of the term "system" in WPS's mantra for creating a PCBS led to a significant shift in how the district adopted and adapted the HRS framework. The original framework (Marzano et al., 2014) presents competency-based education as HRS level 5, and its hierarchical structure can give the impression that competency-based education is achievable only after reaching the four preceding levels. However, WPS leadership believed that the principles of the WPS personalized competency-based approach should permeate every level of the HRS framework.

For example, at HRS level 1, WPS added indicator 1.9 to emphasize the importance of student efficacy and agency in fostering a safe and collaborative environment within a PCBS. At HRS level 2, WPS adopted the Westminster Instructional Model, a competency-based instructional model implemented across all schools in the district. Moving to HRS level 3, teacher teams developed proficiency scales for every performance level and content area, which determine all students' academic progression. At HRS level 4, the district adopted a genuinely competency-based LMS, centered on student needs, making competency-based learning both practical and more effective. Finally, in the WPS context, HRS level 5 focuses on the distinctive elements of classroom grouping, pacing, and scheduling inherent to a PCBS. Figure 6.4 illustrates WPS's internal interpretation of the five HRS levels, highlighting its unique approach to integrating a PCBS across all aspects of the educational framework.

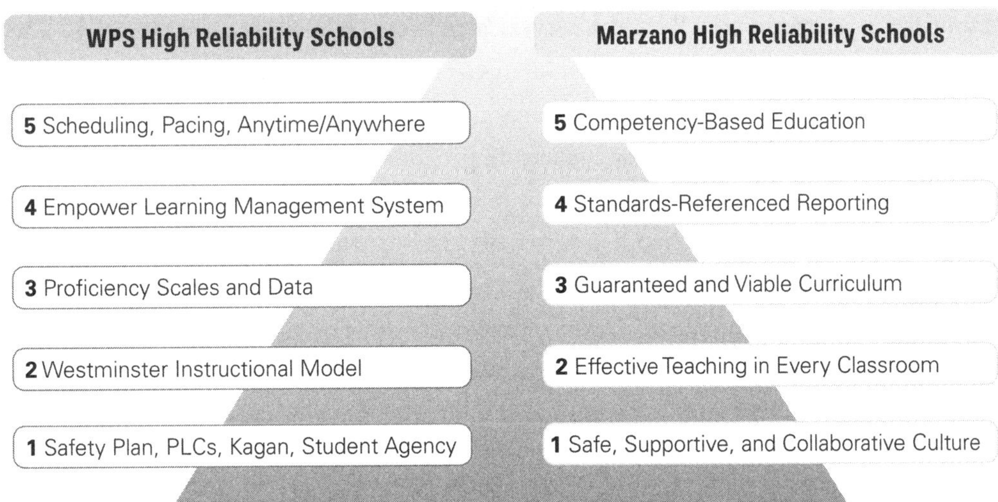

Source: © 2024 by Westminster Public Schools, adapted from Marzano et al., 2014. Used with permission.

FIGURE 6.4: Comparison of the original HRS levels with the Westminster version.

As a result of WPS district leadership's commitment to creating a unified framework, school teams now operate with a single set of leading indicators that guide their daily work. This effort paid off when Cognia conducted the comprehensive accreditation review of WPS in the fall of 2022. Because all Cognia standards were seamlessly integrated into the WPS HRS leading indicators, principals were no longer required to juggle multiple, disparate sets of standards or expectations. By focusing on the WPS HRS indicators, they effectively met all Cognia's requirements, making the 2022 accreditation review far less burdensome than the original 2016 process, which had consumed significant principal time over several days.

Creating the WPS HRS Playbooks

Initially, principals were given the autonomy to create their own monitoring systems for the HRS indicators. However, this approach resulted in a diverse range of practices that, while innovative, lacked uniformity and made districtwide analysis challenging. Recognizing the need for a more systematic and cohesive approach, WPS sought to consolidate these varied practices into a single, unified documentation system. Drawing from the exemplary practices observed among the different school leaders and through several rounds of refinement, WPS developed a comprehensive playbook tool. This playbook synthesized the most effective strategies across all WPS schools, refining them into an electronic format that supported both the specific needs of school-based leadership and the broader oversight requirements of district leaders.

The primary users of the playbook are school staff, school leaders, and district leaders, who utilize it to systematically address every aspect of the WPS HRS framework. The playbook serves multiple purposes: it facilitates a transparent and consistent approach to meeting the high reliability indicators, enables the sharing of best practices across schools, and provides a clear framework for evaluating progress toward established targets. This tool supports the direct application and monitoring of PCBS principles and enhances collaboration to maintain reliability across all levels of the WPS educational system. Through this unified electronic template (see figure 6.5 and figure 6.6, page 182), WPS fosters an environment of continuous improvement where every member of the educational community is aligned in their efforts to deliver a personalized competency-based learning experience. This alignment ensures a solid academic foundation for all students, as outlined in the district's strategic plan, Destination 2030.

WPS High Reliability Schools Playbook

Certification Date:												**Current Average Rubric Score:**					
1.1		1.2		1.3		1.4		1.5		1.6		1.7		1.8		1.9	

Level 1: A Safe and Orderly Environment that Supports Cooperation and Collaboration
(Rubric Descriptors)

HRS Commitment – "Being accountable for ensuring what you do is working… and addressing operational errors before they become system failures."

Leading Indicator 1.1: The faculty and staff perceive the school environment as safe and orderly (Cognia LL 11, GL26, CBE 2, CDE Principal II.A, IV.A) *Sub-indicators for 1.1* Reference list		**Rubric Level:** ☐ S ☐ A ☐ D ☐ B ☐ N ☐ U
Leading Indicator Systems or Processes	**Lagging Indicator Targets**	**Lagging Indicator Evidence and Data**
Conditions that are in place in the form of systems, processes, or programs (provide a description or a link to your school process) ☐ 1.1.1 ☐ 1.1.2 ☐ 1.1.3 ☐ 1.1.4 ☐ 1.1.5	What results do you expect to see if the system or process is successful? Often in the form of SMART Goals	Data or concrete artifacts of practice that provide evidence for the degree to which the leading indicators are present and working in your school's operations • Concrete artifacts of practice • Criterion scores for performance

Source: © *2024 by Westminster Public Schools. Used with permission.*

FIGURE 6.5: Sample HRS level 1 playbook with leading and lagging indicators.

Level 1: Leading Indicator Sub-Indicators

HRS Leading Indicator 1.1: Staff Perception of Environment (Back to 1.1)

- 1.1.1 When asked, faculty and staff generally describe the school as a safe place.
- 1.1.2 When asked, faculty and staff generally describe the school as an orderly place (such as efficiency, lunchroom procedures, and so on).
- 1.1.3 Clear and specific school rules and procedures (such as Code of Conduct, Standard Operating Procedures, Flow Charts, and adherence to suspension and expulsion procedures).
- 1.1.4 Faculty and staff know the emergency management procedures and how to implement them for specific incidents.
- 1.1.5 Evidence of practicing, updating and reflecting on emergency management procedures for specific incidents is available (such as a crisis plan, drills, contacting local sites for emergency release).

4 Sustaining	3 Applying	2 Developing	1 Beginning	0 Not Attempting
The school continually cultivates information through quick data sources to monitor faculty and staff perceptions of the safety, supportiveness, and orderliness of the school environment, and it takes proper actions to intervene when quick data indicate a potential problem.	The school has developed and implemented well-defined, schoolwide routines and procedures that lead to faculty and staff perceptions of a safe, supportive, and orderly environment, and it can produce lagging indicators to show the desired effects of these actions.	The school has developed and implemented well-defined, schoolwide routines and procedures that lead to faculty and staff perceptions of a safe, supportive, and orderly environment.	The school is in the beginning, yet incomplete, stages of developing and implementing well-defined, schoolwide routines and procedures that lead to faculty and staff perceptions of a safe, supportive, and orderly environment.	The school has not attempted to develop and implement well-defined, schoolwide routines and procedures that lead to faculty and staff perceptions of a safe, supportive, and orderly environment.

HRS Leading Indicator 1.1 - Adjustments, Reflections, and Quick Data
If unreliable lagging indicator data are present, follow adjustment steps to modify systems, processes, or implementation. If data are reliable, what quick data will be used to monitor long term to serve as an alert to possible declines?

Source: © *2024 by Westminster Public Schools. Used with permission.*

FIGURE 6.6: Sample HRS level 1 playbook with sub-indicators and adjustments.

To streamline the process of tracking and supporting the implementation of the HRS framework across the district, all playbooks are housed in Google Drive, accompanied by a comprehensive supporting website. This website is structured to display all five levels of the WPS HRS framework for each school, creating a transparent and accessible dashboard of practices and progress. This approach allows for dynamic interaction among stakeholders—teachers, coaches, coordinators, school leaders, and district leaders—enabling them to provide guidance, feedback, and support to school and district leaders. Additionally, it offers principals the opportunity to see how their peers across the district are approaching the same school-level goals. The sharing of systems, targets, and lagging indicator evidence and data has accelerated the pace of continuous improvement across WPS.

In addition, learning services directors play a pivotal role in monitoring and leveraging the WPS HRS playbooks. Each director is responsible for closely overseeing specific indicators within the WPS HRS framework that fall under their area of expertise. For example, the executive director of integrated services is tasked with monitoring all schools' HRS indicators 1.9, 3.6, and 3.7, which relate to intervention and mental health services. This oversight provides critical insights into the effectiveness of the WPS integrated services model at both the district and school levels, allowing for real-time data monitoring and enabling quick adjustments when necessary. Such targeted oversight is crucial for identifying areas where schools may be facing challenges or require additional support. The indicators serve as a guide, signaling the learning services directors to deploy resources, expertise, or intervention strategies tailored to the needs of each school.

By leveraging the capabilities of the Google Drive platform and the supporting website, WPS has not only enhanced the visibility of each school's journey through the WPS HRS framework but also fostered a culture of continuous collaboration and improvement. The direct involvement of learning services directors in monitoring progress ensures support is both timely and relevant, addressing the unique needs of each school. This systemic approach underscores the district's commitment to ensuring all schools have the guidance and resources necessary to thrive within the Westminster learning model, leading to improved outcomes for all students.

Using the WPS HRS Playbooks to Drive Continuous Improvement

The WPS HRS framework now stands as the cornerstone of the district's approach to continuous improvement, embodying a systematic and structured methodology for enhancing educational outcomes. This process involves a comprehensive evaluation of current practices, with every aspect of the system being scrutinized, optimized, and aligned with the latest research and best practices in education. The model's tiered approach facilitates targeted improvements, strengthening the foundation for student growth and school reliability through both leading and lagging indicators. By leveraging the HRS framework and the PDCA cycle (see Navigating Initial Implementation and Learning Opportunities, page 146 in chapter 5), WPS fosters a culture of continuous improvement, actively seeking feedback, addressing challenges proactively, and building on successes.

This methodical approach is composed of four key action steps.

1. **Identify your systems and processes:** Understand the conditions that are in place in the form of systems, processes, or programs.
2. **Set your targets or goals:** Establish what results you expect to see if the system or process is successful, often in the form of SMART goals.
3. **Collect evidence:** Gather data or concrete artifacts of practice that provide evidence of the degree to which the leading indicators are present and effective in your school's operations.
4. **Adjust systems and processes when necessary:** Engage in a six-step review and adjustment process to refine systems and processes.

These four action steps serve as guiding questions for school leaders as they work on completing their WPS HRS playbooks, a tool designed to organize and document school leading and lagging indicators. Step 2 marks a pivotal change in practice by addressing the challenge of being "data rich and information poor." By defining success metrics at the start, school leaders establish a basis for meaningful data analysis, prompting the right questions about whether realistic targets are met. This proactive approach ensures WPS can analyze data with a clear purpose rather than merely observing it. Figure 6.7 captures these four action steps and serves as the foundational template for the playbooks, which are explained in the next section.

Leading Indicator Systems and Processes	Lagging Indicator Targets	Lagging Indicator Evidence and Data
Conditions in place in the form of systems, processes, or programs.	What results do you expect to see if the system or process is successful? Often in the form of SMART goals.	Data or concrete artifacts of practice that provide evidence for the degree to which the leading indicators are present and working in your school's operations (concrete artifacts of practice or criterion scores for performance).

Source: © 2024 by Westminster Public Schools. Used with permission.

FIGURE 6.7: Initial structure to support principals in documenting leading and lagging indicators.

The final step in the WPS HRS continuous improvement process involves school leadership teams engaging in a "Review and Adjustment" process, which includes additional steps if the targets set in review step 2 are not met. Review step 3 is particularly crucial, as it requires analyzing whether the continuous improvement effort needs to focus on the system and process design or its implementation. Often, the system and process may be well designed, but the execution at the school or classroom level might require adjustments.

The complete WPS six-step review and adjustment process is as follows.

1. Share results with relevant stakeholders.
2. Conduct a root cause analysis with relevant stakeholders.
3. Identify problematic leading indicators by asking the following questions.
   + Which leading indicator was not effective?
   + Does it need to be designed differently?
   + Does it need to be implemented differently?
4. Create a plan of action and implement it based on the findings from step 3.
5. Collect lagging indicator evidence to determine efficacy.
6. Wash, rinse, repeat.

Figure 6.8 illustrates the review and adjustment process in action for HRS indicator 1.2 at John E. Flynn A Marzano Academy. Initial survey results fell significantly below the target, with only 33 percent of middle school students responding favorably to the question, "In your class, how much does the behavior of other students hurt or help your learning?" This is far short of the 75 percent favorable response rate goal set in the school's HRS level 1 playbook. This prompted the initiation of the adjustment process. By conducting a thorough root cause analysis, the school was able to identify and address the underlying issues, resulting in a dramatic improvement, with 76 percent of students responding favorably in the end-of-year survey administration.

Step 1: Share results with relevant stakeholders.
• Principal discussed survey with each classroom. • Principal invited teachers and students into the solution process.
Step 2: Conduct root cause analysis with relevant stakeholders.
• Teachers conducted **fishbone** activity with associated **"5 whys"** with students, finding: + That not enough social time is embedded into the school day + That learning is boring + A lack of student ownership in school day

FIGURE 6.8: Example of the six-step adjustment process from John E. Flynn A Marzano Academy for HRS indicator 1.2.

continued ▶

Step 3: Identify problematic leading indicators.
• Students wanted more voice in class (Lack of student ownership in school day). + Student-generated SOPs (1.1.3) were identified as being in place but not having desired effect. + Students discussed desire for more co-creation of learning opportunities (3.1 and 3.7). • Students wanted more social time with friends.
Step 4: Create a plan of action and implement based on step 3 findings.
• Introduce findings to Building Leadership Team (BLT) • Identified new student-led classroom SOP process for each team and implementation dates • Created Synergistic Learning Model (middle school team; cross-curricular PBL with heavy emphasis on co-creation of learning) • Students wanted more social time with friends; new student-generated SOPs included: + Increased passing period by two minutes + Increased recess by five minutes + "Friday Fun" with friends from other classes for good behavior
Step 5: Collect lagging indicator to determine efficacy.
Step 6: Wash, rinse, repeat.

Source: © 2024 by Westminster Public Schools. Used with permission.

Using the Playbooks for Principal Succession Planning

Similar to other districts, WPS has faced challenges during transitions to new leadership at the school level. Often, when a principal departs, a significant exodus of teachers follows within a year or two of the new leader's tenure. This staff turnover typically leads to a notable decline in school performance scores. This trend is especially pronounced in schools that have strongly embraced a collective efficacy model, where staff collaboratively contribute to the development and implementation of systematic practices. Teachers in these environments become deeply invested in established processes, which are tailored to their school's shared vision of student success. Consequently, when a new leader arrives and disrupts these carefully crafted processes and systems, it undermines the sense of ownership and leadership among the existing staff.

Recognizing this pattern, district leadership understood the need for a robust framework capable of withstanding inevitable leadership changes. The WPS playbook template was perfectly suited to encapsulate the core processes, systems, targets, and evidence that underpin the school's operational and educational strategies, guided by the WPS HRS indicators. By providing a comprehensive record of the school's current practices and achievements, the playbooks offer incoming principals a clear overview of the school's strategic direction, the rationale behind existing processes and systems, and the progress made toward specific targets.

The district now provides new principals with their school's current HRS playbooks and expects the documented systemic processes and practices will be sustained.

While new leaders are permitted to propose changes to existing practices and processes, they must first demonstrate the ineffectiveness or redundancy of the current ones using the playbook's lagging indicator evidence and data. Additionally, any proposed changes must adhere to the WPS six-step review and adjustment process, ensuring stakeholder involvement is maintained, and a thorough analysis of existing practices is completed. This approach prevents the indiscriminate replacement of effective or promising practices based solely on personal preference or previous experiences. Moreover, new principals are limited to adjusting no more than one system per WPS HRS level in their first year, ensuring stability and the thoughtful implementation of changes. This practice helps existing staff feel their previous collective efforts are respected by the new principal, helping mitigate the previously high staff turnover rates experienced before.

Using the playbooks not only facilitates a smoother transition for new leaders but also ensures continuity in the school's strategic direction, minimizing the disruption to teachers and students. Furthermore, it safeguards the investments made by staff in developing and implementing effective educational practices, thereby maintaining the collective efficacy model even amid leadership changes. By embedding the essence of the school's operational and educational strategies within these WPS HRS playbooks, a legacy of sustained improvement and success is created, regardless of changes in individual leadership positions.

Aligning Principal Evaluation to HRS Leading Indicators

In finalizing the WPS HRS playbooks, WPS addressed two crucial elements to eliminate redundancy and streamline processes for principals: principal evaluation and the school unified improvement plans. As highlighted in chapter 3 (page 53) regarding teacher evaluations, a similar challenge arose in evaluating principals based on state standards designed for leaders in traditional school settings. This disconnect created a significant gap between the existing accountability measures and WPS's PCBS.

To resolve this, WPS engaged in discussions with the state department to demonstrate that the indicators detailed in the WPS HRS leading indicators not only aligned with but also surpassed the state standards outlined in the Colorado Principal Model Evaluation System (Colorado Department of Education, 2019). After extensive review and dialogue, the state approved the WPS-adapted version of HRS for use in principal evaluations. Consequently, a new evaluation tool was integrated into the Empower LMS that complements and aligns with the teacher evaluation tool. This alignment underscores WPS's commitment to a coherent and unified approach to leadership evaluation within the Westminster learning model.

In parallel, WPS also sought to streamline the school UIPs, a strategic planning process mandated by the Colorado Department of Education (2025b). The UIP framework helps schools and districts identify strengths and areas for improvement, set goals, and monitor progress. Recognizing the overlap between the UIP process and the WPS HRS framework, district leaders initiated discussions with the state department to explore how the detailed planning and monitoring articulated in the WPS HRS playbooks could satisfy the UIP requirements. By leveraging the comprehensive nature of the HRS framework, WPS was able to align the UIP goals with the existing high reliability indicators, further reinforcing the district's commitment to a coherent and unified approach to continuous improvement.

This approach also addressed concerns about how principals would manage the extensive monitoring requirements associated with the HRS playbooks, which cover all five levels and their twenty-nine indicators. The solution involved having principals and school leadership teams select one indicator from each WPS HRS level. Using data and insights from recent prioritized school improvement initiatives, school leaders identify specific WPS HRS indicators for focused review within a given year, which become the major improvement strategies embedded inside the school's UIP. This process of continuous improvement balances the need for comprehensive oversight with the practicalities of managing workload, ensuring both state requirements and district goals are met simultaneously.

High Reliability District

The WPS Board of Education has consistently demonstrated its support and confidence in the HRS framework as a core component of the Westminster learning model, as evidenced by its annual PCBS resolutions, which were discussed in chapter 1 (page 11). Furthermore, HRS certification has been fully integrated into the district's strategic plan, Destination 2030. The plan outlines specific goals: a short-term goal that all schools achieve HRS level 2 by the end of 2024, which the district did achieve; a midterm goal for 85 percent of schools to reach HRS level 5 by 2027; and a long-term goal for all schools to attain all five HRS levels by 2030. These goals clearly convey the district's commitment to upholding its values and priorities, as outlined in the shared vision.

The implementation of HRS began in line with the district's approach of testing initiatives on a small scale before wider application. The principal and team at John E. Flynn A Marzano Academy set a precedent by becoming the first school ever to achieve HRS level 5 certification in January 2022. The insights gained from this pioneering effort were invaluable, significantly influencing the strategies and initiatives as WPS applied HRS principles across all schools. As school leaders progress through the five certification levels, their leadership development and growth become increasingly evident. The rigorous nature of the HRS process has led principals to report feeling more capable and confident in their leadership roles.

Adopting High Reliability Organization Principles

As the HRS process took root across the district, WPS recognized that the principles of high reliability could extend beyond the school setting and be applied to various district departments. This realization prompted an exploration of how the HRS framework could be expanded districtwide, with the goal of evolving into a high reliability district. WPS adopted the high reliability organization principles, which assert that organizations operating in high-stakes environments—where failure leads to catastrophic outcomes—must develop systems that ensure a high degree of success. School districts, like operating rooms, aircraft carriers, or nuclear power plants, carry an equally critical responsibility: the day-to-day work of educating students to realize their full potential.

Initially, it was believed that achieving HRS level 5 certification for every school in the district would qualify WPS as a high reliability district. However, further investigation into the high reliability organization model revealed that this alone was insufficient. It became clear that the roles of various departments and divisions, which support the work of school leaders and teachers, are crucial to ensuring every student attains academic success. While the HRS framework addresses certain aspects of this work, it does not fully encompass what constitutes high reliability in nonacademic departments, such as human resources or maintenance and operations. In response, WPS developed an additional level within its HRS framework—High Reliability District Level 6—which focuses on identifying leading and lagging indicators specific to each department. See figure 6.9.

HRS Levels	Westminster Public Schools' Indicators
High Reliability District Level 6. District Level Systems of Support	6.1 Board of Education 6.2 Superintendent 6.3 Learning Services 6.4 Human Resources 6.5 Finance 6.6 Communications 6.7 Student Services 6.8 Maintenance and Operations 6.9 Custodial 6.10 Transportation 6.11 Logistics 6.12 Technology 6.13 Principal Professionalism 6.14 Athletics and Activities 6.15 Education Foundation

Source: © 2024 by Westminster Public Schools. Used with permission.

FIGURE 6.9: Westminster Public Schools High Reliability District Level 6 indicators based on departments.

Drafting High Reliability District Leading and Lagging Indicators

HRS leading indicator 1.8 serves as a good example of why the HRS framework alone is not sufficient when considering what constitutes a high reliability district. At first glance, it might seem logical to apply WPS HRS indicator 1.8, which states, "The school allocates human, material, technological, and fiscal resources in alignment with the school's identified needs and priorities to improve student performance and organizational effectiveness (time is a resource)," as a leading indicator that could encompass multiple district-level departments—such as human resources, finance, and operations. However, this WPS HRS indicator is specifically focused on the principal's role in managing resources at the school level, not on the broader responsibilities of chiefs, directors, coordinators, and managers within the entire system. This distinction raised a critical question: What are the leading indicators that define a high reliability finance department, human resources department, or operations department?

Answering this question led WPS to identify leading and lagging indicators for thirteen district-level departments, enabling each to apply the same continuous improvement process that WPS schools use through their WPS HRS playbooks. Unlike at the school level, where the HRS levels and associated leading and lagging indicators were already established, the WPS district indicators had to be created from scratch, requiring each WPS department to draft its own indicators.

For example, in the maintenance and operations department, a leading indicator might focus on the timely completion of maintenance requests to ensure school facilities remain safe, functional, and conducive to learning. This indicator could be measured by tracking the percentage of maintenance requests resolved within a set time frame, such as forty-eight hours. A corresponding lagging indicator could assess the overall condition of school facilities based on regular inspections and feedback from school leaders, linking the department's efficiency to student and staff satisfaction with the learning environment.

In the human resources department, a leading indicator might involve the recruitment and retention of high-quality staff, with a specific focus on reducing turnover rates in key positions. This could be measured by the percentage of new hires who remain with the district beyond their first year. A lagging indicator might evaluate the long-term impact of human resources initiatives on overall staff satisfaction and performance, using data from employee surveys and performance reviews to gauge the effectiveness of recruitment and retention strategies.

The finance department might have a leading indicator related to the accuracy and timeliness of budget reports, ensuring all financial statements are completed and reviewed by relevant stakeholders before set deadlines. A lagging indicator could measure the fiscal health of the district, tracking key metrics such as budget variances, fund balances, and audit findings to ensure the district's financial practices support long-term sustainability.

Consistent with the approach outlined in the WPS Leadership Toolbox in chapter 2 (page 35), the goal was to engage those most directly impacted in the authoring of these indicators. Consequently, during the creation of department-level leading and lagging indicators, department heads convened their teams to assess proposed indicators and seek feedback and assistance in drafting the initial indicators. The final selection of department indicators was agreed on by each team. This refinement process ensured the indicators were both manageable and closely aligned with the strategic goals of each department, as outlined in Destination 2030. Examples of a district department completed leading and lagging indicators can be seen in figure 6.10, and figure 6.11 (page 193) reflects a complete set of district indicators.

HRS Indicator 6.8: Maintenance and Operations	
Leading Indicator Sub-indicators:	**Lagging Indicator Samples:**
☐ **6.8.1 Preventive Maintenance Schedule Adherence:** The percentage of scheduled preventive maintenance tasks completed on time. High adherence rates can predict reduced breakdowns and longer asset life.	☐ **6.8.1 Equipment Downtime and Failure Rates:** Measure the frequency and duration of equipment downtime and failures, reflecting the impact of preventive maintenance on operational continuity. ***Target:*** Reduce equipment downtime and failure rates by 15–20% annually.
☐ **6.8.2 Work Order Submission Rate:** The rate at which new work orders are submitted. An increase might indicate potential issues with facilities, while a decrease could suggest improvements in maintenance.	☐ **6.8.2 Work Order Resolution Time:** Assess the average time taken to resolve work orders, indicating the efficiency and responsiveness of the maintenance team. ***Target:*** Resolve 90–95% of work orders within a 5-day average time frame for non-urgent requests and within 24 hours for urgent ones.
☐ **6.8.3 Inventory of Critical Spare Parts:** Monitoring the availability of essential spare parts for critical equipment. Adequate inventory levels can predict reduced downtime in case of equipment failure.	☐ **6.8.3 Parts Availability Rate at Time of Need:** Track the percentage of times critical parts were available when needed, reflecting the effectiveness of inventory management. ***Target:*** Maintain a 85–90% availability rate for critical spare parts when needed.
☐ **6.8.4 Energy Usage Monitoring:** Regular tracking of energy consumption across facilities. Early detection of spikes or irregular patterns can indicate potential issues or opportunities for efficiency improvements.	

FIGURE 6.10: Leading and lagging indicators for the Westminster maintenance and operations department.

continued ▶

HRS Level 6.8: Maintenance and Operations	
☐ **6.8.5 Staff Training and Certification:** The frequency and coverage of training and certification programs for maintenance staff. Well-trained staff can predict more effective and efficient maintenance work.	☐ **6.8.4 Energy Cost and Consumption Trends:** Evaluate changes in energy costs and consumption over time, indicating the success of energy management and conservation efforts. ***Target:*** Achieve a 5–10% annual reduction in energy consumption and related costs.
☐ **6.8.6 Vendor and Contractor Performance Reviews:** Regular assessments of the performance and reliability of vendors and contractors involved in maintenance and operations. Positive reviews can predict smoother and more reliable maintenance processes.	☐ **6.8.5 Maintenance Quality and Efficiency Metrics:** Assess the quality and efficiency of maintenance work post-training, reflecting the impact of staff development on service delivery. ***Target:*** Improve maintenance quality and efficiency by 10–15% following staff training and certification programs.
☐ **6.8.7 Safety Inspection Frequency and Protocols:** The number of regular safety inspections conducted and ongoing processes, drills, inventories. A higher frequency can predict a safer environment and potentially fewer accidents or compliance issues.	☐ **6.8.6 Vendor Reliability and Performance Metrics:** Measure the reliability and quality of work provided by vendors and contractors, indicating the effectiveness of external partnerships. ***Target:*** Achieve an 85% or higher satisfaction rate with vendor and contractor performance and reliability.
☐ **6.8.8 Technology and Equipment Upgrades:** Tracking the implementation of new maintenance technologies or equipment upgrades. Up-to-date technology can predict improved efficiency and effectiveness.	☐ **6.8.7 Safety Incident and Compliance Rates:** Track the rate and severity of safety incidents and the compliance with safety regulations, reflecting the effectiveness of regular inspections. ***Target:*** Reduce safety incidents by 10–125% annually and achieve 100% compliance with safety regulations.
☐ **6.8.9 Facility Condition Assessments:** Regular evaluations of the physical condition of school buildings and facilities. Early identification of issues can lead to timely repairs and better facility management.	☐ **6.8.8 Operational Improvement Metrics:** Evaluate improvements in operational efficiency and effectiveness post-upgrade, indicating the impact of technological advancements. ***Target:*** Demonstrate a 10–15% improvement in operational efficiency and effectiveness following technology and equipment upgrades.
☐ **6.8.10 Feedback Mechanism for Maintenance Services:** The establishment of a system for receiving and addressing feedback from school staff and students regarding maintenance issues. A responsive system can predict better service and satisfaction.	☐ **6.8.9 Facility Repair and Upgrade Needs:** Track the frequency and extent of repairs and upgrades needed postassessment, reflecting the actual condition of facilities. ***Target:*** Reduce the frequency and extent of needed repairs and upgrades by 10–15% through proactive facility maintenance.
	☐ **6.8.10 Service Satisfaction Rates:** Aggregate satisfaction rates and feedback from school staff and students regarding the timeliness and quality of maintenance services. ***Target:*** Achieve an 85% or higher service satisfaction rate from school staff and students.

Source: © *2024 by Westminster Public Schools. Used with permission.*

WPS High Reliability Schools Framework

HRS Level 1: Safe, Supportive, and Collaborative Culture (Safety Plan, Collaborative Teams, Student Agency)	**HRS Level 2:** Effective Teaching in Every Classroom (Westminster Instructional Model)	**HRS Level 3:** Guaranteed and Viable Curriculum (Proficiency Scales and Data)	**HRS Level 4:** Standards-Referenced Reporting (Empower Learning Management System)	**HRS Level 5:** Competency-Based Education (Schedules, Pacing, Anytime-Anywhere Learning)	**High Reliability District Level 6:** District Level System of Support
1.1 The faculty and staff perceive the school environment as safe and orderly. 1.2 Students, parents, and the community perceive the school environment as safe and orderly. 1.3 Teachers have formal roles in the decision-making process regarding school initiatives. 1.4 Teacher teams and collaborative groups regularly interact to address common issues regarding curriculum, assessment, instruction, and the achievement of all students.	2.1 The school has adopted the Westminster Instructional Model, which is used to provide feedback to teachers regarding their status and growth on specific pedagogical skills. 2.2 Support is provided to teachers to continually enhance their pedagogical skills through reflection and professional growth plans. 2.3 Predominant instructional practices throughout the school are known and monitored.	3.1 The school has adopted the WPS Proficiency Scales for all levels and courses taught which adhere to national, state, and district standards. 3.2 The school curriculum is focused enough that it can be adequately addressed in the time available to teachers and flexible in time available to meet student needs. 3.3 All students have the opportunity to learn the critical content of the curriculum.	4.1 Clear and measurable goals are established and focused on critical needs regarding improving achievement of individual students within the school. 4.2 Data are analyzed, interpreted, and used to regularly monitor progress toward achievement goals for individual students.	5.1 Students move on to the next level of the curriculum for any subject area only after they have demonstrated competence at the previous level. 5.2 The school schedule is designed to accommodate students moving at a pace appropriate to their background and needs.	6.1 Board of Education 6.2 Superintendent 6.3 Learning Services 6.4 Human Resources 6.5 Finance 6.6 Communications 6.7 Student Services 6.8 Maintenance and Operations 6.9 Custodial 6.10 Transportation 6.11 Logistics 6.12 Technology 6.13 Principal Professionalism 6.14 Athletics and Activities 6.15 Education Foundation

FIGURE 6.11: Complete set of the Westminster Public Schools high reliability indicators.

continued ▼

HRS Level 1: Safe, Supportive, and Collaborative Culture (Safety Plan, Collaborative Teams, Student Agency)	**HRS Level 2:** Effective Teaching in Every Classroom (Westminster Instructional Model)	**HRS Level 3:** Guaranteed and Viable Curriculum (Proficiency Scales and Data)	**HRS Level 4:** Standards-Referenced Reporting (Empower Learning Management System)	**HRS Level 5:** Competency-Based Education (Schedules, Pacing, Anytime-Anywhere Learning)	**High Reliability District Level 6:** District Level System of Support
1.5 Teachers and staff have formal ways to provide input regarding the optimal functioning of the school. 1.6 Students, parents, and the community have formal ways to provide input regarding the optimal functioning of the school. 1.7 The success of the whole school, as well as individuals within the school, is appropriately acknowledged.	2.4 Teachers are provided with clear, ongoing evaluations of their pedagogical strengths and weaknesses that are based on multiple sources of data and are consistent with student achievement data. 2.5 Teachers are provided with job-embedded professional development that is directly related to their instructional growth goals. 2.6 Teachers have opportunities to observe and discuss effective teaching.	3.4 Clear and measurable goals are established and focused on critical needs regarding improving overall student achievement and growth at the student, class, and school level. 3.5 The school engages in a continuous improvement process that produces evidence, including measurable results of improving student learning and professional practice.		5.3 Students who have demonstrated competence levels greater than those articulated in the system are afforded immediate opportunities to begin work on advanced content and/or career paths of interest.	

HRS Level 1: Safe, Supportive, and Collaborative Culture (Safety Plan, Collaborative Teams, Student Agency)	**HRS Level 2:** Effective Teaching in Every Classroom (Westminster Instructional Model)	**HRS Level 3:** Guaranteed and Viable Curriculum (Proficiency Scales and Data)	**HRS Level 4:** Standards-Referenced Reporting (Empower Learning Management System)	**HRS Level 5:** Competency-Based Education (Schedules, Pacing, Anytime-Anywhere Learning)	**High Reliability District Level 6:** District Level System of Support
1.8 The school allocates human, material, technological and fiscal resources in alignment with the school's identified needs and priorities to improve student performance and organizational effectiveness (time is a resource). 1.9 The school has programs and practices in place that help develop student efficacy and agency.	2.7 The school procures online resources and engages teachers in activities that help them develop and integrate online resources for score 2.0, 3.0, and 4.0 on proficiency scales.	3.6 Appropriate school- and classroom-level programs and practices are in place to help students meet individual achievement goals when data indicate interventions are needed. 3.7 The school has well-articulated domains and accompanying proficiency scales for cognitive and metacognitive skills that are systematically taught and assessed throughout the curriculum.			

Source: © *2024 by Westminster Public Schools, adapted from Marzano et al., 2014. Used with permission.*

By developing these tailored indicators, WPS not only enhanced accountability within each department but also ensured all aspects of district operations were aligned with the principles of high reliability. These examples demonstrate how WPS adapted the HRS framework to meet the specific needs of its nonacademic departments, creating a cohesive system that supports continuous improvement across the entire district.

Final Thoughts

In conclusion, WPS's journey of continuous improvement has been a transformative process. The district's commitment to continuous improvement, coupled with its innovative adaptation of the HRS framework, led to the creation of the unified system of WPS leading indicators that ensures high standards across all schools and departments. The development of the WPS HRS playbooks and the integration of High Reliability District Level 6 have provided a comprehensive and systematic approach to managing resources, evaluating progress, and fostering a culture of excellence. Following its commitment to continuous improvement, undoubtedly, WPS will continue to iterate and expand its high reliability practices as it works to achieve its long-term goals as outlined in the Destination 2030 strategic plan.

Epilogue

The journey of WPS chronicled in this book is a testament to the power of vision, leadership, and a relentless commitment to continuous improvement. From the initial stages of creating a shared vision to the adoption of a PCBS, WPS has navigated challenges, embraced innovation, and remained steadfast in its mission to provide every student with a meaningful and personalized education.

This book has explored the intricate process of transforming a traditional educational model into one that is responsive, equitable, and focused on student outcomes. WPS's evolution is marked by strategic planning, thoughtful leadership, and a willingness to learn from both successes and setbacks. The district's embrace of HRS and high reliability organization principles underscores its commitment to creating a system that is not only effective but also sustainable over time.

A Digital Companion: The Westminster PCBS Website

To further support educators, leaders, and readers of this book, a website has been developed to provide practical examples and resources aligned with each chapter. The Westminster PCBS website (available at https://sites.google.com/wps.org/westminster-pcbs) serves as a digital companion to this book. It offers a wealth of resources, including real-life examples from WPS, tools, templates, and instructional guides that bring the concepts discussed in each chapter to life.

This website is designed to be a living resource, regularly updated to reflect the ongoing developments within WPS. It provides users with the opportunity to delve deeper into the practices and strategies that have been key to WPS's success, offering a practical guide for those looking to implement similar systems in their own districts. By bridging the theoretical concepts in this book with concrete, actionable examples, the website enhances the learning experience and provides a valuable tool kit for continuous improvement.

Continuing the Journey: Thoughts and Recommendations

In the introductory chapter, this book sets out to answer the question, How can an entire school district make the shift from a traditional K–12 education system to a PCBS? Throughout the book, we provided detailed insights and strategies that have guided WPS on this transformative journey. The hope is that the information presented will inspire and encourage other school districts across the U.S. to embark on similar paths, tailored to their unique circumstances and values.

As you reflect on the ideas and experiences shared in these chapters, consider some thoughts and recommendations: Embrace the process of continuous improvement, maintain a clear and shared vision, and foster collaboration at all levels of the organization. These elements have been critical to the success of WPS and can serve as guiding principles for other districts striving for transformative change.

The story of WPS is not an end point but a living example of what is possible when a district commits to innovation and excellence. The hope is that the lessons learned and shared in this book, along with the resources available on the Westminster PCBS website, will serve as valuable tools for educators and leaders as they work to create educational systems that truly meet the needs of all learners. The journey of transformation is ongoing, and with the right strategies and a unified vision, the possibilities are endless.

References and Resources

Advance CTE. (n.d.). *The National Career Clusters Framework*. Accessed at https://careertech.org/career-clusters on September 30, 2024.

Anderson, L. W., & Krathwohl, D. (Eds.). (2001). *A taxonomy for learning, teaching, and assessing: A revision of Bloom's taxonomy of educational objectives*. Allyn & Bacon.

Bernhardt, V. L. (1998). *Data analysis for comprehensive schoolwide improvement*. Eye on Education.

Colorado Association of School Boards. (2006, December). *Reinventing our schools*. Presented at the 66th Annual Convention, "Lead Locally. Think Globally." Denver, CO.

Colorado Department of Education. (2016, August 11). *Curriculum overview samples*. Accessed at www.cde.state.co.us/standardsandinstruction/samplecurriculum on September 30, 2024.

Colorado Department of Education. (2019, August 29). *State model evaluation system for principals/assistant principals*. Accessed at www.cde.state.co.us/educator effectiveness/smes-principal on September 30, 2024.

Colorado Department of Education. (2025a, February 27). *Office of Standards and Instructional Support*. Accessed at www.cde.state.co.us/standardsandinstruction on March 31, 2025.

Colorado Department of Education. (2025b, January 28). *Unified improvement planning.* Accessed at www.cde.state.co.us/uip on March 31, 2025.

Cowen Institute for Public Education Initiatives. (2010). *The state of public education in New Orleans: Five years after Hurricane Katrina.* Tulane University. Accessed at www.coweninstitute.com/our-work/the-state-of-public-education-in-new-orleans/ on September 30, 2024.

Darling-Hammond, L., Wei, R. C., Andree, A., Richardson, N., & Orphanos, S. (2009). *Professional learning in the learning profession.* National Staff Development Council.

Davidson, N. (Ed.). (2021). *Pioneering perspectives in cooperative learning: Theory, research, and classroom practice for diverse approaches to CL.* Routledge.

De Feo, J. A. (2017). *Juran's quality handbook: The complete guide to performance excellence* (7th ed.). McGraw Hill Education.

Deming, W. E. (1986). *Out of the crisis.* MIT Press.

Desimone, L. M. (2009). Improving impact studies of teachers' professional development: Toward better conceptualizations and measures. *Educational Researcher, 38*(3), 181–199.

Deslauriers, L., Schelew, E., & Wieman, C. (2011). Improved learning in a large-enrollment physics class. *Science, 332*(6031), 862–864. https://doi.org/10.1126/science.1201783

Edmondson, A. C. (2019). *The fearless organization: Creating psychological safety in the workplace for learning, innovation, and growth.* Wiley.

Evans, C. M., Landl, E., & Thompson, J. (2020). Making sense of K–12 competency-based education: A systematic literature review of implementation and outcomes research from 2000 to 2019. *Journal of Competency-Based Education, 5*(4), Article e01228. https://doi.org/10.1002/cbe2.1228

Feldman, J. (2024). *Grading for equity: What it is, why it matters, and how it can transform schools and classrooms.* Corwin.

Freeman, S., Eddy, S. L., McDonough, M., Smith, M. K., Okoroafor, N., Jordt, H., & Wenderoth, M. P. (2014). Active learning increases student performance in science, engineering, and mathematics. *Proceedings of the National Academy of Sciences, 111*(23), 8410–8415. https://doi.org/10.1073/pnas.1319030111

Fullan, M. (2001). *Leading in a culture of change.* Jossey-Bass.

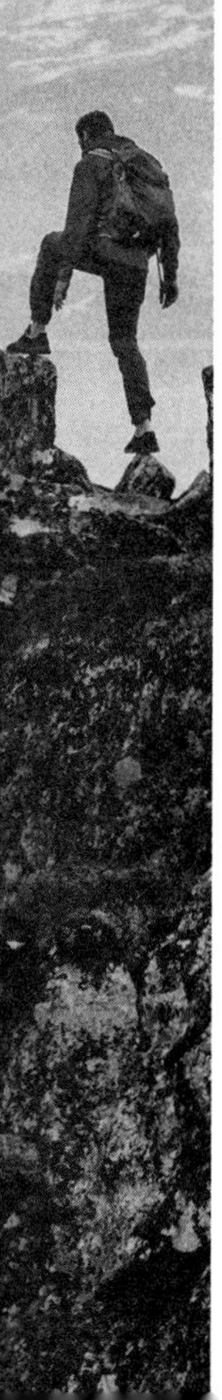

Fullan, M., & Quinn, J. (2016). *Coherence: The right drivers in action for schools, districts, and systems.* Corwin.

Harris, D. N., & Larsen, M. F. (2018). *The effects of the New Orleans post-Katrina school reforms on student academic outcomes.* Education Research Alliance for New Orleans.

Heifetz, R., Grashow, A., & Linsky, M. (2009). *The practice of adaptive leadership: Tools and tactics for changing your organization and the world.* Harvard Business Press.

Hess, K. (2025). *Applying depth of knowledge and cognitive rigor: An educator's guide to supporting deeper learning.* Teachers College Press.

Hill, W. E. (1915). *My wife and my mother-in-law* [Illustration]. Puck.

Johnson, D. W., Johnson, R. T., & Smith, K. A. (2014). Cooperative learning: Improving university instruction by basing practice on validated theory. *Journal on Excellence in College Teaching, 25*(3–4), 85–118.

Kagan, S. (1994). *Cooperative learning.* Kagan.

Kotter, J. P. (1996). *Leading change.* Harvard Business School Press.

Kotter, J. P. (2012). *Leading change.* Harvard Business Review Press.

Larson, N. (2004). *Saxon math 3: An incremental development.* Saxon.

Liker, J. K. (2004). *The Toyota way: 14 management principles from the world's greatest manufacturer.* McGraw-Hill.

Lou, Y., Abrami, P. C., Spence, J. C., Poulsen, C., Chambers, B., & d'Apollonia, S. (1996). Within-class grouping: A meta-analysis. *Review of Educational Research, 66*(4), 423–458.

Marzano, R. J. (2007). *The art and science of teaching: A comprehensive framework for effective instruction.* ASCD.

Marzano, R. J. (2017). *The new art and science of teaching.* Solution Tree Press.

Marzano, R. J. (2018). *Making classroom assessments reliable and valid.* Solution Tree Press.

Marzano, R. J., & Abbott, S. (2022). *Teaching in a competency-based elementary school. The Marzano Academies model.* Marzano Resources.

Marzano, R. J., Dodson, C. W., Simms, J. A., & Wipf, J. P. (2022). *Ethical test preparation in the classroom.* Marzano Resources.

Marzano, R. J., & Kendall, J. S. (1998). *Awash in a sea of standards*. Mid-continent Research for Education and Learning.

Marzano, R. J., & Kosena, B. J. (2022). *Leading a competency-based elementary school: The Marzano Academies model*. Marzano Resources.

Marzano, R. J., Norford, J. S., Finn, M., & Finn, D., III. (2017). *A handbook for personalized competency-based education*. Marzano Resources.

Marzano, R. J., Rains, C. L, & Warrick, P. B. (2021). *Improving teacher development and evaluation: A guide for leaders, coaches, and teachers*. Marzano Resources.

Marzano, R. J., Warrick, P., & Simms, J. A. (2014). *A handbook for high reliability schools: The next step in school reform*. Marzano Resources.

Marzano, R. J., Waters, T., & McNulty, B. A. (2005). *School leadership that works: From research to results*. ASCD.

Marzano Resources. (n.d.a). *The critical concepts*. Accessed at www.marzanoresources.com/educational-services/critical-concepts on September 30, 2024.

Marzano Resources. (n.d.b). *The Marzano compendium of instructional strategies*. Accessed at www.marzanoresources.com/online-compendium/intro on January 9, 2025.

McGraw-Hill Education. (2005). *Open court reading* (2005 ed.). Author.

National Governors Association Center for Best Practices & Council of Chief State School Officers. (2010a). *Common Core State Standards for English language arts and literacy in history/social studies, science, and technical subjects*. Authors. Accessed at https://corestandards.org/wp-content/uploads/2023/09/ELA_Standards1.pdf on September 30, 2024.

National Governors Association Center for Best Practices & Council of Chief State School Officers. (2010b). *Common Core State Standards for mathematics*. Authors. Accessed at https://corestandards.org/wp-content/uploads/2023/09/Math_Standards1.pdf on October 28, 2024.

New York State Education Department. (n.d.). *EngageNY*. Accessed at www.engageny.org/ on September 30, 2024.

NGSS Lead States. (2013). *Next Generation Science Standards: For states, by states*. The National Academies Press.

Patrick, S. (2021). Transforming learning through competency-based education. *State Education Standard, 21*(2), 23–29. Accessed at https://files.eric.ed.gov/fulltext/EJ1315095.pdf on January 9, 2025.

Puentedura, R. R. (2006). *Transformation, technology, and education.* Accessed at http://hippasus.com/resources/tte/ on September 30, 2024.

Pyc, M. A., & Rawson, K. A. (2009). Testing the retrieval effort hypothesis: Does greater difficulty correctly recalling information lead to higher levels of memory? *Journal of Memory and Language, 60*(4), 437–447.

Reeves, D. B. (2004). The case against the zero. *Phi Delta Kappan, 86*(4), 324–325.

Renaissance Learning, Inc. (n.d.). *Star Assessments.* Accessed at www.renaissance.com/products/star-assessments/ on September 30, 2024.

Rhoney, D. H., & Meyer, S. M. (2024). Competency-based education: The need to debunk misconceptions and develop a common language. *American Journal of Pharmaceutical Education, 88*(2), 100637. https://doi.org/10.1016/j.ajpe.2023.100637

Schneider, C., & Paul, J. (2015, September 16). Education chief Arne Duncan: U.S. is falling behind. *The Indianapolis Star.* Accessed at www.indystar.com/story/news/politics/2015/09/16/education-chief-arne-duncan-us-falling-behind/32533827/ on October 28, 2024.

Seddon, M. (2019). Context-dependent memory: Do changes in environmental context cues affect student recall? *Teacher Education Advancement Network Journal, 11*(3), 25–34.

Shingo, S. (1989). *A study of the Toyota production system from an industrial engineering viewpoint* (Rev. ed.; A. P. Dillon, Trans.). CRC Press.

Slavin, R. E. (2010). *Instruction based on cooperative learning.* In R. E. Mayer & P. A. Alexander (Eds.), *Handbook of research on learning and instruction* (pp. 344–360). Routledge.

Stanford, L. (2024, September 17). All states allow competency-based learning. Will it become a reality in schools? *Education Week.* Accessed at www.edweek.org/technology/all-states-allow-competency-based-learning-will-it-become-a-reality-in-schools/2024/09 on January 9, 2025.

Sturgis, C. (2015, June). *Implementing competency education in K–12 systems: Insights from local leaders* (CompetencyWorks Issue Brief). International Association for K–12 Online Learning. Accessed at www.competencyworks.org/wp-content/uploads/2015/06/iNCL_CW IssueBrief_Implementing_v5_web.pdf on August 9, 2016.

TNTP. (2021, May 23). *Accelerate, don't remediate: New evidence from elementary math classrooms.* Accessed at https://tntp.org/publication/accelerate-dont-remediate on January 9, 2025.

Tomlinson, C. A., & Moon, T. R. (2013). *Assessment and student success in a differentiated classroom*. ASCD.

University of Chicago School Mathematics Project. (2007). *Everyday mathematics* (3rd ed.). McGraw-Hill.

University of Oregon. (n.d.). *DIBELS 8th edition*. Accessed at https://dibels.uoregon.edu/ on September 30, 2024.

Webb, N. L. (2002). *Depth-of-Knowledge levels for four content areas.* Accessed at http://ossucurr.pbworks.com/w/file/fetch/49691156/Norm%20web%20dok%20by%20subject%20area.pdf on September 30, 2024.

Weick, K. E., & Sutcliffe, K. M. (2007). *Managing the unexpected: Resilient performance in an age of uncertainty* (2nd ed.). Jossey-Bass.

Wellman, B., & Lipton, L. (2004). *Data-driven dialogue: A facilitator's guide to collaborative inquiry.* MiraVia, LLC.

Westminster Public Schools. (n.d.). *Learner-centered classrooms.* Accessed at https://cbs.wps.org/about-cbs/learner-centered-classrooms on September 30, 2024.

Westminster Public Schools. (2017). *WPS annual report 2017.* Accessed at https://issuu.com/westminsterpublicschools/docs/digital_annual_report_17 on January 9, 2025.

Index

R

S

T

U

V

W

Y

Marzano Academies Series
The Marzano Academies series presents a blueprint for success with competency-based education from experts and educators who have done this work. Leaders and teachers at the elementary and secondary levels will gain innovative, equitable, and effective practices for schools and classrooms.
BKL056, BKL055, BKL054, BKL053

Five Big Ideas for Leading a High Reliability School
Robert J. Marzano, Philip B. Warrick, and Mario I. Acosta
Success as a high reliability organization requires leaders who understand the five big ideas shared in this book. With data-driven approaches and research-backed strategies, the authors demonstrate not only how to help schools thrive but also why their methods succeed.
BKL074

A Handbook for Personalized Competency-Based Education
Robert J. Marzano, Jennifer S. Norford, Michelle Finn, and Douglas Finn III
Ensure all students master content by designing and implementing a personalized competency-based education (PCBE) system. Explore examples of how to use proficiency scales, standard operating procedures, behavior rubrics, personal tracking matrices, and other tools to aid in instruction and assessment.
BKL037

Beyond Reform
Lindsay Unified School District
Learn how Lindsay Unified School District took action to improve student learning by shifting from a traditional time-based education system to a learner-centered performance-based system. By adopting and tailoring Lindsay Unified's instructional model, you and your team can embark on your own district's transformation.
BKL036

MARZANO Resources

Visit MarzanoResources.com or call 888.849.0851 to order.

LEARN MORE at MarzanoResources.com/PD
Parking Lot